The Veiled Vale

Mike White spent over three decades actively investigating the paranormal, both with *Cotswold Paranormal Investigations* in the south of England and the *Association for the Scientific Study of Anomalous Phenomena* nationwide, before opting for a life that doesn't involve spending nights in draughty cellars and windswept hilltops. These days he favours chasing ghost stories rather than ghosts and much prefers chatting to folk about folklore than trying to identify Unidentified Flying Objects. He has been writing about the strange and mysterious ever since his days as a columnist for the *Ley Hunter* magazine but *The Veiled Vale* is his first book. He lives in the heart of South Oxfordshire and is married with two adult children. Many years ago he had ambitions to be a classical musician but settled for a career in IT when he realised that his Bach was worse than his byte.

ALSO PUBLISHED BY TWO RIVERS

Before & After: Reminiscences of a Working Life by Edith Morley, edited by Barbara Morris
Silchester: Life on the dig by Jenny Halstead & Michael Fulford
The Writing on the Wall: Reading's Latin Inscriptions by Peter Kruschwitz
Caught on Camera: Reading in the 70s by Terry Allsop
Plant Portraits by Post: Post & Go British Flora by Julia Trickey
Allen W. Seaby: Art and Nature by Martin Andrews & Robert Gillmor
Reading Detectives by Kerry Renshaw
Fox Talbot & the Reading Establishment by Martin Andrews
Cover Birds by Robert Gillmor
All Change at Reading: The Railway and the Station 1840–2013 by Adam Sowan
An Artist's Year in the Harris Garden by Jenny Halstead
Caversham Court Gardens: A Heritage Guide by Friends of Caversham Court Gardens
Believing in Reading: Our Places of Worship by Adam Sowan
Newtown: A Photographic Journey in Reading 1974 by Terry Allsop
Bikes, Balls & Biscuitmen: Our Sporting Life by Tim Crooks & Reading Museum
Birds, Blocks & Stamps: Post & Go Birds of Britain by Robert Gillmor
The Reading Quiz Book by Adam Sowan
Bizarre Berkshire: An A–Z Guide by Duncan Mackay
Broad Street Chapel & the Origins of Dissent in Reading by Geoff Sawers
Reading Poetry: An Anthology edited by Peter Robinson
Reading: A Horse-Racing Town by Nigel Sutcliffe
Eat Wild by Duncan MacKay
Down by the River: The Thames and Kennet in Reading by Gillian Clark
A Much-maligned Town: Opinions of Reading 1126–2008 by Adam Sowan
A Mark of Affection: The Soane Obelisk in Reading by Adam Sowan
The Stranger in Reading edited by Adam Sowan
The Holy Brook by Adam Sowan
Charms against Jackals edited by Adam Stout and Geoff Sawers
Abattoirs Road to Zinzan Street by Adam Sowan

The Veiled Vale

Strange Tales from South Oxfordshire

Mike White

First published in the UK in 2016 by Two Rivers Press
7 Denmark Road, Reading RG1 5PA
www.tworiverspress.com

© Two Rivers Press 2016
© in text Mike White 2016
© in illustrations Peter Hay

The right of the author to be identified as the author of the work has been asserted by him in accordance with the Copyright, Designs and Patents Act of 1988.

All rights reserved. No part of this publication may be reproduced, stored in or introduced into a retrieval system, or transmitted, in any form, or by any means (electronic, mechanical, photocopying, recording or otherwise) without the prior written permission of the publisher.

ISBN 978-1-909747-17-3

3 4 5 6 7 8 9

Two Rivers Press is represented in the UK by Inpress Ltd and distributed by BookSource, Glasgow.

Cover design by Sally Castle using an illustration by Peter Hay
Illustrations by Peter Hay
Text design by Nadja Robinson and typeset in Bembo and Parisine

Printed and bound in Great Britain by CMP (UK), Poole

This book is dedicated to Jackie, Adam and Bec.
With thanks for putting up with some of my weirder interests.
And a thank you to all those who provided advice, corrections
and, most important of all, their personal tales and experiences.

The illustrations for this book are selected from Two Rivers' collection of Peter Hay rubber stamp images. Peter, who founded the Press, began making these images around 1994 and over the next 9 years he created around 1000 of them. They evolved out of his interest in lino-cut and woodblock printing and he used ordinary 1¾ × 1¼ inch erasers from a high street stationer for the job. The Press now has an archive print and digital copy of each image and, thanks to the author's and artist's shared love of this particular landscape and its inhabitants, it was easy to select illustrations that fitted with Mike's text. We decided against tidying up the images digitally as the imperfections in the printing seemed to complement the atmosphere evoked by the mystery in the stories.

Introduction

> Before the gods that made the gods
> Had seen their sunrise pass,
> The White Horse of the White Horse Vale
> Was cut out of the grass.
> —*The Ballad of the White Horse*, G.K. Chesterton

Chesterton's 1911 epic poem tells a magnificent (if fictionalised) tale of Alfred's struggles and eventual victory over the Danes, with the White Horse playing a strongly symbolic role, much as the carving still serves as a powerful emblem for South Oxfordshire (and for books such as this one about the area) today. The White Horse of Uffington is known to be Britain's oldest hill figure, dating back over 3,000 years to the Late Bronze Age, and it sits at the centre of a landscape consisting of a large number of other prehistoric sites of varying ages which, taken together, make up one of the most densely packed sacred landscapes in the country.

Running across the country just above the White Horse is the Ridgeway, probably Britain's oldest long-distance trail; just along the Ridgeway to the west of the Horse sits the Neolithic long barrow of Wayland's Smithy. On the hill above the carving is the hillfort of Uffington Castle, one of a series of similar fortifications along this stretch of the Downs which includes Alfred's Castle at Ashdown and Segsbury Camp at Letcombe; there is even a 'hillfort' down in the marshes of the valley at Charney Bassett, with the low-lying marshy ground offering just as much protection to Cherbury Camp as any steeply rising downland slope.

In amongst all these archaeological sites this part of the country offers a wealth of historical oddities: ghost stories, both old and new; natural prodigies, witches, UFOs, and even the occasional monster. While I have alluded to the Vale of

White Horse in the title of this book, the area these pages cover much more closely resembles the region once known as North Berkshire – the part that was ripped from its native county and transferred wholesale into the waiting arms of Oxfordshire in the administrative reorganisations of 1974.[1] Roughly bordered by the county boundary with Wiltshire to the west, the River Thames in the east and north and by the line of the Ridgeway to the south, you can find all the places mentioned in this volume on the OS map Explorer 170. I hope some of what you read here inspires you to get out and about exploring the histories and mysteries of South Oxfordshire for yourself.

A note on names: some of the stories in this volume were told to me quite openly and the narrators saw no need to hide their identity in any way, while others have been taken from publications and newspaper clippings where the identity of the various protagonists is already public. Many others, however, were whispered almost furtively and only revealed on the promise of strict anonymity. Given these different circumstances, I have tried to adopt a uniform policy throughout this book. Consequently, where a name is already in the public domain, or where a witness has specifically said that they have no objection to their real name appearing, I have used it; where someone has requested a degree of anonymity (or where in some cases I simply don't know the name of a contributor) I have used pseudonymous forenames to disguise their identity.

---

[1] Author Adam Sowan (who was also editor for this book) uses the term 'Occupied North Berkshire'.

Wallingford

The flow of this book takes us in a generally westerly direction and it seems appropriate to start our canter through the county at Wallingford, since there has been a settlement here for as long as anywhere in the region we will be covering; Stone Age flint tools, Bronze Age weapons and Iron Age fortifications have all been found in the area. King Alfred (we may well encounter the occasional reference to the Anglo-Saxons along the way) fortified the original settlement and made it a *Burh* (the origin of our modern 'borough') and the remains of the original defences can still be traced today – sadly they were not *entirely* effective as the Danes under Sweyn Forkbeard breached the walls and burned the town to the ground in 1006. King Stephen and Queen Matilda made war over and around the town and, while there are no ghosts dating quite that far back, we can find a tale dating from four centuries ago which is quite old enough to get us started.

The George Hotel, originally called the George and Dragon, dates back to 1517 and, as you might expect from a coaching inn of such a pedigree, it has many secrets in its past; a previous landlord whose footsteps can still be heard pacing the upstairs hallways being one, and two small children who appear occasionally beside the washbasin in one of the bedrooms another. In terms of notoriety, the most famous guest that The George can lay claim to having entertained has to be the infamous highwayman Dick Turpin who, it is said, made many a daring escape from the law by leaping from his room down onto the back of his faithful steed Black Bess before disappearing into the night. However, dashing lawbreakers aside, The George is best known for a more tragic tale: that of the Teardrop Room.

This sad story starts in the seventeenth century, in 1626 to be precise, a year after King Charles I had ascended to the throne and at a time when the tensions that would eventually lead to the Civil War were beginning to stir across the country. Naturally Wallingford, a major local market town as well as a strategic river crossing, was not immune to unrest, especially as a significant number of soldiers were billeted in the town, their cavalier attitudes[2] doubtless causing friction with the people of the area. Of course not all the soldiers were of the rougher sort – step forward one such officer and gentleman named John Hobson.

Hobson was engaged to the daughter of the then landlord of The George, a local man by the name of Francis Smith. Unlike his daughter, who was reputed to be both virtuous and beautiful, Smith was known to be a man who sailed rather close to the wind in his dealings with the law, and there are historical documents which detail his continual refusals to submit to the authority of the local Commissioners for Brewing to back up this assertion. It is possible that the very belligerent qualities that made him such a problem to local officials might have been useful on the evening of March 3rd when John Hobson came to call on his fiancée at The George but, alas, for all his faults, Smith was a conscientious innkeeper and was working elsewhere in the building at that moment. The exact events of that fateful night are unclear but it seems that one of the local ruffians picked an argument with Hobson and, after the dispute became more impassioned, produced a knife and stabbed him through the heart before fleeing the ensuing uproar.

Rushing to the scene, the Smiths were horrified to find Hobson lying dead in a pool of his own blood and the young girl was so distraught that she had to be taken to her room and sedated. Sadly, the loss of her lover upset the balance of her mind and over the following days she did nothing but draw

---

2 Sorry.

an extensive pattern of teardrops across the wall of her room, using makeshift ink made of soot from the fire moistened with her own tears. Having completed this dolorous task she allowed herself to pine away and join in death the man who was destined never to be her husband in life.

Life, of course, must carry on and the business of the hotel continued despite the tragedy that had occurred within its walls; but perhaps some echo of the drama remained. Many visitors who slept in what became known as the Teardrop Room reported hearing strange sighing during the night, seeing glimpses of shadowy forms and, most significantly, being awoken by an overwhelming sense of sadness permeating the room. This phenomenon was first described by writer T. C. Lethbridge, who used the unfortunate term 'ghoul' to describe how strong feelings, usually of sadness or fear, can persist and be perceived by sensitive individuals at a later point in time.

In the case of the Teardrop Room there was far more to the haunting than simple emotional residue, as one traveller in late Victorian times discovered. This gentleman stopped at The George to break his journey, doubtless enjoyed a meal and was eventually shown to the Teardrop Room to settle himself down for the night. Some hours later, a terrible storm unleashed thunder and lightning on Wallingford and the traveller awoke. In the light of intermittent lightning flashes he was perplexed to see the ghostly silhouette of a young girl crouched beside the fire tracing out shapes on the wall. The man leapt out of bed in shock and went to move towards the girl who, clearly sensing his presence, turned towards him a beautiful face framed with dark hair and cheeks stained with the unmistakable tracks of tears. Lightning flashed, the thunder rolled one more time and then the girl was gone.

How the traveller slept after this is not recorded, but we can probably assume that after an encounter of this nature it was not at all well. Perhaps he eventually managed to convince himself that it had all been a dream but, as the morning began to illuminate his room, such fancies were quickly dispelled by the trails of soot to be found across the walls and floor around the fireplace. Visitors to The George today can see one wall still preserving the sad evidence of a young girl's grief.

It is not just above the ground that The George is haunted. Down below in the cellars some members of staff have reported hearing strange delayed echoes while working there alone. One night the barman went down to tap the bungs on the barrels and as he left and was locking the door behind him, he heard the unmistakable sound of that very same activity coming from the dark, empty cellar. There are tales of tunnels radiating outwards underneath the town from these subterranean vaults, so perhaps this may begin to explain how these odd echoes occur, but it has to be said that those working alone in the shadows find other, less rational, explanations to be far more persuasive…

In years gone by, Wallingford was frequently visited by wandering tradesmen and the arrival of one particular group became entrenched in local folklore. Artist George Leslie wrote to the magazine *Folklore* that:

> The people here at Wallingford have an odd belief about the wandering German bands that visit at times. It is said that they invariably bring rain. When they see them crossing the bridge they say, 'There come the Germans: it will rain tomorrow.' My gardener firmly believes in this.[3]

---

3   Why the Germans should be singled out in such a particular way is not explained, though my money is on a misunderstanding of the term Rhinelanders.

Not all of Wallingford's ghost sightings are hundreds of years old, as an encounter from 1966 illustrates. One autumn evening in that year three teenage boys were playing in a small copse known locally as Gypsy Wood, making a fire and just generally messing  about, when, out of the corner of his eye, one of the boys became aware of a grey robed figure striding silently through the bushes nearby. Startled, he turned and called out to his friends to look but when they did so the figure was nowhere to be seen. Mystified as to where he could have gone, the woods being too sparse to allow anywhere for a man to hide, one of the boys hit upon the idea of an experiment to determine whether the apparition had been in any way supernatural.

No sooner had the idea been suggested than it was put into action and soon a glowing stick from the fire was standing upright, wedged into the branches of a tree near where the figure had appeared. Nervously, one of the three exclaimed: 'If there be any spirits in the wood then set the stick on fire!' – and the boys all jumped in shock as the smouldering stick burst into flames.

Their curiosity aroused, the trio decided to see how much more they could coax from whatever spirit they had contacted. 'If the spirit is friendly, break off five sparks.' Five sparks obediently drifted into the air but, as they did so, a large grey shape materialised off to the side. Eyes wide with shock the boys realised that, even in the dying light, the figure was not entirely solid and the outlines of trees could be seen through its body.

'If we can have the stick back, strike two sparks off it.' Two sparks jumped out, and the boys summoned up enough courage to move towards the reddish glow ahead of them in the twilight. As they approached, the figure drifted away from them and slowly faded away.

Had they imagined the whole incident, was this a case of collective hallucination or had they had a genuine encounter with something truly other-worldly? At first the three boys were unsure but, as they retrieved the still-glowing stick they became aware that something was not quite right: despite giving all the appearance of burning, the embers gave out no heat; they just gradually faded to black and followed the grey figure into nothingness.

Brightwell-cum-Sotwell

Brightwell-cum-Sotwell was originally two distinct villages (well, three if you count the southern hamlet of Mackney) but, unusually, it seems that Sotwell almost entirely bisected the larger Brightwell, presumably to such an extent that the local inhabitants grew tired of trying to identify exactly which village they were actually standing in and opted for the current double-barrelled naming arrangement. Whatever their disparate origins there is obviously a long-standing sense of combined community as this old verse illustrates:

> There's Brightwell and Sotwell,
> And merry Mackney,
> But lousy old Cholsey
> Is worse than all three.

From the 1930s the village was the home of the celebrated homoeopath Dr Edward Bach, inventor of the famous flower remedy system, which, like all homeopathic medicines, is said to derive its efficacy from potions which are diluted to the point where they don't actually contain any part of the flowers from which they are prepared. Apparently piles of empty spirit bottles were a common sight piled up outside Mount Vernon, the house in Bakers Lane where he lived and worked: before you leap to the wrong conclusion I ought to stress that dilution with brandy formed part of the production process.

There are a number of wonderful place names scattered around the area near Brightwell-cum-Sotwell. There is a field here known as Cuckoo Pen, the name referring to an old tradition that if a cuckoo could be trapped within a ring of greenery and so prevented from flying away as autumn approached, then summer could be extended forever. Needless to say such attempts always ended in failure but similar stories are common throughout the country. A stream nearby, which goes by the colourful name of Bloody Mere, is said to commemorate the time that blood from a great battle on the hills above the village made the stream run red, and the very last bustard, a large native bird which was hunted to extinction in the UK by the 1840s, is said to have been killed at Bustard Piece. (There is currently a project running on Salisbury Plain to reintroduce the bustard so this splendid bird may one day once again grace the field that bears its name.) And finally there is a field intriguingly called The Evils. This is widely thought to have attained its name and reputation because sheep kept there were more likely to develop foot rot than anywhere else, but in fact the name is more likely to derive from *ea-wills* or 'water springs' (nearby Ewelme has the same derivation). Of course, sheep kept in a waterlogged field are quite likely to develop foot rot so the name is still entirely appropriate.

I only have a few tenuous ghost stories from the village. One of the houses in Mackney Lane was once thought haunted, as was Dobsons, one of the oldest houses in the village and, allegedly at least, once the hideout of a band of local smugglers. One can only wonder if the story of the haunting was created to dissuade curious local people from investigating too closely when they noticed strange lights flitting around the cottage at night. The Old Priory can boast two ghosts seen in fairly recent times by a number of members of the family who lived there; one a man on the stairs and the other a grey lady who would make occasional appearances in the dining room, a habit detrimental to the digestion I should think. One final piece of local folklore: Stonor Hays, the old village manor house, has a pond, probably part of an old moat, which was once thought to be bottomless. In the interests of accuracy I checked this out: it isn't.

North Moreton

The pretty village of North Moreton has much to offer those in search of the strange. Take for example the case of Anne Gunter, a most extraordinary young girl who may, or may not, have been cursed by witches, and of her brutal and embittered father whose machinations eventually brought the community to the notice of the highest authority in the land.

In the early years of the seventeenth century young Anne lived in the village with her father Brian Gunter, a country gentleman of both wealth and local influence, at least by the standards of the time. Or so he would doubtless have described himself. To be honest, the term country gentleman did not really suit Brian Gunter, for although he had connections to Exeter College in Oxford (his elder daughter was married to the Professor of Divinity) he was something of an interloper in Moreton, not having been born locally. Worse still, he had made his wealth by buying up *impropriated tithes*, effectively taking the profits from church tithes under his wing for later distribution as he saw fit. He was also clearly a man of some temper; in 1598, while he was part of the crowd watching a football match a brawl broke out and, seeing his sons being beaten in the ensuing ruckus, he attacked two local men, the brothers John and Richard Gregory, with such violence that they later died. The Parish Register for 1598 states:

> These two men were killed by ould Gunter. Gunter's sonne and the Gregories fell together by the ears at footeball. Oulde Guntre drew his dagger and broke booth there heads and they died booth within a fortnight after.

The boys' family tried to have him convicted of their murder but the case failed in the courts. Even though it had been he who had committed the murders, Gunter vowed revenge upon the Gregories, although (doubtless thinking that some dishes are best served cold) he bided his time, awaiting the right moment to strike.

In the year 1604 Brian Gunter was taken ill and sent to Exeter College to convalesce. It was around the time of his absences from Moreton that Anne, at that time fourteen years of age, began to suffer a series of strange fits and periods of paralysis during which she constantly railed against three local women – a certain Elizabeth Gregory, the sister-in-law of the two men killed by her father six years before, and two other members of the extended Gregory family, Agnes Pepwell and her daughter Mary. While today we might wonder whether Anne had been suffering from epilepsy or possibly a violent allergic reaction of some kind, a local witch-hunter from Newbury by the name of John Wendore diagnosed sorcery (by the unusual method of examining Anne's urine),[4] and for Brian Gunter this was clearly an opportunity not to be missed.

On his return from Oxford, presumably restored to health and wishing to support his afflicted daughter, Gunter reported suffering pains in his shoulder, which, he claimed, had mysteriously vanished when he scratched Mistress Gregory on the head, a clear sign that she was guilty of witchcraft. Following this accusation Anne's symptoms intensified; she now frothed at the mouth and became at times completely insensible to pain, which was perhaps just as well since she was frequently seen to exude pins from her mouth, fingers and breasts. During this period she was visited by various clergymen who seem to have had little luck in curing her – quite the reverse, in fact, as she was said to have impudently tugged thirty hairs from the beard of the vicar of Brightwell

---

4 In the nineteenth century, Warlock Manning (more about Manning later) would recommend filling a bottle with the victim's urine and turning it upside down. If bubbles rose upwards then the victim was suffering from some kind of curse. Conversely, a suspected witch's urine would be boiled; if this caused pain to the suspect they were certainly a minion of Satan.

when he came to call. On another occasion the Rev. Gilbert Bradshawe from North Moreton attested that he had watched as

> her undergarments loosened without human aid and her shoes, stockings and garters came from beneath her clothes, crept along like worms, then returned again.

Doubtless a highly entertaining spectacle for all concerned.

Obviously, Anne's condition caused considerable interest and she was examined by a number of Oxford scholars including John Prideaux and Thomas Winniffe, both Fellows of Exeter College (and therefore presumably acquainted with her father), all of whom pronounced her bewitched. The case against the three women seemed watertight and they were consequently dragged off to be prosecuted for witchcraft at the Abingdon Assize.

Almost certainly Brian Gunter was well pleased with this development, especially so when Agnes Pepwell made the surprising announcement that she had actually been a practicing witch for the past fourteen years and had her own familiar in the shape of a black cat. She also claimed that the other women had familiars of their own in the forms of a bearded mouse called Sweat and a white toad which went by the name of Vizitt. Why she suddenly made this confession is open to debate; perhaps she was planning to throw herself onto the mercy of the court by this action and so avoid being hanged; certainly she admitted responsibility and publicly expressed regret for bewitching Anne.

Luckily, not everyone had been caught up in the witch-hunting frenzy and one of those who approached the case with caution was a Wiltshire gentleman called Thomas Hinton. Hinton had originally joined the crowds as an interested spectator but after observing matters for a while had begun to have doubts about how genuine Anne's symptoms really were.

Some reports say he was actually a Cunning Man, one of those odd combinations of hedge wizard, witch-finder and general wise man and wonder-worker who could be found in most parts of the country until very recent times, in which case it seems likely that his attendance was due to more than simple curiosity. Hinton secretly marked some pins in the Gunter household and was then able to demonstrate trickery when Anne subsequently spat them out during one of her seizures. Once this incident with the pins had punctured the certainty of the case, other clear heads began to look at the evidence and, with Hinton constantly using his connections at the Assize to encourage restraint, no proof of witchcraft could be found. The three women were acquitted. The acquittal was not actually an entirely unexpected verdict since only around half of witch trials in England ever ended in a hanging (England being relatively relaxed about such things compared to either Scotland or the continent) but it does highlight the question of how many convicted witches in Europe may have been nothing more than victims of aggrieved neighbours. In any case, Brian Gunter and his case were both discredited.

We might expect the story to end here but there were still some further plot twists to come: Brian Gunter was down but not out. During a visit of King James I to Oxford, he managed to gain a royal audience during which he took the opportunity to display his 'bewitched' daughter and, knowing the King's interest in the subject, plead for royal intervention. James had written a treatise on witchcraft called *Daemonologie* in 1597, but his views had mellowed somewhat by the time of his visit and consequently he passed the case over to Archbishop Richard Bancroft to investigate. The Archbishop was sceptical on the question of witchcraft so his inquiry was very thorough and, as it turned out, highly critical. Gunter's shameful treatment of his own daughter was exposed for all to see; he had apparently forced her to drink wine and salad oil (*'sack and sallet oil'*) and another unknown *'green mixture'* in order to promote convulsions. The Archbishop also discovered that Brian Gunter had used a combination of drugs and induced trances to allow Anne to demonstrate her immunity to pain, had coached her on spitting pins and had bullied her so mercilessly that she had on more than one occasion threatened suicide. Although he did not mention it in his report, given the account of the undulating underwear from the Vicar of North Moreton there was clearly a degree of hysteria from others involved in the case too. Faced with such a damning conclusion, Brian Gunter was hauled up before the Star Chamber, the most feared (semi-)legal court in the land and, although the final verdict has been lost, it seems unlikely that he would have been able to resume his prosperous and settled existence. He did, however, live (fractiously of course) into his eighties. Anne (probably quite willingly) disappeared into obscurity, although some storytellers assert that she married a servant of the Archbishop who had tried her father and lived happily thereafter.

Moving swiftly on to the year 1900 and one of the odder items to appear in these pages. In that year a later vicar of North Moreton wrote in *Nature Notes*, the magazine of the Selborne Society, that:

On July 20, while some repairs were being carried out in our church, a skeleton was discovered at a depth of about six feet under the pavement, and in the skull a large yellow toad. The theory of the man who found it is that the creature was there in the man's lifetime and grew after his death!

Judging by the tone used in the letter it is clear that the vicar held little sympathy with the opinion of the toad's discoverer;

it is nice to find that at least some of the priesthood of North Moreton across the ages have been fairly level-headed individuals. Of course, even discounting the grown-in-the-head theory, it is still a mystery how a toad managed to find its way into the skull of a man interred six feet underground, let alone survive for any length of time.

South Moreton

One dark night in 1804, William Field hanged himself in his barn at South Moreton. While one might suppose this to be the end of the story for the unfortunate William, it seems that his spirit was unable to find rest and numerous passers-by were, over the next few years, terrified by the sight of his ghost appearing in the stackyard to the south side of the barn. One young boy called George Hall told of his terror when a grinning ghoul peered at him from behind a tree and another, Thomas Money, described how he had been watering horses at a trough when a white apparition had appeared above the yard, causing the horses to stampede in panic. Clearly the situation could not be allowed to continue and so around the year 1850 eleven, yes eleven, priests were assembled and this cadre of padres was dispatched to the scene to banish the troublesome spirit.

It was obvious that this was going to be an exorcism of some spectacle and the lure of it proved too much for two local brothers named John and James Parkes, who hid themselves under a pile of straw in the barn just before the banishment was due to begin.  The ceremony was duly started and after a while the ghost manifested itself to the collective clergy and demanded, as the price for his departure, either 'the cock on the dunghill or the two mice under the straw'. The priests suggested that the cockerel would be most appropriate and it was instantly torn into pieces by the ghost: one can only imagine the state of mind of the two 'mice' watching from under their hiding place! The spirit was then ceremonially staked to the bottom of the farm pond and was never seen again.

Another tale from the village records how sometime before 1820 one cottage was plagued by the troublesome attentions of a poltergeist, which would throw gravel into the bedrooms at night, cause the family bible to leap off its shelf and candles to either go out or, more worryingly, explode with a blue flash. Many observers confirmed that these manifestations were genuine and eventually two brave men, Job Lowsley and Thomas Humphrey, decided to investigate the phenomena and offered to stay overnight at the property to see if they could get to the bottom of the mystery. To make their vigil easier they stipulated that they must be alone in the house but, somewhat to their surprise, the owners of the cottage were uneasy at this, saying that although the ghost had never made any attempt to harm them they could not guarantee the same would apply to the intrepid pair. The would-be Ghostbusters were adamant, however, and eventually got their way, shuffling the family out to stay with friends while they settled down for a long night in the haunted house.

As it turned out, their night was uneventful to the point of being dull, but it did at least give them the chance to make a thorough examination of the property and this turned out to be the key to the mysterious phenomena that had been reported. Far from any infestation of ghosts they discovered loose floorboards under the matting in the bedroom, which would allow a person standing on a table downstairs to throw gravel into the bedroom unseen. Furthermore, they noticed that the wall behind the shelf which supported the Bible was pierced by small wooden pegs which, when knocked from the other side of the partition,

would cause the Bible to seemingly jump off the shelf. Their suspicions now fully vindicated, they looked closely at the candles and found that some had been cut open and filled with gunpowder!

The reason for all these shenanigans? The family believed that landlord was planning to raise the rent and they wanted to make it unlikely he would find another tenant in the event they threatened to leave. Amazingly, there are numerous contemporary examples of tenants using identical tactics today to 'persuade' the local authority or landlord to rehouse them. Plus ça change?

And now, the sad tale of one Felix Maggs, a farmer who lived at Fulscot Farm and who, one fateful day in 1894, decided to consult with the local wise woman to enquire as to what the future might hold. She informed him that she had seen a vision of him being 'struck down by a great black horse' and that he should stay alert and try to avoid his fate. We can be fairly sure that Maggs took great care to avoid horses from that point onwards but alas the warning, as is so often the case, turned out to be more metaphorical than exact: in 1909, possibly while on the lookout for runaway horses, he stepped onto the railway line just outside the village and was killed by a train. Irony... It is also a valuable lesson on the subtleties of soothsayers and the perils of prophecies.

Aston Tirrold

It is not often that a small village plays a pivotal role in the creation of a rock album but, thanks to one particular cottage, Aston Tirrold can lay claim to exactly that. In the year 1967 musicians Steve Winwood, Chris Wood, Jim Capaldi and Dave Mason met in Birmingham and, finding that they had much in common musically, decamped to the Gamekeeper's Cottage in the village to play, write and put together an album. (For those unacquainted with 1960s music, Traffic, as they became known, eventually produced seven studio albums over the next few years, albeit with some changes in band members.)

The interesting thing about the cottage was that it turned out to have a resident ghost, as evinced by footsteps proceeding (always in one direction) along the upstairs landing and small objects going missing or being moved about the property. In the creative atmosphere (the cottage was visited by a number of musical luminaries from the period including Eric Clapton and Pete Townsend) stories to explain the haunting blossomed, the most memorable of which attributed the haunting to a young student who had hanged himself by the cottage well; indeed some visitors reported being able to hear the anguished howls of the suicide victim's dog! One of the group's songs entitled 'Mr Fantasy' was supposedly written about the ghost and another, 'House for Everyone', was certainly a homage to the cottage itself. One of Traffic's live bootleg albums is another tribute to the band's time at Aston Tirrold: it is called *A Group, a Dog, a Ghost*.

As a final piece of music trivia, it is worth noting that another group just starting out at around the time Traffic was formed were dismayed when they heard the name chosen by these established musicians, so much so in fact that they decided that their own band name – Traffic Jam – was just too similar and needed to be changed. The name they eventually settled upon was Status Quo.

Musical goings-on at the cottage notwithstanding, there are other phenomena to be found in the village, most notably a silent phantom coach and horses that can be glimpsed on the Turnpike Road (or, in an alternative version of the story, heard but never seen). It is also said that Thorpe Farm has a peculiar haunting in that the ghost, a little old lady who is said to come and sit by the fire, is only visible to members of the Slade family who have owned the property since 1521.

Grim's Ditch

No-one is entirely sure why Grim's Ditch (alternatively, Grim's Bank) was constructed but, given that its maximum height from ditch to mound is 6 ft (1.8 m), it can hardly have been used as a major defensive fortification, especially since it may never have been one continuous earthwork. Since a number of parish boundaries follow the line of the structure, it probably pre-dates such relatively recent administrative constructs and may well indicate that the original purpose of the ditch was also as some kind of older boundary marker. Although estimates vary it is likely that it was constructed in the late Iron Age period. There are various disconnected parts of this earthwork along the line of the Downs, the main sections being near Aston Upthorpe and Blewbury (where it is also known as Dragon's Ridge),[5] Ardington and Hendred.

In legend the ancient earthwork was supposed to have been created by the Devil (possibly with the assistance of two demons) in a single night and the Scutchamer Knob barrow is what remained after the Devil had scraped the mud from his satanic spade. In another story the Devil created Grim's Ditch by ploughing along the Ridgeway, although what he intended to plant is not stated. Hellebores perhaps.[6] It was also said that Grim's Ditch was made by the Romans, served no purpose at all, and that it went all the way to Wales.

Given the pervasive Anglo-Saxon influence in the vicinity it is possible that the construction also has associations with the Norse god Odin/Woden, since one of his many aliases was Grimir. One plausible suggestion is that Christian missionaries

---

[5] Possibly an association with the St Michael Line – see Ley of the Land later.

[6] There is an increasingly rare local wildflower called the White Helleborine (actually an orchid) which can be found in Frying Pan Wood near Blewbury. Coincidence?

linked the name Grimir with the Devil in order to, quite literally, demonise the earlier gods worshipped in the area. The name Grimir sometimes also meant a masked person or one who concealed his identity, which may well relate to the unknown provenance of the Ditch.

Cholsey

Finding the pagan Saxons of the seventh-century Thames Valley in need of conversion, the Frankish missionary St Birinus came calling at the court of King Cynegils at Cholsey and petitioned to be allowed to preach to the local people with a view to saving their souls. Unwilling to anger his neighbouring Christian kings, especially the expansion-minded Mercians, Cynegils realised that allowing the Saint his day would be the most politic action and so gave his permission. The wily king, however, decided that the best location for Birinus to preach would be Churn Knob near Blewbury; admittedly a natural platform but, additionally, a reminder to all the listeners of their pagan roots and culture.

Despite the location, Birinus's rhetoric carried the day and a number of his listeners were converted on the spot: Cynegils was not himself sufficiently convinced to join the Christian communion at that time, though he was eventually baptised a few years later. Of course, the reasons for his eventual conversion owed far more to politics than faith since one of his attempts to fight off the Mercian threat involved forming an alliance with the pre-eminent monarch of the time, King Oswald of Northumbria. Oswald vehemently declared that he could not enter into a treaty with a heathen and so Cynegils not only converted on the spot but also packed his daughter off to be married to the Northumbrian king. In gratitude for his assistance in cementing this alliance, the king allowed St Birinus to build an abbey across the river at Dorchester. On the way to examine the site so many courtiers expressed an interest in joining the new faith-of-choice in the kingdom that Birinus stopped off at the village of Brightwell (now -cum-Sotwell) and performed an impromptu mass baptism in the nearest stream.

Cholsey is haunted by a number of ghosts from various periods of history. On Station Road several witnesses have reported seeing a man wearing shoes with prominent buckles (a sartorial detail that does little to help with dating the figure) and a poltergeist once plagued the attic of a now-demolished cottage in the 1930s with assorted banging noises and other nuisances. Once the family summoned up the courage to beard the poltergeist in its lair by breaking into the attic,  they discovered a pair of reading glasses and some official-looking paperwork, possibly legal documents of some kind. Unfortunately, since none of the family could read, they simply destroyed the papers, after which the haunting ceased.

A lady by the name of Miss Walters who lived in another Cholsey cottage in the early years of the twentieth century was not so lucky with her poltergeist. At first it was content to simply throw stones at her front door like some kind of deceased delinquent but it later progressed to major disruptions such as hurling the table and chairs around the kitchen. This seems to have been something of an intermittent haunting since the disturbances would stop for months or even years at a time, before suddenly starting up again for no apparent reason. One wonders how she managed to put up with such an inconsiderate phantom: perhaps she didn't for this cottage is no longer extant – something which, unfortunately, makes any further investigation impossible.

One house that is still standing is Broadlands, which was haunted by the ghost of a girl or young woman. The spirit was exorcised by the local vicar but sometimes just a trace of her presence has been noted by some particularly sensitive visitors.

The Great Western Railway passes Cholsey to the south and, as part of an agreement with local landowners, bridges were built across the new cuttings to allow farmers access to their newly partitioned land. One such bridge is known locally as Silly Bridge, the name deriving from the fact that shortly after its construction local enclosures removed any right of way across the railway, thus rendering it useless to most local people. However, Silly Bridge may have more than an odd name to recommend it, or so one local man discovered in the mid-1980s. On a warm December evening he was walking his dog in the hills above Cholsey and, as the sun had set, was in the process of returning home via the path across the bridge. Just as he was halfway across the structure began to vibrate and he heard the unmistakable sound of a steam engine passing underneath: heard but not saw, for despite the noise and slight shaking of the bridge no train could be seen, nor was there any sign of smoke or steam. A check with the stationmaster at Cholsey revealed that no steam engines had passed that way all day although the line did, and still does, play host to numerous pleasure trips hauled in the traditional steam-powered fashion. To add to the mystery the witness's collie dog subsequently started to display signs of agitation on approaching the crossing and would growl and stare at something unseen on the bridge itself. Whether the two events are connected is an open question, but it is clearly always worth keeping an ear open if you happen to be crossing Silly Bridge at sunset.

Before we leave the village, something for the record books: Cholsey Tithe Barn, erected in the fifteenth (some sources say thirteenth) century and often referred to as Cowper's Barn was, for a brief period, the largest aisled barn in Europe with a height of 51 ft (16 m) and a length of over 300 ft (91 m). A local man named John Lanesley was a thresher at the barn and documents record that, incredibly, he continued working there until he was 92. An inscription commemorated his work:

> In this barn John Lanesley threshed for Mr Joseph Hopkins 5 quarters, 7 bushels and a half of wheat in 13 hours on March 15 1747.[7]

Sadly, you cannot go to visit this outstanding piece of mediaeval architecture because it was demolished in 1815.

---

7   By my reckoning this equates to about 76 kg or 170 lbs.

Cursus, foiled again!

If you ask anyone to think about prehistoric monuments they will almost certainly call to mind Stonehenge, Avebury and, quite possibly, the Uffington White Horse, but most people are unaware that all these monuments sit surrounded by a landscape of other earthworks, often of earlier build, most of which are unknown outside of archaeological, er, circles. Stonehenge, for example, has a strange construction of roughly  parallel ditches almost 3 km long to the north of the main site, called, unsurprisingly, the Stonehenge Cursus, which is actually hundreds of years older than even the earliest phases of the main Stonehenge monument. The term *cursus*, coined by antiquarian William Stukeley in 1723, simply refers to the similarity between these objects and Roman chariot race-tracks.

As you might expect from an area steeped in prehistory, the Vale and surrounding areas can boast their own cursus monuments every bit as impressive as their Wiltshire cousins and there are in fact a whole series of these cursuses marching like giant's footsteps across the local landscape. Just over the River Thames, and therefore outside the self-imposed area covered by this volume, are the Dorchester, Benson and North and South Stoke Cursuses but, as we move westwards into the Vale, we encounter the two halves of the mysterious earthwork known as the Drayton Cursus.

The Drayton Cursus runs from the Mill Brook approximately north-east across the B4016 Drayton to Sutton Courtenay road for at least a mile – and possibly further though no-one has been able to definitively identify the far end. It consists of two ditches approximately 75 m apart, joined at the south but, as far as anyone can tell, open at the northern end and, curiously, is aligned to point directly towards Abingdon Abbey, although whether this is sheer coincidence or not is open to debate.[8] Because it is divided by the road (and the site of a much later Saxon village) the two halves tend to be referred to separately as the North and South Drayton Cursus and they may never actually have been physically joined, although they are generally assumed to be part of a single unit. The southern part was first discovered by a Major Allen in 1933 and the northern segment was spotted from crop marks some forty years later in the 1970s.

The cursus was excavated and extensively documented, first by E. T. Leeds, then by a team from the Abingdon Archaeological and Historical Society. Later followed work by the Oxford Archaeological Unit and another, more newsworthy, dig was undertaken in June 2009 by the Channel 4 programme *Time Team*. As a result of these investigations, radiocarbon dating indicated that it had been constructed somewhere between 3635 and 3385 BC, which fixes its construction towards the end of the Neolithic period. For comparison, Stonehenge is thought to have been built starting in 3,000 BC, meaning that the Drayton Cursus is considerably older than Britain's most famous ancient monument!

There is another possible cursus within the town of Abingdon itself just to the side of Caldecott Road but, as you might expect, the development of the town has completely obscured any evidence that might help determine whether this is a genuine site or not. If this is a bona fide cursus it would be interesting to know if it was also aligned towards the site of the present abbey. Other disputed examples of similar structures can be found at Charney Bassett and Buckland, although the latter has most recently been redefined as a *mortuary enclosure*. Less contentious is the cursus at Buscot Wick, which nestles between the River Cole and the Thames and is aligned with the open end pointing south-east, though not towards any significant landmark. Moving further north and leaving the Vale behind there is another confirmed cursus at Lechlade and a smattering of other possible candidates at Ducklington, North Cerney and even East Adderbury near Banbury.

---

8   This isn't as surprising as it sounds considering that many churches are built over pre-Christian sites, in which case the cursus is actually aligned towards whatever existed before the abbey was built.

No-one is entirely sure why cursuses were built and what they were actually used for, in fact some archaeologists have proposed that the act of constructing the earthwork might have been more important than the finished monument itself. Another suggestion is that they were used as proving grounds of some sort, possibly as part of initiations or some such (so Stukeley may not have been far wrong when he compared them to racecourses), but probably the most likely option is that they served a ritual purpose as procession-ways at particular times of the year.

Most cursuses are not especially straight so they may not really have been built to align with any particular point at all; the NNE–SSW direction of the Drayton Cursus means that it cannot have been pointing towards any sunset or sunrise points, even at mid-summer or mid-winter, so the direction of any possible alignment (if there is one) must have been either a star-rise or set or towards something on the horizon which has disappeared today. Equally perplexing are the gaps in the ditches that make up the outline of these puzzling constructions. Some are paired as if to indicate that a path crossed the outline but others seem to be placed randomly at points along the sides. Curiouser and curiouser.

So, to summarise our knowledge of these enigmatic constructions: we know where some of the cursuses are (doubtless many more have been lost forever), and when they were dug out of the ground, but we do not know who built them or, more critically, what they were for. Just some more mysteries to add to the list the Vale has to offer.

Wittenham Clumps

Rising above the landscape to the east of the Vale are the twin summits of Wittenham Clumps. Technically, the term *Clumps* only refers to the wooded summits, the hills themselves being known more properly as the Sinodun Hills, the name deriving from the Celtic *Seno-Dunum* meaning 'old fort'. Certainly there is an Iron Age hillfort atop Castle Hill (its partner is known as Round Hill) and this was built over the remains of an even earlier Bronze Age fortification, but an alternative suggestion for the source of the name suggests that it may be a pun on the Latin *sinus*, meaning breasts. An alternative local name for the Clumps might support this theory; prior to county boundary changes the name Berkshire Bubs was both geographically correct and suggestively accurate. Continuing with the rather dubious symbolism is the amusing alternative of Mother Dunch's Buttocks, a name which refers to a lady of the Dunch family who owned Little Wittenham Manor in the seventeenth century. Just to add to the confusion of names, the pair were in the past often called the Dorchester Clumps and I have seen the individual hills referred to as Sinodun and Harp hills – the latter alternatively as the Welsh Harp, from its similarity to the instrument from a certain angle. Just to extend this discussion of idiosyncratic local place-names, down beside the river below the Clumps is a small landing place formerly, and somewhat mysteriously, known as the Devil's Steps. Perhaps this is to stand in contrast to the healing spring called St Anthony's Well, which emerges nearby.

The Clumps are thought to be home to the oldest stand of beech trees in the country and the larger circle is sometimes known as the Cuckoo Pen (see p.9), another reference to attempts to trap cuckoos and prolong the summer.

The artist Paul Nash spent much of his life drawing and painting the Clumps and local maltster and poet Joseph Tubb (whose twin careers may well explain what follows) spent two summers in 1844 and 1845 carving a twenty-line poem into the bark of one tree on Castle Hill. Sadly the poem is scarcely legible today, but a plaque nearby commemorates the event and displays the text from his original carving.

> As up the hill with labr'ing steps we tread
> Where the twin Clumps their sheltering branches spread
> The summit gain'd at ease reclining lay
> And all around the wide spread scene survey
> Point out each object and instructive tell
> The various changes that the land befell
> Where the low bank the country wide surrounds
> That ancient earthwork form'd old Mercia's bounds
> In misty distance see the barrow heave
> There lies forgotten lonely Cwichelm's grave.
> Around this hill the ruthless Danes intrenched
> And these fair plains with gory slaughter drench'd
> While at our feet where stands that stately tower
> In days gone by up rose the Roman power
> And yonder, there where Thames smooth waters glide
> In later days appeared monastic pride.
> Within that field where lies the grazing herd
> Huge walls were found, some coffins disinter'd
> Such is the course of time, the wreck which fate
> And awful doom award the earthly great.

I could almost use these lines as a trailer for stories to be found in this book: the ancient earthwork refers to Grim's Ditch, and Cwichelm's grave, better known as Scutchamer Knob, is a site we will be visiting later. Note how Tubb refers to the excavations which were even then taking place and which have been on-going ever since.

Not all of the aforementioned digging at the Clumps has been officially sanctioned. There is a story of a local man who, on hearing tales of buried treasure in the unsubtly named Money Pit, decided to do a little excavation of his own and spent many hours digging a deep hole, hoping to find gold, gems or other valuable items. To his delight he uncovered a large iron-bound chest and was about to attempt to break it open when a raven alighted nearby and croaked 'he is not yet born!' Understanding this utterance to mean that he was not the person destined to benefit from the buried hoard he promptly reburied the chest and went home!

Long Wittenham

The house now called The Manor in the High Street in Long Wittenham, formerly Willington's Farm, dates back to the late sixteenth century but there has been a building at the same location for very much longer and, in earlier times, the ubiquitous Abingdon Abbey had a rest house on the site until it was claimed by the Steward to the Abbey and given to his daughter Beatrice de Braose in 1295. Does the lady still retain an interest in the property over seven hundred years later? An encounter early last century might suggest so.

Henry Hewett who owned the manor at that time awoke one night in September 1919 to find his bedroom bathed in moonlight. While he was entranced by the beauty of the night-time scene he was equally taken by the loveliness of the strangely-glowing female figure who suddenly, and unexpectedly, appeared walking past his bed towards the door. The figure was garbed in a grey dress in the style of the thirteenth or fourteenth century and had brown wavy hair, but the most noticeable thing about her was the look of extreme sadness on her face and the way her hands were clasped tightly together as if in deep sorrow. Well, perhaps not the single most noticeable thing, because when the apparition reached the door she disdained to open it and walked right through without even slowing down. So was this enigmatic sorrowful lady Beatrice or some other past inhabitant of the manor? The description of her clothes would indicate that the period would fit correctly but what could have caused her such distress that she should revisit the house after all these years? Perhaps only another visit will tell.

Outside the manor there are ghosts as well, and far more terrifying ones at that. Take for example the ghostly coach drawn past the house at breakneck speed by four spectral horses – it is said that anyone unlucky enough to see this frightening apparition late at night should hastily cover their ears for to hear the sounds of its passing is an omen of certain death. An unknown apparition also haunts the nearby fishponds; unknown because local people were too terrified to approach closely enough to even identify its gender. It was supposedly laid to rest in the ponds by eleven priests in the eighteenth century, a story almost identical to one we encountered earlier at South Moreton. Is this an example of a single incident being displaced to a new location or is it possible that there was there a coven of clerics roaming the area and banishing the undead around two hundred years ago? I know which *I* think is more likely but you are free to make your own mind up on the matter.

In the second decade of the nineteenth century one of the thatched cottages in the village gained a reputation for being haunted due to the rapping sounds which could sometimes be heard in the building. Fearing the worst, the owner, an elderly lady by the name of Mrs Wernham, arranged for a priest to come and perform an exorcism on the building to cleanse it of any possible evil influences. After the ceremony she was doubtless much relieved though as it turned out she need not have worried, since her niece, who was living at the cottage with the old lady, eventually admitted that she had been making the noises herself by knocking her elbow against hollow brickwork by the chimney.

Unfortunately not all the ghost stories associated with this beautiful and historic village can be placed in the comfortably distant past and one dating back just a few decades to the beginning of the Swinging Sixties caused severe disruption to the lives of a local shop manager and his staff. The month was November and the year was 1962.

Like many such rural areas, Long Wittenham could once boast a range of local businesses from blacksmiths and carpenters to Post Offices and village stores, each of which contributed directly to the local economy and gave a sense of community to the villagers. Of central importance was the village store, in this case the local Co-operative Society managed by Mr Derek Bird, a careful and conscientious man who was described by his staff as logical and level-headed. Mr Bird had worked late one Monday night arranging a display in the window, locked up the shop at around 7 pm and gone home for some tea. Being, as we have already noted, a conscientious man, he had later returned to the premises to undertake some repairs on the decorative lights surrounding the store window. To his surprise on his return that evening he found that the lights were ablaze but, assuming that he had simply forgotten to switch them off before leaving, or that he had somehow knocked the light switch as he passed, he worked on the decorations and went back home for the night. Had he suspected that this was to be the start of a couple of highly disturbing weeks he may well have decided to take a holiday, but the delights of hindsight were at that point unavailable to him and he doubtless slept soundly.

The following night, Mr Bird, this time accompanied by his wife, was once again working late in the shop when they both sensed 'a gush of nothing' come out from behind the counter and move across the shop floor. Although they both simultaneously sensed this presence, neither actually saw anything out of the ordinary. Then at 9.15 pm the decorative fairy lights suddenly went out. Rather unsettled the couple decided that they had worked *quite long enough thank you* and went home.

Next morning when he opened the shop Mr Bird and an assistant, Mrs Joyce Stanier, who also lived in the village, found two boxes of breakfast oatmeal cereal neatly stacked neatly in front of the storeroom door: needless to say they had not been there when Mr and Mrs Bird had left the previous evening. As they glanced around they noticed other oddities: three further cereal boxes had been piled in front of the cleaning materials counter and a number of tins of bicarbonate of soda were scattered on a window sill near the section of the shop selling children's books.

That evening a mystified Mr Bird gathered his whole staff together at 9 pm to try and solve the mystery before things got out of hand. At 9.10 pm they switched off all the lights except for the window decorations and retired to the back room to wait. Sure enough, as had happened on Monday, the fairy lights went out at 9.15 pm exactly, except that in this case Mr Bird sternly told them to come back on at once – and they did! Then, as they all stood outside the empty store to lock up, the staff heard distinct noises of movement from inside. No-one went to investigate; even to the sceptical Mr Bird it was obvious that someone or something was playing tricks in the Co-op that night.

The following day was Thursday and it seems to have been a rather strained day at work, with more minor poltergeist effects being noticed, most notably a customer order book being repeatedly moved by an unseen hand, in one case in full view of witnesses. Mrs Stanier commented that by that point she had begun to think she was going mad and, in the interests of staff sanity, the shop closed early to give everyone a break. Apparently Mrs Stanier went off to bingo to calm her nerves and doubtless the other staff members relaxed as best they could until the evening, when everyone assembled once again at the front door. As the nervous staff entered the shop everything seemed normal and the relief must have been palpable – until they noticed two cereal boxes placed neatly by the storeroom door... They bravely repeated the experiment of the previous night and were rewarded by the sight of a decorative star above the sweet counter swinging wildly when the lights went back on.

At this point, after almost a week of unexplained phenomena, Mr Bird decided that he had had enough and called his regional head office in Oxford. The Area Grocery Manager, Mr Styles, came with a group of security guards who checked locks and windows but could find no way that anyone could have gained entry into the building from outside. An electrician examined the wiring but could find no reason for the strange behaviour of the lighting and a photographer had no luck in capturing the ghost on film.

Doubtless the weekend came as a welcome break for Mr Bird and his team. 'I don't know what is happening' he said, 'we are not hysterical but the co-incidences are uncanny'. Mrs Stanier had clearly reached her limits: 'If it is a practical joker at work then he is a despicable coward but I don't see how it can be. There are so many things happening for which there is no logical explanation. I don't know how I will carry on if it does not stop.'

However, she did think she might have an explanation for what was happening and related a folk-tale from the village of an old lady who could be seen walking from one of the houses, past the back of the store and into the church. Recent roadworks had disturbed part of her usual route and Mrs Stanier thought that the old lady might have been making a detour through the shop and causing mischief as she passed. In any case, in a final desperate attempt to confront the ghost, Mr Bird and Mrs Stanier returned to the shop on the Saturday evening and challenged the ghost to break a cuckoo clock that was hanging on the wall behind the counter. When nothing happened they smiled to themselves in a relieved kind of way and went home.

On Monday morning the clock was found shattered in pieces on the floor. Despite this setback business carried on as usual, but when Mrs Stanier's 15-year-old daughter Adrienne was startled by shuffling footsteps behind her and fainted on the spot, it was clear that things could not go on as they were. Consequently the shop was closed early and the local vicar, the Rev. Roberts, arrived to perform a short exorcism. He spoke briefly for ten minutes and, just as he was finishing the final prayer from the service, there was a flash of blue smoke from one of the newly fitted florescent lights. 'I should call your electricians; that is definitely an electrical fault' commented the vicar, dryly.

After the ceremony Derek Bird went on record as saying he considered the matter closed and that it was 'business as usual' from now on. His superiors at head office evidently thought the same as he was ordered not to speak to the press again, although he did say that he considered that many of the effects he observed could well have been caused by electrical malfunctions in the old Co-op building.

And there the matter rested: the saga had made headlines for a week and was quickly forgotten. This was not the end of the story though. Adrienne, the young assistant who had fainted with shock on hearing the ghost, took two weeks off work to recover before resuming her daily duties. All went smoothly for almost a year and then she began to notice an old woman with white hair and a smiling expression appearing in the shop. After the old woman's third appearance Adrienne suddenly realised where she had seen the woman before, in a portrait of her great-grandmother hanging on a bedroom wall in her house. Any fear the girl had felt on seeing the apparition vanished. 'I know she wouldn't do me any harm,' she commented.

Sadly the story really does end there. The Co-op was closed in 1972, Mr Bird retired and Adrienne married and now lives in Australia. Of course her identification of the old woman does not explain the why, or more importantly the how, of what happened and so as usual we can only wonder as to the motive and method of this particular series of events. However not all is lost: while there are no longer road works in the village there is still the story of the old lady walking towards the church to invite our investigation. And perhaps next time the road is disturbed the old lady will take another route to her nightly service. Do feel free to call me if she does.

There is a final, even more recent, ghostly sighting from Long Wittenham, which happened in one of the older cottages in the village one night in 1981. According to the witness the head and shoulders of an elderly Victorian lady appeared in mid-air in the owner's bedroom but, as if to add an extra layer of oddness to the apparition, it was clear that this was a ghostly reflection because the image was bordered by an equally spectral oval wooden frame. The lady was wearing

> a very dark grey dress, with many pin-tucks leading from the neckline, which had a small stand-up collar with white frilling inside it... She had very straight dark hair, parted in the middle and scraped back, small alert grey eyes and a tight-pursed mouth. Her complexion was completely pale, with no colour in the cheeks.

It appears that the image in the ghostly mirror was equally aware of the witness because she turned her head to look directly outwards at her, but it seems as if neither party to the encounter was unnerved by the experience; in any case once the two women broke eye contact the ghostly mirror and its occupant vanished. Perhaps the mysterious Victorian lady subsequently went away to report the appearance of a strangely dressed woman appearing on the other side of *her* mirror.

Clifton Hampden

Clifton Hampden is the setting for one of the most romantic tragedies the Vale has to offer: the story of Sarah Fletcher. A number of writers have covered the story in detail, first and foremost Maude Ffoulkes in her book *True Ghost Stories*, but I will shamelessly plunder their research and summarise the details here.

In the year 1799, at the extensive Georgian house named Courtiers in Watery Lane, lived Sarah, twenty-nine years old and married to a dashing but dastardly naval officer. While she may have considered the marriage suitable, her husband, Captain Fletcher, clearly did not as he had secretly made plans to bigamously marry a local heiress, all the while pretending to his poor wife that he had been lost at sea.  Somehow Sarah was alerted to his scheme and arrived at the church just in time to stop the wedding; he returned to sea in a rage, she returned to Courtiers and hanged herself from the marital four-poster bed. Sarah was buried at Dorchester Abbey, something which would not normally be possible for a suicide but, as *Jackson's Oxford Journal* reported,

> the derangement of her mind appearing very evident, as well as from many other circumstances, the jury, without hesitation, found the verdict – Lunacy.

Half a century passed and eventually Courtiers was rented by the Crake family (at a suspiciously cut-price rate) and was converted into a boarding school; it was at this point that it became apparent that Sarah had not left her old home.

Mystifying footsteps were heard in the corridors, inexplicable cold spots appeared on the stairs, doors were slammed and a wardrobe was opened and closed in plain sight by an unseen hand. More eerily still, a teacher in the house reported that on one occasion the ghostly footsteps had been accompanied by a strange translucent cloud that seemed to mirror their passage. And then one night the mysterious presence made an appearance. Young Edward Crake, son of the headmaster and then aged about 17, awoke one night to the sound of footsteps approaching his room and watched in amazement as a beautiful young woman, dressed in a long black silken cloak and with a purple-red ribbon adorning her curly auburn hair, moved towards his bed. The apparition stood gazing down at Edward with tears in her eyes and then, suddenly, was gone. He saw her again on the anniversary of her death, 7 June 1864, and this time she seemed to see him as well because she smiled sadly in his direction and moved into another room. He followed her, begging her to stop and speak to him for he had somehow convinced himself that he had fallen in love with this forlorn figure, but when he stepped through the door he found that the room was empty: once more, Sarah had gone. After this incident the footsteps became heard less frequently and eventually ceased to bother the school at all.

Things remained quiet for over a decade, during which time Edward Crake moved away and became an ordained priest while his brother assumed the mantle of headmaster at Courtiers. However, at some point something clearly disturbed Sarah's rest and the footsteps began once again. Edward was called upon in his professional capacity and he attempted to perform an exorcism on the restless Sarah, but either he misspoke part of the ceremony or the spirit was simply irritated by the attempts to banish her because he singularly failed to do anything other than make things worse. Following his attempted intervention the supernatural activity grew progressively more active: terrible crashes were heard and door handles rattled themselves in the darkness; an empty room resounded to the sound of a terrifying scratching (as if iron talons were being drawn across the floor, according to one description); at one point witnesses heard the sound of a body being dragged up the stairs. Given that these phenomena coincided with an outbreak of an unidentified fever in the village, it is doubly understandable that the school relocated to a new home on the south coast shortly afterwards.

The building lay deserted for a while before being converted into a number of smaller apartments and it was during this period that Maude Ffoulkes, the journalist who first researched Sarah's tragic tale, saw her ghost herself during a visit to Courtiers, dressed in her trademark black. The story of Sarah Fletcher certainly doesn't end here though, as in 1968 a landscape gardener from Bournemouth reported being haunted by a silent shade who visited his bedside each night. While at first disturbed by this presence, he later underwent some sort of revelation and became convinced that his nocturnal visitor had been buried at Dorchester. After first visiting Dorchester in Dorset and finding nothing to support his intuitions he eventually came to Dorchester Abbey by the Thames, where he was able to visit her grave and identify the ghost as Sarah Fletcher. After this he seems to have viewed her as something of a guardian angel and ceased to be concerned by any occasional visits she made from that point onwards.

These days it seems that Sarah restricts her appearances to the village and her ghost has frequently been seen in the (less-than romantic) location of the car park at the Barley Mow Inn, not far from her old home. The figure reported by witnesses can only be Sarah taking a nocturnal stroll, as her description always tallies with that given by the young Edward Crake; that of a young woman dressed in a black cloak with a violet ribbon in her red hair.

Down from the Barley Mow, as the Thames meanders past Clifton Hampden, it encounters a strip of very hard sandstone, parts of which break the surface in a series of *aits* or little islands, making navigation particularly difficult and causing endless frustrations for the local ferrymen. As a consequence there is now an impressive brick-built six-arch bridge, which was designed by architect George Gilbert Scott Senior (better known for his designs for St Pancras Station and the Albert Memorial) and erected in 1864. Local folklore has it that Scott was dining one day with local landowner Henry Hucks Gibbs, who complained that many of his staff lived across the river in Long Wittenham and were therefore often late for work because of problems with the ferry. On hearing of his host's problems Scott whipped off his starched white shirt cuff and sketched out the plans for the new bridge across the river there and then.

The sandstone gravel riverbed makes the water hereabouts particularly clear and an ideal spot for fish to sun themselves in the shallows. Today the fish you can see in the Thames are very modest in size[9] but this was clearly not always so. Writing in *Athenae Oxonienses* in 1813, Anthony à Wood, as part of his notes of significant events in 1677, comments:

> About midsummer a sturgeon eight foot long was taken up at Clifton Ferry in [the County of] Oxon by some of the family of Dunch of Wittenham. Dr John Lamphire eat some of it and Hen. Price of the Blue Boar dressed it.

---

9   Notwithstanding the monstrous pike 'the size of a gatepost' and 'so large that no-one present had a wire long enough to slip over its head' which was landed at Bampton in the 1800s.

By my estimates a fish of this size would have weighed at least 125 kg (275 lbs), not a record breaker but certainly a spectacular and unusual catch and the nearest thing to a river monster that the Upper Thames has to offer. It probably also presented something of a challenge for the poor innkeeper tasked with preparing the beast.

The Barley Mow is not the only haunted pub in Clifton Hampden and, in a nice piece of coincidence, this story comes from an article in the *Oxford Mail* by a reporter also called Anthony Wood. The Plough has long been said to be haunted by the ghost of John Hampden, the cousin of Oliver Cromwell, who stayed at the inn during the time of the Commonwealth, in the room which now bears his name, though whether it was actually his restless spirit or that of another which disturbed the peace of the pub is a question that cannot be answered.

What is known is that landlady Mrs Helen Maund told Wood how she and her husband often felt that they were being watched as they worked alone behind the bar at the Plough but neither shared their experiences for fear that the other would laugh. When they finally discussed the matter it turned out that not only had they both felt unseen gazes but they had both sometimes also been nudged from behind even though no-one was ever close enough to have touched them. It was not just odd feelings either, since both of the Maunds had, on several occasions, noticed a weird blue glow coming from behind the door to the bar at night. Mr Maund also described how he had been working in the back kitchen one winter morning when he heard the door latch open and someone come into the bar; when he came out to find out what the visitor wanted the room was empty.

As in so many cases no-one was ever able to offer an explanation for these strange events and the Maunds were forced to accept that they would just have to live with some odd things happening around them. However, they were probably not expecting one final, and quite dramatic, incident which occurred one night after closing. As was their custom they liked to spend some quiet time after the regulars had left and on this particular evening they settled down beside the bar for a relaxing drink before bed. Mr Maund poured a small glass of whisky for his wife and placed it on the counter before turning back to the optics to pour one for himself but, the moment he did so, the full glass raised itself up into the air, turned itself upside-down and emptied itself all over the surface! I wonder what could possibly have upset the spirits that night...

Didcot

Didcot is generally thought of as little more than a modern commuter town, but there has actually been a settlement in the locality since the Iron Age. The name of the town in Saxon times was Wibaldeston, the name Didcot (Dudcotte to be precise, Dudda being the father of St Frideswyde), not being recorded until around 1200. In the grounds of All Saints Church stands a venerable yew tree which is said to be among the oldest in the country, having survived more than 1200 years of uneventful growth followed by a spate of recent arson attacks. It is notoriously difficult to date yew trees but if this age is correct then the churchyard specimen may well have been planted before the birth of King Alfred. Yew trees are often associated with churches because of their legendary link to eternal life and renewal but there are also pragmatic reasons for their appearance: a statute from the time of Edward I stated that yew trees were to be planted in churchyards to protect the church from high winds. Staves from the tree were also used for longbows and, more prosaically, to create fences around the churchyard to keep out straying cattle.

The footpath leading from the town to nearby Sutton Courtenay is cheerfully known as Corpse Lane; perhaps this is connected with local legends telling of human sacrifices taking place on a burial mound to the west of the town.

Notwithstanding the dominating presence of the power station cooling towers,[10] Didcot has, over the last hundred years anyway, been primarily a railway town and so it is fitting that the town has a railway ghost story, albeit a rather sad one. This tale dates back to the 1950s and relates to a certain Mr Crossley who lived in a small house in Long Lane. One

---

10 Three remain at time of writing.

night, sometime around midnight, he was restless and unable to sleep and while lying awake in his bed he suddenly heard a regular clanging noise coming in through his open window from the street below. After a while the sound stopped, only to start a short time later even louder than before. Mr Crossley got out of bed and looked out of his window to see a small boy dressed in old-fashioned clothes standing by his front door. Hurrying downstairs he opened the door to discover… no-one.

Returning to bed, he eventually fell asleep only to be wakened by the same sound as before. It was now 3 am and, perhaps anticipating what he might find, he moved downstairs at once and opened the front door just in time to see the strangely dressed boy gazing in his direction. Clearly this was no normal child (for one thing, Mr Crossley noticed that his face was slightly transparent) but before he had time to come to terms with this peculiar sight the boy turned away and made off towards the railway level crossing. Mr Crossley was suddenly aware that an old-style steam train was approaching the crossing and that the gates were open. To his horror the boy stepped in front of the train but, before he was forced to witness a terrible tragedy, both boy and train simply disappeared. Mr Crossley ventured out to the crossing to investigate the mysteriously vanishing accident: the gates were closed and nothing was in sight on the line.

I am entirely unsure what to make of this story. As far as I have been able to discover there are no recorded incidents of children being killed on level crossings near Didcot (though, given the possible era of the mystery child, perhaps this isn't surprising) but, more relevantly, I can find no record of a street called Long Lane in the town. Street names do change over time, of course, and Didcot has been extensively redeveloped over the years so this is hardly a major flaw in the account, but it would help to locate the scene of this incident. Still, the uncertainty of the setting only serves to heighten the mystery of the tale.

Didcot has more than just railway stories to share and the events which took place in the PetFare shop in the High Street back in 1984 show some startling similarities with the Long Wittenham case of two decades earlier. It all started when two shop assistants, Michael McGibbon and Trevor Read, were startled to hear a female voice calling out their names when there was no-one else in the building. Thinking that this was just a practical joke, they were puzzled but hardly worried, although when the voice was succeeded by ghostly footsteps from the upstairs storeroom that were loud enough to shake the whole building it was clear that something very unusual was happening to say the least. To add to the strangeness the sound of someone sawing wood was also heard coming from the rear of the shop, though there was never any sign of the unknown carpenter when they went to investigate.

PetFare owner, Mrs Ira Wright, took a sceptical view of these strange events until she was working late one night and heard the footsteps walking across the upstairs part of the empty premises herself. At first she was sure that an intruder had broken into the shop and she crept cautiously upstairs to investigate, finding nothing but echoes. Still unwilling to acknowledge that anything paranormal could be happening, Mrs Wright called in the police to investigate (a fairly common first response to unidentified footsteps in a building) but, despite a meticulous search, they could find no sign of forced entry, nor was anything missing.

Perhaps whatever had decided to move into PetFare took offence at the police visit, or perhaps it was a logical next step in the haunting; in any event things began to heat up. Firstly, items began to turn up on the wrong shelves or even in the middle of the floor and later the contents of bins of dried pet food was found scattered around the room. In a more sinister development Mrs Wright arrived at work one morning to find that the aquaria had all been drained and the fish left dying in dry tanks, even though there was no sign of the missing water and the floors were completely dry. On another occasion she arrived to discover that all the animal cages had been opened and the shop was overrun with newly liberated gerbils and other small animals.

Fearing that something worse was on the way, Mrs Wright contacted local medium Katrina Rivers who came to spend a night at PetFare in an attempt to contact whatever entity had moved in. Perversely, the night when Mrs Rivers stayed at PetFare nothing out of the ordinary happened at all, which was doubtless deeply frustrating for all parties but at least led to a slight hiatus in the problems that had been plaguing the staff and a considerable improvement in the beleaguered atmosphere in the shop.

Perhaps Mrs Rivers' day job as the local traffic warden was of some help in moving the troublesome poltergeist along; unfortunately traffic wardens have no powers of arrest and, sure enough, although it had relocated itself for a while, the mischievous spirit eventually returned. Faced with more footsteps and more dead fish, Mrs Wright contacted the local vicar, the Rev. Ian Randall, who agreed to come and offer what assistance he could, although he drew the line at performing a full exorcism. On the day of his visit he actually performed a simple blessing ceremony and, as if by magic, the phenomena ceased and never returned – an abrupt end to a mystifying and disturbing couple of weeks for the PetFare team.

East and West Hagbourne

Here is a lovely piece of local folklore, almost gossip really, from the early nineteenth century. At that time in Hagbourne there lived a local character called Robert Appleford, a pig dealer who was widely known in the local accent and dialect as Bob Applevord. In a wonderful example of early public relations he let it be known that he would present his marvellous prize pig free, gratis and for nothing, to any man who could prove that he *always strictly minded his own business*. At first a few hopefuls came forward to claim the pig but Appleford always knew of a time that they had interfered in someone else's business and so they were denied the prize.

There was, however, a highly taciturn individual living in Didcot at the time and his neighbours (who presumably did most of the talking) persuaded him that he was the ideal man to take ownership of the prized animal, so he decided to pay a visit to Appleford's pig-yard to state his case. You will have to work through the transliteration as it sounds so much better in the original.

'I be the man as minds my own business,' began the Didcot claimant, 'an' be come vor that ther pig.'

Bob Appleford looked at him appraisingly and, clearly unable to dismiss his claim out of hand, said, 'Well, I be glad to zee 'e then. Come an' look at 'un.'

The two men went over to the sty in which the pig was kept. Appleford stroked it and remarked, "E be a fine 'un jus' as I zed, be'ant' 'e?'

'Eese a rayly be,' answered the visitor. 'Zurely a remarkable vine pig. Might I ax 'e what 'e have fed un on?'

Doubtless a small glint shone in Appleford's eye as he answered, 'That be my business an' not yours – good marnin' to you!'

No-one ever tried to claim the pig after that and for many years anyone displaying an unhealthy interest is the affairs of another was likely to be told 'Yo'rl never get Bob Applevords pig!'

If the prospect, or more likely not, of a free pig fails to excite there are still a couple of ghosts to be found in the Hagbournes. The first is a dramatic headless horseman who has been observed riding through East Hagbourne on New Year's Eve. There is no accepted explanation for this decapitated apparition but some suggest that it may date from the time of the Civil War when some 6,000 horses were quartered in the area by the Parliamentary forces. Others, however, hold that the haunting was caused by the opening of a burial mound in 1803 that was found to contain the body of a local chieftain along with his horse and chariot.

Local celebrity Thomas Phillips, who was royal carpenter to Kings George I & II, died in 1736 and was buried in the village churchyard. Local rumour has it that if you run around his grave four times at midnight a ring of ghosts will appear, holding hands and dancing around the church. If there was ever a haunting worth making the effort to reproduce, that would certainly be very high on my list.

Paws for thought

What is the largest wild animal one could reasonably expect to encounter when out and about in the Vale? Foxes perhaps, or maybe a badger. Possibly a deer, especially in the wooded parts of the area, but nothing more exotic, not to mention frightening, surely? Well, a surprisingly large number of people have actually reported encounters with animals no-one could reasonably expect to see in our leafy countryside.

Take the case of anglers Peter Jones and Nigel Meehan who were on a fishing trip to Oday Hill Lake near Abingdon back in May 1998. Mr Meehan told the *Oxford Mail*:

> We were walking along beside the lake when we heard a noise but we couldn't see anything. I was cracking jokes, like 'This is like something out of a B movie – any minute now it's going to jump out and get us'. There was a tree overhanging the water and we could see something. We thought it was someone's teddy bear because we could see a head with two little round ears. Then it turned its head and licked its paw – it was like a large, black cat. We didn't hang around, we ran.

Large, unidentified paw prints were found by the lake on Sunday afternoon – and a lot of feathers where there had once been a family of geese. To quote one of the men, 'they had obviously been lunch for something.'

Large cats had been reported around the country before this incident made the news but, apart from one possible sighting around the Downs to the south of Wantage in the 1960s and a series of brief sightings of a seven-foot long black cat near Culham in 1997, this is the first detailed report from the Vale.

A couple of years later, in May 2000, reports had moved south-west to the village of Westcot, where a cat 'the size of a Doberman dog' was seen repeatedly over a period of weeks.

A spokesman for the Lonsdale Estate, in Kingston Lisle, said they had heard a rumour about the cat but said that none of their gamekeepers had seen anything unusual. They could not confirm the sighting, nor had any of their game or livestock been killed in unusual circumstances. Thames Valley Police cautioned the public about approaching the big cat but noted that there was little that they could actually do apart from informing the wildlife liaison department, which holds full records of confirmed and possible sightings.

In March 2005, just to the north of the Vale, the Cotswold Wildlife Park offered a £5,000 reward for the capture of a cat dubbed the Beast of Burford. This followed numerous big-cat sightings and the discovery of a large feline paw print in countryside near the perimeter of RAF Brize Norton. The reward caught the interest of an ex-game warden from Tanzania who arrived with considerable publicity, expressing a desire to trap the animal (and who subsequently left with little fanfare after having singularly failed to do so).

I only mention this because in the very same month Stephen Thompson of Ickleton Road in Wantage discovered a decapitated goose in his back garden and publicly speculated as to whether another big cat might have been responsible. He may have been influenced by publicity from the Burford sightings or he might have been thinking back to an incident of his own in January, when he reported pulling into his driveway at about 6 pm and seeing an animal about 10 yards in front of him. The animal, which looked like a big black cat, then jumped over a four-foot fence and made off into the distance.

Mr Thompson was sure the animal was definitely not a deer or a dog, because the way it jumped was just like a cat – only larger of course. 'It looked like a panther to me,' he said. 'It gave me a shock. I have never seen anything like it.' Brushing the January sighting aside, Graham Scholey, conservation team leader for the Environment Agency in Wallingford, said it was most likely that the goose killing was the action of a domestic dog and that there was no reason to suggest there was a rogue predator at large in the area.

Whether the one or more big cats in the vicinity were impressed with this logic or not, sightings in the Vale continued. In the spring of 2006 a mysterious animal was spotted on an Abingdon housing estate prowling around the black bags which had been put out for the dustmen. Mrs Porter, who made the sighting, explained:

> I often wake up in the night and it was about two or three in the morning. I looked across the garage and saw what looked like a dog. Then I looked closer and it was definitely a cat.

Her husband confirmed that he had also seen the animal before:

> It was out in the front of the garages across the road. It certainly wasn't a domestic cat and wasn't a dog. We've had dogs and you can tell a dog from its silhouette and it had a longer tail than a dog. It was black and about the size of a springer spaniel.

Their house borders onto fields at the edge of the estate, which may explain the presence of the animal in such an urban setting.

Shortly afterwards in April, local researcher Brian James twice encountered large cats while driving; firstly near Blewbury and secondly not far away at Moulsford, after which he commented:

> A very obvious large feline leapt out of the hedgerow to the left of the road, bounded across the road in four to five bounds, then leapt off into the verge on the other side of the road. On both occasions the look of a big cat was obvious with the long s-shaped tail held out behind the dark brown and grey animal. The two sightings have been within 1 km of each other, so it is more than likely this was/is the same animal.

Some months later, one day in early October in fact, Mrs Jo Naylor of Carswell, near Faringdon, went to close her daughter's bedroom window and spotted a big cat-like creature skulking in fields near her house. 'When I first saw the animal I thought it was a big dog, but the tail was much longer and it looks like a big black cat,' she said. She watched the creature prowling around for about 15 minutes until she suddenly thought she ought to capture a photograph of the magnificent moggy. By the time she had found a camera the animal had moved closer and conditions seemed ideal, but when she actually went to take her picture, the camera flash frightened the beast, which promptly disappeared off into the woods leaving Mrs Naylor with nothing more than a grainy image of what she had seen. The next morning she and her husband went out to try to track down the animal and both of them saw what looked like a pair of the creatures in the distance. The couple also showed their picture to friends who told them that there had also been a recent big-cat sighting in Longworth.

Explanations for these black cat sightings vary from the supernatural to the mundane. When black cats were first reported in the Home Counties in the 1960s, some writers speculated that the Surrey Puma as it became known could have been teleported from foreign climes or even just miraculously appeared as if to magically fill an ecological niche. A more prosaic explanation posited that all these animals were escaped pets or zoo animals. Certainly the Dangerous Animals Act of 1972, which made it illegal to keep wild animals without the appropriate licences, may have led to some animals being released into the wild, but that would mean that these animals would have to have mated and produced a viable population to explain the continued sightings up to the present day. According to big cat experts, cross-species mating is quite possible for these animals (tigrons and ligers, crosses between lions and tigers, can be found in zoos around the world, after all) so this is not an entirely unlikely explanation.

A Freedom of Information request in 2007 revealed that Oxfordshire residents alone were keeping six lions, one jaguar and an undisclosed number of leopards as well as assorted bears, crocodiles and venomous snakes, so perhaps roaming big cats might actually be the least dangerous of all the possible escapees.[11]

And still the sightings kept coming. In 2008 a woman who had pulled

---

[11] If you need convincing of this then reflect on the major panic in the 1930s when three wolves escaped from Oxford Zoo. Two of the animals were quickly shot but one remained on the loose for several days and was responsible for the slaughter of much livestock before it too was killed.

over to the side of the road to use her mobile phone watched as a large cat strolled casually past and in July 2011 a large cat was photographed at Hill Farm near Steventon just after the Truck music festival (even though the Stray Cats did not play that year) and there was another sighting in the Faringdon area in 2014. Most recently a local radio station made much fuss of the Beast of Berkshire and a sighting was recorded in Steventon. A few years previously there had been also sightings in Wantage and West Hagbourne, with Rebecca Lowe from Abingdon reportedly seeing a big cat crossing the A34, near Lodge Hill. She commented:

> It was massive and I could tell it was a cat from the way it was walking.
> I was going to go back and check, but thought better of it.

Probably the best decision all round for anyone who might have a similar encounter in the future.

Surprising as they might be, big cats are by no means the most exotic animals to have been spotted around the Vale. A few years ago I was told by a friend, in deeply embarrassed tones, of the time she had glanced out of a train window as it pulled out of Didcot towards Reading and spotted a kangaroo beside the track. I now feel rather guilty at writing this off as a misperception because other people have encountered similar animals over the last few years and it seems as if Oxfordshire had a small, if transient, population of wallabies to call its own. For example, back in June 2002 a dead wallaby was found beside the M40 north of Oxford and in 2005 another was found beside the A34 to the south of the city. More locally Jon Taylor, a scientist at AERE Harwell, spotted a live wallaby hopping around in a nearby field in 2003, though whatever happened to it after that is anybody's guess.

All attempts to trace where these animals came from have so far been unsuccessful, but one police spokesman joked: 'We have carried out extensive inquiries to find relatives, but so far we are not doing very well.' There are a number of wildlife parks in the area and it can only be assumed that if there is a breeding population somewhere nearby then they are descended from escapees from one or more of these parks.

Certainly escapes of this kind are sometimes reported in the press, the latest at the time of writing was on the Black Isle in Scotland in 2011, so this idea is not totally implausible. Wallabies are shy and largely nocturnal so it is not surprising that, even if this is the case, sightings are rare.

Finding big cats and wallabies may be unlikely but badgers are a common sight in the more rural areas of the Vale, even if they are most often to be found lying at the side of a major road. The average weight of an adult male badger may be as much as 26 lbs (12 kg) so what are we to make of the specimen trapped north of Tubney in the nineteenth century, which weighed it at a massive 50 lbs (23 kg)? Badgers were believed to be able to live over a hundred years so the gamekeeper who caught it might not have considered this entirely unexpected in a very old animal, but he would probably have treated it with considerable caution given the prevalent local belief that a badger was able to puff out its skin making it so hard that it was impermeable to bites and invulnerable to weapons. The unfortunate chink in this natural amour-plating ability was that the nose remained vulnerable, so a blow to this unprotected area would be the only way to kill the animal. Whether this particularly magnificent specimen was dispatched in this manner is not recorded.

I am not sure how common it was to trap badgers, but a local saying from Milton must have made life very difficult for local grass snakes: 'Kill the first grass snake you see and you will kill all your enemies for the year'.

And now a brief excursion into the occasionally exciting world of that most iconic of our local farm animals – the sheep. The Vale and the

Downs above it are home to not inconsiderable numbers of these placid ruminants, whose lives generally run entirely without major incident. Of course, the word 'generally' invites exception and it is certainly true that sheep in the Vale do occasionally show signs of somewhat unusual behaviour.

Take for example the night of Saturday 3 November 1888, probably sometime around 8 pm, when flocks of sheep across a broad swathe of countryside between Faringdon and Henley-on-Thames seem to have been seized by an epidemic of mass panic, sufficient to cause them to break down the fences of their enclosures and flee into the surrounding fields: quite literally going on the lam. The wayward animals were found the following morning cowering in a state of terror under hedges and whatever other cover they could find. A correspondent to the *Oxford Journal* commented that 'the occurrence was far too universal to have been the work of any evil-disposed persons'. It was estimated that it would have taken over a thousand men acting simultaneously to release and chase away so many animals, not to mention the fact that holding pens had clearly been battered down from inside, so these hypothetical sheep-scarers would have had to perform their mischief from within the folds themselves. In fact, human agency seems even less likely when we consider a note in the *Sheffield Independent* newspaper a few days later, which extends the range of the panic from Wallingford to Twyford near Reading. According to this report the night of the 3rd was exceptionally dark but, significantly, was lit by occasional flashes of lightning. Could the passage of a particularly frightening storm along the Thames Valley have caused such widespread ovine over-reaction? The *Independent* didn't think this likely and proposed that an earth-tremor might have been responsible.

Symons's Meteorological Magazine reported that the panic had covered an area 25 miles long and eight miles wide, but when the case was investigated for the *Journal of the Royal Agricultural Society* by O. V. Aplin, he found that the phenomenon had actually extended all the way into Warwickshire and Gloucestershire. Aplin attributed the mass terror to the total darkness of the night of the 3rd; he theorised that sheep are usually able to perceive something of their surroundings even in what, to us, would seem total darkness, but on this occasion low cloud swept across the area totally blinding the animals and causing the ensuing frenzy, especially among those packed tightly into pens. This theory would appear to be corroborated by a witness describing 'an extraordinary black cloud travelling from north-west to south-east which appeared to be rolling along the ground'. Given the incredible geographical range of this evening of terror, it is not surprising that it later became known as the Great Sheep Panic.

Perhaps we shouldn't be surprised by this behaviour: after all, smaller scale incidents of this type are far from uncommon and the word 'panic' itself derives from the Greek god Pan who was said to take particular pleasure in spooking flocks of sheep and goats. There was, however, another, broadly similar and almost as widespread, incident mentioned not many years later by a correspondent to the *London Standard* who wrote that on the night of 4 December 1893 sheep across the county from Wantage to 'the borders of Oxfordshire' behaved exactly as had their antecedents five years earlier and hightailed it into the distance. There was no mysterious black cloud this time (although the possibility of an 'earth wave' was raised) but the writer also stated that he had been awakened by a bright light to the south and he suggested that the passage of a bright meteor may have been the cause of the incident on this occasion.[12]

Scared sheep, out-of-place pumas and wandering wallabies may be interesting but they are not especially supernatural, so let us finish this zoological roundup with something far more eerie. Back in the early 2000s a young woman called Jenny, a self-avowed pagan and mystic, was walking along the Ridgeway from Wayland's Smithy towards the White Horse Hill car park one early winter evening (after performing a meditative ceremony of some sort at the tomb) when she became aware of something following her:

---

12 For more on meteors over the Vale see Hatford and Baulking.

I suddenly realised that I had company in the form of a large dark shape behind me. It was a clear night with a full moon so there was enough light to see clearly, but whenever I turned to catch a glimpse of whatever it was behind me it always seemed to be in shadow. From the impressions I did get it seemed to me to be a large shaggy hound, at least as tall as my chest and very broad. I wasn't at all frightened as I knew that it was just a guardian spirit making sure I was safe on my trip back home. It didn't make a sound and when I reached the road [back to the car park] it either stayed on the Ridgeway or just vanished away.

This is a fascinating story. I make no assumptions about Jenny's state of mind after her 'meditation' at Wayland's Smithy but she has described a classic encounter with a guardian Black Dog which parallels similar stories from other parts of the country. Comparable dogs are known as Shuck in Norfolk, Barguest and Padfoot in the north of England, and even Hairy Jack in Lincolnshire, but I am unaware of any particularly notable local legends which might give Jenny's Ridgeway dog a local name. If some of the more frightening stories are to be believed then Jenny was lucky to encounter one of the more benign variants of the breed; some of its brethren have weirdly glowing red eyes or are entirely headless – even worse, Black Shuck is said to be a portent of imminent death.

There are rumours of a similar ghostly dog further to the east on the Icknield Way, so there may be some connection there, and a black dog is said to appear below the Ridgeway at Letcombe, although this is supposedly a normal-sized animal rather than the enormous creature Jenny described.

The location of Jenny's experience is especially interesting as there is said to be a golden coffin buried somewhere along the Ridgeway near Uffington. I have been unable to unearth many details of this intriguing story but many black dog apparitions are said to be guardians of hidden treasure so, if there is a kernel of truth behind this account, it might help explain why this particular dog was out haunting the Ridgeway that night.

Blewbury

Is superstition dead and gone in the Vale? I suspect not if an episode from 1996 is anything to go by. Blewbury Antiques, run by Sheila Richardson, was a small but thriving business in the village with a shop-front spilling iron implements, china and brassware out onto the pavement. Of course, such an environment is an invitation to some and one day in June a brass Buddha, which was hanging outside the shop and was said to have been placed there to ward off bad luck, disappeared. Mrs Richardson was understandably upset and hit upon a novel solution to encourage the return of her property: she spread a rumour that the figure was jinxed and would bring misfortune to whoever had taken it. Whether or not this had any genuine effect on the thief, a couple of months later the Buddha reappeared outside the shop.

Encouraged by the success of this ploy, Mrs Richardson, who it must be stressed never claimed to be any kind of witch, placed a mock protection curse on all the merchandise in her shop. Sometime later a valuable cast iron kettle was stolen but, as before, whoever had taken it was unable to resist the putative curse and abandoned the item on the Downs, where it was found by a dog-walker who realised that it could only have come from Blewbury Antiques and returned it to its rightful owner. Mrs Richardson was obviously delighted. 'I had joked about the jinx but when I got the kettle back I thought it was a bit strange.'

Which begs the question, was the curse effective enough to cause some misfortune to the crooks who had made off with Mrs Richardson's merchandise or did the simple thought of the supposed jinx prey on their minds until they returned their ill-gotten gains? Certainly it was not universally successful; a sundial that disappeared the same year was never returned. We can but hope that it, and the garden of whoever took it, have been shrouded in cloud ever since!

On a more conventional note, if conventional is entirely the right word to use when discussing a haunting, the New Inn in Blewbury suffered an outbreak of minor poltergeist activity in 1953 when landlord Charles Spriggs undertook a series of modifications to the structure of the building. The (by now familiar) disturbances, noises in the night, footsteps descending the stairs to the bar and small objects disappearing were blamed on a previous landlord, usually identified as 'Old Edwin',[13] objecting to the changes. The activity ceased after a medium was asked to perform a cleansing ceremony at the pub. Sadly the building is now a private house; one can only wonder what Old Edwin would have made of that.

Blewbury seems particularly prone to poltergeist phenomena. The sculptor Langford Jones once rented a house in the village and was plagued by similar problems, even to the extent that he described watching a washbasin fly across the room right in front of him. Needless to say he did not stay in the property any longer than he had to.

Now sadly no longer a hostelry, the Load of Mischief used to have a pub sign copied from the Hogarth painting *A Man Loaded With Mischief*, which featured a man carrying a monkey and with a bird perched on one shoulder. This would probably not have been too inconvenient but the poor gentleman was further weighed down by having to give a woman a piggyback while she cheerfully drank from a full glass of gin or wine. The sign was accompanied by the caption: 'A monkey, a magpie, and a wife, is the true emblem of strife'.

The first inn to use this motif was the Man Loaded with Mischief, Oxford Street, London, but there were subsequently a number of copy-cat taverns across the country; apart from Blewbury there was a also a similarly-themed Mischief Inn at Wallingford.

---

13 Edwin Fry, who ran the pub in the 1950s.

Blewbury landlords were clearly an interesting bunch and one of the more memorable was Malachi Grace, landlord of the Blewbury Inn during the 1860s. Malachi was not only the local landlord but also a carter, driving a cart to and from Newbury and, not infrequently, arriving back from his trips roaring drunk, for it was widely known that he was a man who liked a drink. One night he overdid his drinking to such an extent that he was forced to pull his cart over to the side of the road where he promptly passed out. Some time later a group of local lads came across him snoring contentedly away and decided that a practical joke would be in order. Consequently, they unhitched his horse and led it out of sight and then pushed the sleeping Grace and his cart into a nearby barn and hid themselves away in the hayloft. After some time Grace began to stir, sat up and looked around, and finally registered both his position and lack of horse. 'Be I Malachi Grace?' he is said to have asked rhetorically, 'Be I Malachi Grace? If I be I've lost a horse and if I 'baint I've found a cart!'

And yet another tale from the village, or on the Downs above it to be precise, where the Pasque Flower grows but only, it is said, where Saxon blood was spilled in times past. Up here on the Ridgeway sits Warren Farm and it is here, so the story goes, that an old shepherd used to see the ghost of his wife dancing around the garden in her nightgown. A subsequent search discovered that a blonde woman had been buried (with little regard for the legalities of the situation) in a home-dug grave at the bottom of the garden. There was no suggestion of foul play in her death, only in the manner of her interment. Could her shade have been protesting at her unchristian burial or was she simply posthumously partying at the place where her body lay?

Finally, to close the section, a gruesome little historical note. In or about the 1860s or 1870s the landlord of one of the hostelries in Blewbury (sadly, the name of exactly which one has been lost) fell under suspicion because a number of his guests had mysteriously disappeared after staying at his inn. Despite some investigations by the local constabulary, nothing was ever proven because the bodies of the missing persons could not be found and so the mystery remained unresolved. The landlord later left the inn, presumably due to an inevitable fall-off in trade because of his unsavoury reputation, and a new landlord moved in and business resumed. Some years later, probably around the year 1900, an old tree in the neighbourhood was blown down in a storm and the workmen who were clearing the wood away found to their horror that there was an adult skeleton nestled amongst the tangled roots. This discovery puzzled the village until one of the older residents remembered the long-departed landlord and also recalled that he had been particularly keen on planting trees around the neighbourhood. Why the police had not been told this at the time is a mystery, but it does raise the question of how many of the old trees around Blewbury might be sheltering a macabre secret...

Blewburton Hill

Blewburton Hill, just outside Blewbury, is topped by a small hillfort which has been reduced to a sorry state by many years of determined ploughing as if in an attempt to rid the area of an inconvenience – which, from the local farmers' point of view, I suppose it is, since unlike nearby Wittenham Clumps, it sits firmly in the middle of a working farm. During excavations on the hill the bones of an Iron Age dog were discovered. Described as a small mongrel, it may well have been used to hunt small prey or used as a rat catcher, much as terriers are used today.

The dog may not have returned as a phantom pooch but Blewburton Hill does have its own ghost, the spectre of a horseman who was struck by lightning while out riding and disappeared in a clap of thunder never to be seen again. In a replay of this event he may sometimes be seen on stormy nights galloping up the side of the hill, only to vanish again as the lightning flashes and the storm rumbles. Sadly, the identity and origins of this unknown rider are shrouded in mystery, as is any possible connection he may have to the mysterious lights which can sometimes be seen as long flashing trails both around the Hill and off towards Aston Tirrold.

Chilton

The Downs above the village of Chilton present a glorious panoramic view across the Thames Valley, including such modern sights as the research facilities of the Rutherford Appleton Laboratory, the Diamond Light Source and what used to be the AERE Harwell facility, now a business park. However, in 1978 this setting was to present three stable lads with a vision of a rather more supernatural nature. The three men were exercising racehorses on the jumps at dawn one morning when a lone horseman crossed their path and then vanished into some unexpected early morning mist.

> It was a sunny morning at first, then it suddenly came over misty,' said Garry Anderson, one of the three. 'The figure of the rider was distorted but I remember he was very tall. There was something strange about him.

> The figure appeared amid an eerie silence and made no sign that he had seen them at all. To make matters stranger still, they waited for him to reappear from the sudden bank of mist but he completely failed to do so: the horseman had vanished as mysteriously as he had appeared. The three lads fled the scene in terror.

> On reporting their sighting to the local paper, another report was forthcoming, this time from 1920 when the witness was a young woman who had been cycling on the Downs early one morning. This report duplicated the description of the stable lads' sighting almost exactly, even down to the detail of the rider disappearing into the mist. Although he admitted that it was purely speculation, local historian Frank Denzey considered the ghost to be that of George Goddard, who has allegedly haunted the village since the eighteenth century since dying after falling from his horse. Despite pleas for further information no other sightings of the Downs

Horseman have been forthcoming and so his identity must remain hidden, perhaps for another 60 years.

Continuing the equestrian theme, there is a spot on the path between Chilton and Upton which seems to spook horses. Some mounts have become agitated as they reach this point on the path, others break into a trembling sweat and some have stopped so suddenly that their riders have been sent tumbling to the ground. Of course there is no way to tell whether this is in any way related to the appearance of the figure on the Downs.

Moving back down onto level ground brings us to the Harwell Business Park. Even before the coming of the Atomic Energy Research Establishment, this was RAF Harwell, a bustling air base initially hosting Wellington bombers and later gliders, all housed in massive aircraft hangars which dotted the site. After the conversion of the facility to the AERE one of the old hangars, then known as Hangar 9, acquired a reputation for being haunted. During the war an RAF airman was said to have been in the habit of climbing up to the steel roof beams of this hangar to find a private place for a nap and, although there is no evidence to link to this airman with the ghost, it was his spirit which was thought to be responsible for the odd noises which could sometimes be heard at night from underneath that end of the hangar. There were also uncorroborated reports of a headless figure in uniform who was occasionally glimpsed at night in the same area, although there is no indication that the napping airman had ever been decapitated. The hangar has now been decommissioned and dismantled and so these reports of sounds and sightings are as much a part of the lost history of the site as the building itself.

Rowstock

There is a local legend in Rowstock village, a small community of houses strung along the Wantage to Reading road near Harwell, which tells of a tragic crash that took place in the early 1700s. It is said that on the anniversary of the crash, should the weather be crisp and clear, a re-enactment of the events of that night can be witnessed by anyone brave enough to venture abroad.

The tragedy was commemorated in the *Didcot Advertiser* in the 1930s by a poet who preferred to remain anonymous (although I would love to credit the author if they or a relative would like to step forward after all this time!) and republished later in *Harlequin*, the local Harwell magazine, in the 1960s. The text of the poem admirably conveys all the relevant details of the crash so all I need to do is reproduce it below:

> Most famous of all Berkshire tales
> Surviving from bygone days,
> Told far and wide on the bleak downside
> Is the tale of the phantom chaise.
>
> This story has been handed down
> Since the time of good Queen Anne;
> Those were the days when the posting chaise,
> And the four-horse mail coach ran.
>
> The Gloster, carrying London mails,
> And drawn by a team of bays,
> From the White Horse Vale to Notting Vale
> Outpaced the swiftest chaise.
>
> 'Twas winter and the year, we're told,
> Was seventeen hundred and nine;
> Through a howling gale of rain and hail
> The Gloster was keeping time.

THE VEILED VALE

Wantage-Reading, the midnight stage,
With quarter the journey done,
Raced with a will down Rowstock hill
As the Harwell clocks struck one.

That self-same night a youthful pair,
Eloping from Newbury Town,
With a team of greys and an eight-post chaise
Were tearing across the town.

The lover, a cornet in Marlborough's horse,
Feared pursuit in the dawn,
And, though the road was bad and the pace was mad,
He shouted the postboys on.

The crash – it came at Rowstock Cross
One dashing north, one east
It was hard to tell in that writhing hell
Which was man and which was beast.

The broadside of the Gloster mail
Had splintered the chaise apart;
Its steel-shod pole took a dreadful toll –
It pierced the maiden's heart.

Still she lay in her lover's arms,
And never a word she said;
He was lifted clear of crumpled gear,
And they found he, too, was dead.

Two hundred winters have come and gone
Since that night of tragic scene,
But ever the tale of the Gloster mail
Bridges the years between.

Stand, if you dare, in Rowstock copse,
A certain night of the year,
At one in the morn you may hear a horn,
And a strange light will appear.

Then it may be your beating heart,
Or was that a muffled cry?
As without a sound o'er the frozen ground,
A phantom chaise glides by.

Alas, poetic licence aside, I am unaware of anyone who has actually seen the phantom chaise glide by...

Steventon

Steventon is the proud possessor of a very odd construction known as the Causeway, a raised pathway almost a mile long running across the oldest part of the village. No-one is exactly sure when it was built; best estimates suggest the thirteenth century but a Court roll of 1418 states, 'By ancient custom the Causeway is repaired by the tenants of the manor', so it may well be even older. If its age is uncertain its purpose is no less so: one suggestion is that it was built to facilitate the passage of merchants through this notoriously marshy part of the Vale, the nineteenth century addition of flat stones or *pitchings* to form a pavement might seem to support this argument; an alternative proposal is that it was erected as the base for an aqueduct serving the local cloth-workers. The causeway was traditionally maintained by a charitable organisation of *Causewaymen,* a group who still maintain the path in fact, but it is now additionally (and rather oddly) a Grade II listed building.

Hard aside the Causeway sits the North Star, an unusual pub in itself since it is one of only nine remaining inns in the country which have no bar – beer and other drinks being dispensed from a back room via a door hatch. Beside the pub sits Tudor Cottage, a misleading name since recent tree-ring dating of the internal beams of the original part of the building revealed that the cottage dates back as far as 1299. As such, it is almost certainly the oldest cottage in the village and, as befits a home of this age, it has some very interesting features, which tell us a great deal about some of its previous inhabitants.

The tale of Anne Gunter demonstrated that there was a genuine belief in and fear of witchcraft amongst the ordinary people of earlier times and physical evidence of this can be found in all sorts of unexpected places. It is obvious that an early resident of the cottage was afraid that some unwelcome supernatural visitor might use the chimney to gain entrance to the property, because there are a series protective 'witch marks' carved onto the beams above the fireplace, which can still be seen today. The current owners John and Diana explained that the beam was originally covered in pitch before being scraped clean, so some of the marks are rather indistinct, but there are two clear instances of the letters *AM*, shorthand for *Ave Maria,* scratched into the wood as well as some intersecting angles which may represent the letters *VV* standing for *Virgin of Virgins.*[14]

These protective gouges are quite common in older buildings, especially in the eastern parts of the country, and range from the prayers found in Tudor Cottage to ornate petal-shaped symbols, known as 'daisy wheels', of unknown meaning. This class of protective etchings are referred to as apotropaic marks, the word *apotropaic* deriving from the Latin for a verse or hymn intended to offer protection from malign forces.

As if protecting the entrances to a house wasn't enough, it was also common to secrete personal items in out-of-the-way places to serve a more general protective function. While socks, stockings and even hats have been found, usually but not always tucked away near the chimney breast, by far the most common items secreted in this way were shoes. Northampton Museum maintains an index of concealed shoes from the UK and has records of nearly 2,000 finds, a list that grows by approximately one find every month.

No-one is entirely sure why shoes should be so popular but it may well be related to the story of John Schorn, who was Rector of the Buckinghamshire village of North Marston in the fourteenth century and was famous for having cast out the Devil, forcing him into a boot. It is possible that shoes, as high value items, were more valuable as 'sacrifices', if one

---

14 Or perhaps anticipating an appearance in *The Veiled Vale?*

can use such a term, or it may be relevant that shoes are one of the few items that retain their shape and therefore, in some sense, the imprint of their owner when discarded.[15] Whatever the reason for their use as protective talismans, they have been found at an assortment of locations across the Vale; a seventeenth-century lady's shoe was found in chimney stack at the Bear Hotel in Wantage and six shoes hidden under a floor in Stanford-in-the-Vale are on display in the Vale and Downland Museum in Wantage.[16]

If hiding shoes in your chimney sounds a little outlandish then best look away now, because during renovation work on one Hanney cottage the residents were more than a little surprised to find a mummified cat behind their chimney breast. Dead cats are  far less common than shoes but do still crop up with startling regularity. Again, they are thought to serve as 'protective spirits' for a house (cats are traditionally associated with witches and were thought to be able to sense ghosts so they make ideal candidates for this role); I ought to point out that the cat would probably have been a much-loved pet and would already have been dead before it was interred.

---

15 This argument might well explain the presence of hats and caps too.

16 Not, alas, in a Brogues Gallery.

Drayton

Drayton is reputed to be haunted by the ghost of a white lady on horseback who rides along Gypsy Lane, but it is probably better known for the 'Great Fire of Drayton' in 1780. This local but tragic conflagration began when one of the villagers threw out some hot ashes on a windy day and was doubtless horrified to see the wind carry the embers into the thatched roofs of nearby cottages, causing them to smoulder and then catch fire. The wind fanned the flames and spread sparks across the whole of Drayton and, despite increasingly desperate attempts by householders to douse the flames, soon more than thirty houses, almost three-quarters of the village at the time, had been burned to the ground. The calamity received widespread press coverage and a national appeal was started to raise funds to finance the rebuilding of the village. Many of the cottages in the village date back to this period and were funded by the appeal.

Just as an aside, in one of those little coincidences that crop up occasionally, I discovered that Market Drayton in Shropshire also boasts a 'Great Fire', which had started in a gingerbread bakery over a century earlier in 1651 and also destroyed three-quarters of the town. Fortunately, it seems that any conflagration contagion seems to have stopped after two occurrences because none of the other British towns and villages with related names have suffered similar disasters. This is not to say, of course, that fires in villages made up of wooden-framed wattle and daub cottages were that uncommon: in 1659 almost the whole of Hagbourne village was destroyed in a similar blaze.

Sutton Courtenay

Sutton Courtenay was a prosperous and important place in Saxon Britain, with an impressive royal palace to match those in Wantage and Faringdon. The Witan, the nearest thing the Saxons had to a parliament, met here in the original manor in 1042 and the village was the first Anglo-Saxon settlement in the country to be professionally excavated and documented.[17] In Norman times the village retained its previous status; indeed Queen Matilda, wife of Henry I, moved there for the birth of her first child in 1101. Sadly, her first daughter died but her second, also born at the manor, survived and went on to become the Empress Matilda. Following the civil war fought between this Matilda and her cousin Stephen, the Empress's son, who later became Henry II, gifted the manor to his close friend Reginald de Courtenay, thus giving the village its name.

The present beautiful Norman hall dates back to the late 1100s when construction was started under the aegis of Reginald's son, Robert de Courtenay. The fortunes of the de Courtenay family improved further a century later as Hugh Courtenay became Earl of Devon and the household promptly decamped to their new higher-status lands in the south-west. Some years later the manor (including the new manor house) was bought by the Bunce family; it then moved into the possession of the Cravens, the Monks and later Robert Lloyd-Lindsey, Lord Wantage, after whose death the estate was sold off piecemeal. It was some subsequent owners of Norman Hall, Major and Mrs Pease, who first began to realise that there was something strange happening in the very oldest parts of their property.

It started one afternoon sometime in the 1950s as Mrs Pease was sitting at a desk writing a letter. As she wrote she became aware of an overpowering floral scent from over her shoulder, in fact so strong was the scent that she turned around expecting

---

17 It was also visited by the Channel 4 *Time Team* programme in 2010.

to see someone behind her – needless to say the room was empty. On another occasion a decorator who was painting one of the rooms in the old wing commented on the powerful aroma of flowers permeating the building; again, there were no flowers in the house that day.

No-one seems to have been able to come up with any kind of explanation or back story for this strange olfactory phenomenon. Local people do seem to have believed that the haunting, if that is what it was, had been experienced by previous residents over the years. And the scents continued to appear for the Peases and subsequent owners. Mrs Doreen Bradshaw, who had taken ownership of the house from the Peases, reported that her mother, who had been visiting the house in the early 1960s, had been awoken by a strong, spicy smell as if someone was baking cakes. Intrigued, she climbed out of bed and went down to the kitchen but the oven was cold and everyone else in the house was asleep in bed. Other visitors have subsequently reported the aroma of incense and the scent of unseasonal flowers, with narcissi in January and jasmine in April but, according to the present owners, the phenomena currently seem to be in abeyance. These unexplained odours are fascinating and there is no generally accepted explanation for what could be causing them. Clearly it is not an ordinary ghost; that would make no scents…

There is another, more confused, story from Sutton Courtenay which tells of a ghost that may be seen on dark and stormy nights in the Hobbyhorse Road area, riding a white horse and brandishing an old-fashioned cutthroat razor. This malicious phantom is said to be seeking victims to slaughter and is generally associated with the

name Dr Sherwood, although the Berkshire History website suggests a more likely identification is that of local man Daniel Grimshaw, who was hanged on 4 March 1825 for the murder of his six-month-old son. Another pair of his reputed favourite haunts are the appropriately named Purgatory Farm and Hell Corner. A priest is alleged to have attempted to exorcise the malevolent, not to mention murderous, spirit and whether his intervention made any practical difference or not, to the best of my knowledge the phantom has not been seen for over a century.

Culham

Although Culham is an ancient settlement with a church dating back to the twelfth century, the main point of interest for us is the Culham Science Centre, home of the Joint European Torus fusion project. Or rather, the site that JET now occupies. Originally this was Royal Naval Air Station HMS Hornbill, an air base operated by the Fleet Air Arm as a centre for naval reservists and after the Second World War it was used as accommodation for No. 1 Parachute Training School, who actually undertook their training at RAF Abingdon. One night in June 1959 trainee Brian Leigh was sleeping in one of the old Nissen huts which served as dormitories, when his slumber was disturbed by the noise of a terrible thunderstorm. As he awoke and sleepily looked around he realised that the hut was dimly illuminated by the light from an old-fashioned stove; this struck him as odd – this was summer after all. He sat up and looked around to see a group of five royal navy men in uniform sitting around the stove. All were clearly injured and wore bandages; four of the men were ratings and, from the look of his uniform, the youngest of the men seemed to be an officer. Leigh let out a gasp of surprise and the sailors, along with the glow from the stove, immediately vanished. Leigh climbed from his bed to look around but, on checking, discovered that the stove which he had seen burning warmly only moments ago was cold to the touch. Perhaps unsurprisingly, after he told his story none of his comrades were especially keen to sleep in that particular hut again.

Abingdon

Abingdon can lay claim to being the oldest continuously inhabited town in the country, with evidence for settlement stretching back 6,000 years. Originally the County Town of Berkshire (the title passed to Reading in 1867, largely because Abingdon had been, quite literally, side-lined by the Great Western Railway), its full name of Abingdon-on-Thames was truncated after the 1974 county boundary changes added insult to injury by moving the town, and indeed the whole of the Vale and North Berkshire, into the county of Oxfordshire. It is now formally Abingdon-on-Thames once again, but however the town is titled, its long history has allowed plenty of time to accrue a few stories and several ghosts along the way.

For as long as there has been written history there has been an abbey in the town and there are many legends about how and when Abingdon Abbey was first established. The most popular claims that a hermit called St Abban founded the abbey shortly after the Romans left Britain, but it seems likely that this story was concocted at some point to enable the abbey to claim it was the oldest monastery in the country and thus enhance its reputation and status. Other colourful legends casually sprinkled around include the story that it had been founded by King Lucius and destroyed by the Emperor Diocletian; that the Emperor Constantine had been educated there as a boy; that the original planned location for the community had been atop a nearby hill, but any building work always collapsed overnight until the site was moved into the town; and, best of all, that five hundred monks lived in the surrounding woods as hermits only emerging from their retreats and returning to the abbey on Sundays and festival days.

What is known for certain is that a monastery on the site of the abbey was in existence by 675 and that it was probably built by a local Saxon Prince called Hean (or possibly by his uncle Cissa) on a site reputedly revealed to the founder in a dream. Before this time the town had originally been known as Scovechesham, but was soon being referred to by the name of Abbendon, 'the town of the abbey'. At the same time Hean's sister, Cilla, set up a nunnery at the site of what is now St Helen's Church and endowed it with a holy relic, a small fragment from one of the nails from the True Cross. This scrap of metal was set into an iron cross and was, amazingly, given the religious value of the item, eventually buried with Cilla after her death. Her grave was subsequently lost along with the priceless relic until it was accidentally unearthed in the tenth century by workmen digging a drain. The Black Cross, as it came to be known, was recovered and moved to the monastery, although what the nuns who actually owned the object had to say about this is not recorded. It was certainly venerated in its new home and accredited with supernatural powers – the *Historia Ecclesie Abbendonensis*, the history of the abbey written in the twelfth century, claims: 'It is so holy that no-one who has taken an oath upon it can affirm a lie without punishment or mortal danger'. Not only that but the cold iron of the cross rejected all attempts to gild it with gold or silver; no matter how magnificent the workmanship the decoration was always shed overnight.

Despite the significance of the Black Cross it seems to have been lost once more, although there is a legend that it remains buried somewhere beneath Abingdon awaiting rediscovery. Given the modern predilection for urban reorganisation it may well turn up again at any time; or, then again, perhaps 'he is not yet born'…

Sadly, nothing of the original abbey buildings remain as they were destroyed by Danes from nearby Reading who sacked the town in 871, and the current abbey buildings were probably rebuilt over a long period starting around 1100. In case you are wondering about the fate of the nunnery, that too is gone, although St Helen's Church remains. It is reputed to be the widest church in England. Incidentally, the scenic ruined arches in the abbey gardens are nothing to do with the original buildings and were erected in the 1920s as a folly, though it is thought that they may contain some of the stonework from earlier structures.

For a community of such age, the abbey has a surprising lack of authenticated ghost sightings. The Long Gallery of the present abbey is said to be haunted by a female ghost but, as far as I am aware, she has not been seen in recent years.

The Old Gaol is an entirely different matter. This imposing edifice was constructed by Napoleonic prisoners of war and opened for business, as it were, in 1811. It had a brief, if bloody, history until 1868 when it ceased to be a prison, fell into disuse until 1874, and was then drafted into use as a grain store. Ownership passed to the Vale District Council in 1975 when it became a leisure centre and it was at this point that strange events began to be reported. Doors would slam for no apparent reason, voices would be heard in the building and shadowy shapes and figures would flit along corridors. In one of the changing rooms hanging clothing baskets would start to swing from side to side and, as staff were leaving for the night, they would sometimes hear ghostly childish laughter drifting along the deserted corridors. Despite some frightening occurrences, the staff at the centre did not feel threatened by whatever was disturbing their peace and quiet and the Centre manager commented at the time:

> They are quite harmless and they only seem to be around when there is building work going on. Perhaps they don't like being disturbed.

Eventually, an explanation was proposed to explain these uncanny events. As the story went, an eight-year-old boy who had been imprisoned for burning down two barns with 'malice, cunning and revenge' in mind had been hanged in the gaol and it was either his ghost or that of his mother which was haunting the building: the only problem with this explanation, according to Abingdon local historian Mieneke Cox anyway, is that there are no actual records of this affair documented in the gaol. I am not sure that an eight-year-old child in prison would have a great deal to laugh about in any case.

Digging into the legend a little further I came across a reference, in the letters of the poet John Milton, to a child arsonist being hanged at Abingdon, which has a striking similarity to this explanation for the gaol haunting. In this letter (which is dated March 1630 and so predates the construction of the current gaol building by more than two centuries) Milton says:

> At Berkshire assizes was a boy of nine years old condemned and executed for example, for burning a house or two; who only said upon the ladder, 'Forgive me this, and I'll do so no more.'

According to *The Annals of Windsor* (the arson attacks were committed there) the boy's name was John Dean and the execution actually took place on 23 February 1629. In a clear link to the usual Old Gaol story, it was said that the judge refused to show mercy because 'it appearing upon examination that he had malice, revenge, craft, and cunning.' It is generally believed that the youngest person hanged in England was a seven-year-old child at Kings Lynn in 1709, but recent research has revealed that the victim in this case was actually 17 so the Abingdon hanging, with John Dean's age given chillingly as 'an infant, between eight and nine years', is in fact a grisly and unwelcome record for the town.

One further point to mention is that in the seventeenth century the town assizes were located beside the entrance to the abbey at the top of Bridge Street near what is now the Roysse Room, a little to the north and east of the Old Gaol site. The legal proceedings took place in a tent especially erected for the occasion and the town pillory and cage were located nearby, whereas executions were carried out in the Market Place opposite.

All these details would seem to introduce considerable doubt as to the accuracy of the conventional explanation for the Old Gaol haunting. It is possible that our pre-pubescent pyromaniac may have taken to haunting the Old Gaol for some unknowable reason but it does seem unlikely (unless, in good horror movie tradition, he was buried on the site of the future building). While all this speculation may cast doubt on the story given to explain the phenomena experienced by the leisure centre staff, it only reopens the question as to the real reasons for the strange happenings in the building.

While personnel at the gaol building were puzzling over unseen voices and childish laughter, invisible footsteps echoing along night-time corridors were also being reported at the old police station. This sat close up against the Old Gaol and, interestingly, the building to the other side of the police station which used to be the tourist information centre also had reports of footsteps and slamming doors at night. These phenomena were so alarming and persistent that some of the staff refused to work alone in the building after dark. Could all these cases be linked by a ghost with a bad case of wanderlust, are they a series of separate hauntings, or is this all just a case of a contagion of jitters in eerie deserted buildings late at night?

Opposite the Old Gaol is the Broad Head pub, which is generally supposed to have acquired its name from the bloated faces of men hanged across the road. The name actually dates back to 1794 (previously the pub had been called the Saracen's Head) and, as such, pre-dates the Old Gaol, but given that hangings in the town were only just up the road in the square,

then the suggested reason for the name may well still be accurate.

A little further down the road towards the river, on the mid-stream island spanned by Abingdon Bridge, is the Nags Head. The river here is haunted by the ghostly head and shoulders of a woman presumably floating in the water; she is alleged to have drowned in the river at some unspecified time, a not-unlikely event as one of the early abbots of Abingdon, Richard de Clyve, was drowned near that very spot in 1315 when his boat overturned in turbulent water with the loss of all on board.

Abingdon can boast another haunted pub in the Crown and Thistle, a sixteenth-century coaching inn which once had a stable block across the road for the convenience of its guests and other visitors. On occasion a phantom coach and horses has been seen leaving the main area of the inn and crossing the road to the stables. The most recent witness to the event was a lady called Mrs Usher who was staying at the Crown and Thistle sometime in the year 1930 and one lady a few years later told the then owners that her parents had once run the inn but had been forced to give it up, because of the constant worry that they might encounter the ghost!

The Abbey Press Group are now based in a modern building on an industrial park on the outskirts of Abingdon, but when the company occupied their old works in Stert Street many of the workforce came to believe that something not of this world shared the building with them.

The ghost first made itself known in the early 1970s when late-night workers began to hear footsteps moving around in the offices above the printing presses. No-one paid any attention to these noises, which generally occurred at two or three in the morning, until it was pointed out that none of the office staff were in the habit of visiting the plant at that time of night... Vernon Whitehead, one of the staff at the Press, became so worried that he brought his dog, a large German Shepherd/Collie cross, to see if the dog would respond to whatever was haunting the building. On hearing the phantom footsteps upstairs he led the animal towards the office only to find that she stopped dead on the landing and resolutely refused to enter the room.

Some years later, another employee named Joe was working alone one night when he heard one of the internal connecting doors slam shut and saw a figure passing behind him, reflected in the shiny metal of the press at which he was working. 'I froze but the reflection continued to move so I am sure it was not coming from me,' he said. 'Then I felt a definite presence behind me... I looked round but didn't see anything... It was really frightening.' This event closely matches another reported occurrence when an office worker was startled to see a shadow fall across his desk from the other side of the window to his office, a window that faced inwards towards the open space of the factory.

There were also reports of presses starting themselves at odd hours, which doubtless helped to fuel the tension in the building, and one of the bookkeeping department was startled to see his electric adding machine start to output random strings of zeros when he was not using the device. He himself blamed this on an electrical fault and in fact many of the staff seem to have been decidedly sceptical about the presence of any kind of ghost on the premises, but others noticed that the building stood on the site of the old Abingdon graveyard and drew their own conclusions. Sadly, once the story had been reported in the local papers, accounts of other-worldly phenomena dwindled away and, in any event, after the factory site was levelled in 1985 the ghost did not accompany the firm when it made the journey to its new home.

At this point, should you fancy a change from ghost stories, let us just mention that in 1998 local man Maurice Ridgeley reported a strange dark blob that he claimed to be a UFO flying across the skies above Abingdon. He managed to take some video footage of the alleged aerial object and a number of UFO groups investigated the incident, but no firm conclusions as to the provenance of the object were ever reached. In local terms at least, Abingdon seems to be something of a UFO hotspot as two sightings were also been reported to the *British Earth and Aerial Mysteries Society* a decade later. The first object appeared in October 2008 and was described as a red and black globular orb, which silently flew approximately 200 ft above the High Street before suddenly disappearing, even though the sky was perfectly clear. A month later, 16 equally silent amber-coloured lights were observed moving northwards towards Oxford at around 10.30 pm. In this instance the two witnesses described the nearest of the lights as appearing to have a jellyfish-like canopy with segments visible, before the formation drifted off into the sky and then rapidly vanished upwards.

While hesitating to jump to conclusions, the last case certainly seems to bear all the hallmarks of a series of Chinese lanterns drifting across the night sky; in fact there was a very similar report from near Wantage in 2010. However, as if to confound our comfortable assumptions, a year later in August 2009, two fast-moving pale yellow lights were observed speeding across the sky in a similar direction but in this case there was no wind to explain their movements[18] and the witness was adamant that they were not aircraft. UFO sightings being particularly contentious, I think it wisest to simply step aside and let the reader draw their own conclusions in all these cases...

---

18 At ground level anyway.

Moving quickly on from stories of UFOs, let us once again turn to the past and contemplate the sad case of Elizabeth Stile. Stile was a 65-year-old widow who was, by all accounts, a rather unpleasant person, 'lewd, malicious and hurtful', according to her neighbours. She lived in Windsor but since her story, along with that of three other women, ends at Abingdon I have featured it here.

Their sorry tale began in August 1578 with the unearthing of three wax dolls with bristles embedded in the hearts, which had been buried in a dunghill somewhere in London. This discovery caused a considerable degree of consternation at the time, both because wax dolls were thought to be a method used by witches to curse their victim and because the discovery was made at a moment of great political tension for Elizabeth I, who at the time had Mary, Queen of Scots, under house arrest, and was alert to any whiff of plot and treason. Elizabeth Stile was arrested and held in Reading Gaol where, apparently entirely unprompted and of her own free will, she made what we can only describe as a fulsome confession of witchcraft.

The testimony she gave claimed that she was a member of a coven of witches led by a woman known as Mother Seidre (who died before she could be brought to trial), with her fellow members being Mother Dutten, Mother Devell and Mother Margaret of Windsor along with a man named Father Rosimond and his daughter.[19] Stile confessed that the coven had committed a catalogue of crimes including numerous magical murders using wax images (in one case when a victim recovered they killed his cow

---

19 Father here is clearly used in the same sense as Mother rather than as a religious title.

instead!) as well as many other 'heinous and villainous practices'. Furthermore, she maintained, each of the women had a familiar in the form of a rat, a toad, a cat and a kitten and that the Rosimonds were shape-shifters who could assume the forms of an ape or a horse at will.

Given these unprompted pronouncements the women were moved to Abingdon where they were tried in February 1579. They do not seem to have presented much of a united front, although after Elizabeth Stile's revelations perhaps this is not entirely unexpected. In any case prison did not treat Mother Stile gently and she caught one of the many terrible diseases that infested the dark, dank, unsanitary cells of the time, causing her hands to become numb and her feet to rot. She accused Mother Devell of bewitching her and, towards the end of the proceedings, her health had deteriorated so badly that she had to be trundled from her cell to the courtroom in a wheelbarrow.

One interesting piece of testimony given at the trial came from an ostler (a stablehand) who testified that Mother Stile often came begging alms from his master's house, but on one occasion, after being turned away empty-handed, she cursed him with 'heaviness and aching of limb'. After trying every possible medicinal remedy, the gentleman of the house eventually consulted a wise man who advised that he scratch the witch who had ensorcelled him and draw blood; this he duly did and shortly thereafter recovered.[20] The name of this wise man? Father Rosimond.

At the conclusion to the trial the judge decided that there had been no treasonous intent from any of the coven, but still sentenced Mothers Stile, Dutten, Devell and Margaret to death for their other nefarious activities. They were finally

---

20 It would be interesting to know whether Brian Gunter was aware of this testimony, since a similar incident formed part of his deception a quarter of a century later in North Moreton.

hanged on 26 February 1579. Perhaps it was because of his actions in aiding the ostler, or perhaps there were other factors that have not been recorded, but Father Rosimond and his daughter were declared innocent and released.

And so back to ghosts. If we think of haunted houses we automatically tend to picture glorious old gothic piles, ivy-clad and shrouded in a spooky mist rolling in from the local graveyard. The truth, of course, is usually considerably at odds with our imagination, as this recent episode from Abingdon illustrates.

The Smith family, as we shall call them, live in a modern three-bedroomed house on the Peachcroft Estate to the north of the town. John and Jane Smith, along with their two teenage daughters, Jenny aged 16 and Josie aged 13, led a perfectly ordinary life, although Jane had a lively interest in a variety of esoteric topics and it may have been this enquiring personality which led her to buy a set of tarot cards from a well-known

online trading site. Pleased with her new purchase, she encouraged the family to try out the fortune-telling cards, something they did in what Jane describes as 'a light-hearted manner' on a number of dull winter evenings, without noticeable results.

They would probably have tired of their new game and quickly forgotten about it had Jenny not mentioned the cards to a family friend she met one day after school. The friend was both outraged and alarmed at the Smiths playing with something she described as 'very dangerous and pagan' and clearly filled Jenny's head full of tales of demonic possession and other terrifying risks. To her credit Jenny was unfazed by their friend's evident distress, they were just playing cards after all, though she did tell her parents and sister about the conversation even though they paid it little heed. Or rather, they paid it little heed at first.

Some days later, on a suitably dark and stormy night, the lights in the house started to flicker inexplicably, something the family pragmatically assumed to be caused by the wind gusting outside. The next day John Smith lost his car keys only to have them reappear, after much frantic searching, exactly where he had left them – again a perfectly normal-seeming event and one which went, at the time, mostly unremarked upon. The family only really started to become alarmed when they began to hear unexplained footsteps moving around the house after they had all retired to bed: on investigation they could find no evidence of a presence either human or otherwise in the property. And then there were the days when the house felt inexplicably cold... Eventually, the cumulative effects of these seemingly mysterious events made the family wonder if there had been anything in the warnings that Jenny had been given about 'meddling with the unexplained' and whether some unseen being was haunting their home. Suddenly the house seemed a far from friendly place.

At which point, through an acquaintance, they contacted a paranormal researcher to ask for advice on how to tackle the problem. As a result of that meeting, the Smiths started to keep a diary of the various spooky events that they observed over the course of the next few weeks and to make a determined effort to find possible non-supernatural explanations for the things they were recording or, at least, which family members were around most often when they happened. Since, according to one theory, many hauntings, and particularly poltergeist effects, are reportedly associated with teenage girls, this diary would have helped identify a possible source of the phenomena but, far from identifying a potential cause of these activities, an interesting pattern emerged – the more they recorded odd happenings, the more mundane they started to appear. Small items went missing but investigation generally found them in unexpected, but entirely logically explainable places: drawers, coat pockets and so on. Cold draughts were revealed to come from leaky single-glazed windows; nocturnal noises never seemed to be quite as frightening when the family considered them in the cold light of day. Much to their relief, and to the chagrin of the paranormal investigator, they realised that rather than identifying the psychic source of their haunting they had in fact rationalised it away. Or, as John put it: 'The closer we looked, the less we found. We're not sure whether to be relieved or disappointed.'

And there the tale just peters out. No doubt odd things still happen around the house but the Smiths no longer worry that they are the result of an unnamed supernatural entity, just memory lapses and the creaking of cooling floorboards. Proof indeed of John Keats's words when he wrote of science (though, as was the custom at the time, he called it natural philosophy):

> Philosophy will clip an Angel's wings,
> Conquer all mysteries by rule and line,
> Empty the haunted air, and gnoméd mine…

Whether you consider this a good thing or not, it was certainly an approach which helped the Smith family a great deal, though I don't know whether they ever used those tarot cards again.

Marcham

When Mr Harpham and his new bride moved into the seventeenth-century Tithe House in Marcham in 1899, they doubtless hoped for a peaceful home in which to raise a family. Certainly it became a family home for they raised three children there in the early years of the following century, but it was not always entirely peaceful. From the very day they moved into the house they were disturbed by the sound of a child crying echoing through the empty rooms. After the births of their three children the disembodied cries often sent them rushing upstairs, only to discover children happily asleep and just the echo of phantom grief fading away into the darkness.

After a few years living in the house it seems some renovation was required and so, in 1905 to be exact, workmen arrived and began the task of repairing and rebuilding large parts of the property. As work progressed there was some excitement as a secret cupboard was discovered walled up below the stairs. Unfortunately, excitement was soon replaced by horror as exploration of the hidden recess revealed the sad remains of a very young child (some accounts say a baby) bundled up into a package inside an old dress.

Needless to say the police were called and they determined that the dress dated from thirty or forty years previously and that the child had suffered head injuries, which had probably been the cause of death. One can only imagine the feelings of the Harphams after this discovery, but they were doubtless much relieved when the child was buried in the local churchyard and the nocturnal crying ceased to disturb their evenings.

Frilford

This is a short tale I was sent by an anonymous young man I will call Dan, who lived at Frilford Heath some years ago. Dan's mother had remarried and the new extended family moved in to the house owned by his new step-father, an old seventeenth-century cottage in the village. Dan always felt a little 'creepy', but could never pin down any particular reason for his unease until one April evening when his mother and step-father were away from the house for the night. At some point in the evening there was a power outage in the area, so Dan lit a dozen or so candles around the living room for light. It was around 11 pm when he heard a car driving along the main road outside followed by the unmistakable sound of screeching tyres, as if the car was braking to avoid hitting someone or something in the road. At that very moment, all at the same time, every candle went out. Then came seven loud thumps on the wall to Dan's right accompanied by a muffled voice saying something not quite intelligible. As the voice ceased speaking the candles spontaneously re-lit themselves! Rather than stay in the house a moment longer than he had to, Dan went directly out to his car and drove off to stay with his father for the night. He was understandably nervous about returning to Frilford but never heard or saw anything unusual in the subsequent six months he lived at the house; a strangely unsatisfying postscript to an undeniably eventful night.

A final note from Frilford: with reference back to Brightwell-cum-Sotwell and Wittenham Clumps, there is another of those Cuckoo Pen fields near the village. Local people must have been really keen to hang on to summer in the Vale.

East and West Hanney

There has always been a considerable degree of rivalry between the two Hanneys, in fact there is a saying locally that 'East is East and West is West and never the two agree over village affairs.' The older West village used to be known as Church Hanney and its partner, sprawling along the old road as it does, was traditionally Long Hanney, but it might not have been so. An old memoir dating from the 1950s published by the Women's Institute describes how, when the village church was originally constructed in the twelfth century, it had been planned to build it on the East Hanney side. In a rather nice twist of the traditional tale of the Devil or fairies moving building materials, the memoir claims that every night villagers from West Hanney crept to the building site and laboriously moved all the stones and tools to their preferred site in their half of the village. Every morning the builders would be forced to move everything back and every night the westerners would repeat their mischief. Eventually the weary workmen accepted defeat and the church was constructed where it stands today.

There is a memorial in Hanney Church to Edward Bowles who died at the remarkable age of 89, and his wife Elizabeth, the most long-lived English woman ever, who lived in (probably) East Hanney and died in 1718 aged 124. This remarkable woman would have seen the sixteenth, seventeenth and eighteenth centuries and lived through the reigns of three queens and six kings as well as two Lords Protector during the Commonwealth, a truly astonishingly long life, especially for so long ago.

The villages can boast a selection of different ghosts, not all of them human. The road from Steventon to East Hanney, for example, has been the scene of encounters with ghostly horses: one lady described how a number of grey and insubstantial animals drifted across the road in front of her car and then leapt over the hedge by the roadside. Another singular sighting from 2006 concerns a driver and passenger who were travelling from Steventon into Hanney and were startled by a lone horse which galloped from a side road and out in front of their car. To avoid panicking the animal further they turned off the headlights briefly, but when they switched them back on it was just in time to watch the apparition vanish before their eyes. There is a field which used to be known as Deadman's Ham close by this point in the road, but this is entirely unrelated to these ghostly sightings, referring instead to the tendency of the field to flood at the slightest opportunity, rendering it 'dead ground' or unfit for regular cultivation.

The most well-known story from Hanney is that of the little old lady of Dandridge's Mill. Dressed in a long white skirt and white bonnet, she comes scurrying along the road keeping her skirts raised to protect them from the mud, climbs over the metal railings at the side of Mill Bridge and jumps into the brook, only to completely vanish from sight. She is thought to have once lived at Hale Cottage and is said to have committed suicide sometime in the late eighteenth or early nineteenth century.

The best individual description of this haunting comes from one of the great characters of the village, the late Bob Brakespear. Bob served in the Home Guard during the war and one evening he and a companion were on guard at the bridge beside Dandridge's Mill (which was, at the time, used as a factory manufacturing aircraft parts) when they were startled to hear the sound of clattering feet coming along the road towards them. Along the road came an elderly woman dressed in old-fashioned clothes and wearing wooden shoes. Both men were very struck by both these points: the clothes were definitely from a bygone age and even in rural Berkshire wooden clogs had gone out of fashion many years before. In any case the old lady passed the two vigilant sentries and moved onto the bridge whereupon she walked to one side and threw herself over the edge into the water below. The two men rushed to her aid but peering into the darkness below them they could see no sign of her body, nor was the surface of the water disturbed by so much as a ripple. As might be expected the two men checked the river but no trace of a body could be found. Even more strangely, when they told their tale to their friends and neighbours many of them reported seeing the very same apparition.

The thatched cottage called Bankside in West Hanney is said to be haunted by the ghost of a man dressed in sixteenth-century costume. He has been described as around 6 ft tall with blond hair and has been seen wearing white breeches, hose and a shirt with a blue diagonal sash. Sweets and biscuits tend to disappear when he is around but always reappear somewhere else in the house, which perhaps indicates that the ghost has a mischievous nature rather than a sweet tooth. Milk-bottle tops (a detail which dates the story) were once observed to fly across the room and he seems to have a curious penchant for opening safety pins. The sounds of footsteps climbing the creaky stairs have been heard at night and there is reported to be an icy cold atmosphere in the house whenever he makes his occasional appearances.

Ley of the Land

During his travels around rural Herefordshire in the 1920s, beer salesman and brewer Alfred Watkins, perhaps influenced by his own journeying (or perhaps after sampling his merchandise), was suddenly struck by a vision of prehistoric straight-line pathways criss-crossing the entire country and serving as markers for ancient traders to make their way from settlement to settlement selling their wares. These lines, as he pictured them, could still be seen marked out by prehistoric burial mounds and other such places; churches built on pagan sites, hilltops, standing stones and a wide variety of other landscape features. He published an in-depth description of this theory in his book *The Old Straight Track* and his ideas were taken up by other enthusiasts across Britain, which eventually led to the formation of the splendidly named Straight Track Postal Portfolio Club. Interest in what  Watkins called 'leys' (after the old English term for tracks) faded in the post-war years but was revived, with a decidedly spiritual twist, in the 1960s, firstly by a group of researchers in France and later, in the UK, by writer and researcher John Michell, among others.

In their new incarnation, leys (now 'ley lines') were designed and engineered by early civilisations to carry mysterious earth energy or even, according to some of the more outré writers, as guidance systems for visiting UFOs. This exuberance eventually faded and modern ley theories tend to concentrate on the folkloric connotations of the alignments and their association with funeral paths. Whatever your views on the reality of leys, examples have been documented in the Vale over the years and it is interesting to follow in their tracks, if only as historical curiosities.

In the original *Old Straight Track*, Watkins notes what he calls a 'White Ley' across the River Thames towards the east of our region. He supposes that this is the relic of an old salt traders' route and traces it from White Hill near the village of Moulsford and then on through the churches in Ewelme, Cuxham, Wheatfield and Whitchurch. There is another ley completely on our side of the river, which starts St Mary-le-More Church in Wallingford, follows a straight line through the earthworks known as the Kinecroft in the town centre, over the village of Brightwell-cum-Sotwell and then on to Brightwell Barrow. After this point the line leads on to Wittenham Clumps and, skirting the edge of Little Wittenham, it reaches its conclusion at another St Mary's Church, this time in Long Wittenham.

It is a rare earth-mysteries researcher who can avoid mention of Uffington and, as you might expect, there is a well-documented ley at the Uffington complex. Paul Devereux and Ian Thompson, writing in *The Ley Hunter's Companion,* described a ley of nearly 10 miles in length, which starts at the Uffington Church of St Mary, runs southwards crossing the summit of Dragon Hill before passing through a barrow on the steep grassy slope and the reaching the summit of the hill at Uffington Castle. From this point the ley switches into overdrive and races across the countryside to a tumulus on Parkfarm Down, passes over two linear earthworks at Farncombe Down and Near Down (through a convenient notch in the structure in the latter case) and finally terminates at a tumulus east of the village of Preston.

While these small-scale alignments are interesting (and fun to explore), some researchers have claimed that a much more significant alignment passes through the Vale: the St Michael Line. The existence of this mega-megalithic construction was first suggested by John Michell, who envisaged it as a magnificent feat of prehistoric engineering, an arrangement of the significant features we have previously noted but especially featuring churches dedicated to All Saints and the martial, dragon-slayer saints, St George and St Michael. This ley, as he describes it, starts at St Michael's Mount in Cornwall and follows the path of the rising sun on 8 May,[21] passing through both Glastonbury Tor and

---

21 Curiously, this is the date on which an apparition of St Michael was seen at Monte Gargano in in Italy in 494.

Avebury as it heads north-east towards the Vale of the White Horse and thence on towards Bury St Edmunds and the East Anglian coast near Lowestoft.

Because of the curvature of the Earth, no perfectly straight line of this length could ever have been constructed, indeed attempts to draw an exact line fitting the description I have just given are doomed to failure, so a modified version of the theory suggests that rather than being one overarching ley, the Michael line is made up of a series of shorter, more accurate, alignments which can be combined to give the impression of a coherent whole.

All these straight lines are all very well but they do tend to ignore another major facet of what tends to be called earth mysteries: dowsing. In 1989 Paul Broadhurst and Hamish Miller published a startling book entitled *The Sun and the Serpent* in which they claimed that the St Michael line was not only laid out to mark the position of a line of earth energy surging across the country, but that it was actually one of a pair of lines (the other being the St Mary line) which wove across the country, following the approximate path we have previously traced but twisted like threads of yarn or, more evocatively, entwined snakes. As with the original St Michael Line, these leys meander through the Vale passing through a range of interesting places, so let's follow them and see where they lead us.

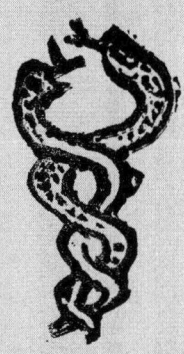

St Michael

The St Michael Line enters the Vale, appropriately enough, from St Michael's Church in Aldbourne, near Lambourn, although, oddly, this church was originally dedicated to St Mary. The first point of call on the way into the Vale itself is a pair of tumuli near South Fawley, up on the Downs above Letcombe. From here it moves on to All Saints Church, Farnborough and then crosses the Ridgeway[22] before reaching Churn Knob (of St Birinus fame) near Blewbury. From here the line crosses Blewburton Hill, moves on to a mound in South Moreton and then to another right next to the church in North Moreton (All Saints again). The next stop is, oddly, considering the line we are following, St Mary's Church in Long Wittenham.[23] Next is the, more predictable, thirteenth century St Michael's Church in Clifton Hampden and then on to Castle Hill at Wittenham Clumps before heading across the river to Dorchester Abbey. If you are following all this on a map you will be aware that this line is anything but straight although, not being a dowser, I am not qualified to comment on the authenticity of its seemingly random path.

St Mary

The St Mary Line starts our way from the Bishopstone Church of St John the Baptist[24] and then to 'The Cathedral of the Vale' – St Mary's in Uffington, with its unusual octagonal tower. Although it is not explicitly stated, I would be very surprised if the line were not to pass through St Mary's in Ashbury along the way. It then moves on to the thirteenth-century Holy Cross Church in Sparsholt, which was built on the site

---

22 Does this explain the name Dragon's Ditch? See the Grim's Dyke section.

23 On an entirely unrelated note, St Mary's is the proud possessor of one of the few remaining lead fonts in the country. This was boarded up during the time of Cromwell to avoid it being melted down by the puritans and then entirely forgotten until its rediscovery in 1839.

24 Those who have been paying attention to some of the coincidences I highlight occasionally throughout this book might be interested to know that the village of Bishopstone near Salisbury also shares this dedication.

of an even earlier eighth-century wooden Saxon chapel. Interestingly, there is a Nine Men's Morris board scratched into the stone by the priest's door at Holy Cross, which might have some significance to the line we are following because Nine Men's Morris was a game played with stones on a grid, the aim being to form straight lines across the board. Is history leaving us messages? Leaving Sparsholt there is no mention of St Mary's in Childrey; instead we move on to St Andrew's in Letcombe Regis, another twelfth-century church with a very unusual memorial in the churchyard commemorating 19-year-old Maori chief George King Hipango, who died in Letcombe in 1871 whilst training to be a missionary. His career was tragically cut short before he even made it out of the UK: he is generally assumed to have died of TB, but one theory suggests that his death was actually caused by a reaction to a smallpox vaccine he had been given, for the sake of his health, before returning home. Another All Saints Church at East Lockinge is next in line, this one complete with a wonderful Norman doorway, followed by another St Mary's at East Hendred. This may well be a decidedly dubious link in the chain, as the church was only consecrated in 1865 so is hardly an ancient monument. On now to All Saints Church in Didcot which, in an appropriate counterpoint to Aldbourne, used to be dedicated to St Michael. After Didcot the St Mary line moves on to cross the St Michael Line twice, once at an unremarked and otherwise unremarkable location somewhere outside Didcot and then again at the far more noteworthy Castle Hill in the Sinodun range, before heading off towards all points north-east.

In following these meandering serpent paths I was sometimes struck by the somewhat irreverent thought that some of the places they miss are more relevant than some of the places they actually visit. We have seen that both lines sometimes show little regard for their primary saint's affiliation, so I was surprised to realise that the St Mary line misses a trick: a short detour would take it through Sutton Courtenay and the George and Dragon pub (near the All Saints Church too) and past the wonderful picture of St George and the Dragon on the side of Gothic House in Drayton, which was painted by Charles Sykes in 1949.

The picture is of a design taken from the original, smaller mural inside the house and commemorates a mumming play featuring St George and the Dragon that used to be performed in the village.[25] Alternatively, the St Michael line could have moved slightly to the west to pass another George and Dragon pub, this time in Upton, or deviated even further to Wallingford where, if you recall, the George Hotel was once the George and Dragon.

Perhaps the failure of these lines to consider pubs as significant as churches and prehistoric mounds is not entirely surprising, but whatever your opinion of the validity of these particular cross-country routes the experience of following them certainly makes for an interesting and scenic trip across the region.

---

25 Sykes was an artist and sculptor who designed the 'Spirit of Ecstasy' figure which graces the front of Rolls Royce cars to this day.

Grove

Authority to begin construction of a new airfield at Grove, on '272 acres of first quality milk producing land' as it was at the time described, was given in May 1941 at one of the darkest times in the Second World War. RAF Grove was built as a Class A airfield with three converging concrete runways in a 'K' pattern and, although only one of the proposed two massive T2 hangars was ever built, by August 1942 the airfield had begun to take an active part in the conflict as a training base for Wellington Bomber crews. Unfortunately, because of a large number of glider flights from the training base at Brize Norton this role was quickly abandoned and the base was transferred to US Air Force control and, as part of the USAF Support Command (34th Transport Group), Grove played a major role in offering support to the D-Day landings on 6 June 1944.

After the Second World War the base returned to the RAF and was later used by the UK Atomic Energy Authority as a storage facility. As years passed, part of the complex, the old No. 2 Communal Site, was acquired by Metal Box (now Crown Cork and Seal), while the rest eventually became a business park. However, even with the passing of the years it seems that not all the servicemen have left the old airfield.

While UKAEA were at the site, the old T2 hangar was used as an irradiation plant and, for obvious safety reasons, was operated and manned around the clock. One summer night in 1969 at around 9pm the duty officer, a Mr Halliday, heard voices outside his office and went to investigate. Since the hangar was supposed to be a secured building, the presence of other people inside would have been a major breach in security but, after a good look around, he realised that no-one else was present and the security man at the gatehouse confirmed that apart from the boilerman he was alone on site. Supposing that the conversation he had overheard had simply been mechanical noise coupled with an overactive imagination, Mr Halliday thought no more about the incident. However, a month or so later he once again heard voices, this time much more clearly, but as before he found that the hangar was deserted. After hearing his tale, other colleagues confirmed that they had also had similar experiences on previous occasions.

There is a generally accepted theory that an American serviceman who had committed suicide by hanging himself in that very building is the source of this haunting, but one thing worries me about this explanation: if he is the ghost, then who are the others he is talking to?

The Crown Cork and Seal site has also been the source of rumours of ghostly activity. Bob, one of the security guards at the plant, had a tale to tell about the site of one the old hangars. In the time between him making one round of checks and the next, a stairwell light and a high-pressure fire hose were both switched on by person or persons unknown. As Bob commented, 'No-one was working and once the gates are locked it is impossible to get inside at night'. Most of the reports are more visual, for example, a figure dressed in an RAF uniform, complete with the oxygen mask of a flyer, has been seen on several occasions near the location of the old chapel and Officers' Mess. Some witnesses have described him as a tall red-haired man and he is sometimes assumed to be a fighter pilot who was killed when his plane crashed on landing and burst into flames. Metal Box were quite keen to play down these reports; to be fair, the Officers' Mess was very close to what later became the staff Social Club and they would not have wanted to encourage the thought that some of their staff might have been slightly the worse for wear when they reported seeing the 'Ghost Flyer'.

An alternative identification of the airman suggests that he was a local man called Symons who was part of the crew of a Lancaster bomber, which crashed at Lyford[26] on 8 April 1945. To add piquancy to the tale, some versions claim that the crewman's father, working at Clarke's Mill in Wantage, watched the struggling aircraft attempting to maintain height as it passed above him without realising that it was his son who was part of the life-and-death struggle overhead. No-one seems to have asked why an aircraft flying south from Grove and struggling to stay aloft would eventually crash half a dozen miles to the north...

As we move south from Grove towards Wantage, pay particular attention as we pass the old Grove Bridge, now marked by traffic lights, where both the Wilts and Berks Canal and the Wantage Tramway once crossed the Letcombe Brook. Grove Airfield expert Colin Appleton reports that there is said to be a horse and cart which drives along the Wantage to Grove road past the old dairy and the canal cottages and off, perhaps, towards the old Wantage Road railway station to the north of the village. I have never come across anyone who has seen this mysterious travelling apparition, but the tale could well be related to the well-known story of Arthur Hitchcock, the man who raced the Wantage tram.

Arthur Hitchcock was born in Eynsham but came to Wantage in the 1890s to work for the Great Western Railway. In 1895, after what would today be called an industrial accident, he lost a leg and by way of compensation the company set him up in business as a chimney sweep, complete with a donkey and cart as transport.

From this point on there are two versions of this intriguing

---

26 Or Fyfield in an alternative version of the tale.

story. In what we might call the mythologised version, Hitchcock kept in touch with his old colleagues (mostly no doubt in the local alehouses) and one night he rashly declared that his donkey and cart could match the tram easily on the Wantage to Wantage Road Station run. Consequently, a contest was arranged between Jane, the engine used by the tramway, and Hitchcock, his cart and, of course, the gallant donkey (whose name is sadly unrecorded). According to witnesses, as the race started the engine let out a great rush of steam, which so scared the donkey that it tore away into the lead and subsequently won. The other, and rather more prosaic, version of the story records that Hitchcock was making his way back home to Grove when the tram passed close by and spooked the donkey, which subsequently raced away despite Hitchcock's frantic attempts to stop it. There is a wonderful postcard commemorating the event with a cartoon depicting both the tram and cart (complete with sweep's brush) and a 1923 ditty by E C Float describing the race:

> A Curious race has come to pass
> Between an engine and an ass
> The Wantage Tram all steam and smoke
> Was beat by Arthur Hitchcock's moke!

Certainly the jaunty wave that Arthur is giving the tram in the postcard would seem to support the first version of the story. Arthur Hitchcock died in 1942 aged 79; is it possible that his ghost occasionally revisits the scene, either to rerun his famous race or simply to retrace his steps home?

Wantage

Wantage, birthplace of King Alfred in 849 and the location of an Anglo-Saxon royal palace (most likely situated near the spring known today as Alfred's Well), is probably best known for its notorious reputation during the Georgian period, when it became known nationwide as Black Wantage. The name was doubly appropriate: the town was well known as the hideout of choice for anyone fleeing the Bow Street Runners in London because of its reputation as a haunt of bandits and vagrants and, additionally, one of the major legitimate industries in the town was tanning, a singularly dirty and unpleasant occupation. The tunnels which run beneath the town square connecting the oldest public houses in Wantage date from this period and there are a number of slightly tenuous stories of apparitions being glimpsed in most of the older inns in the town, but the most impressive hauntings date from the years of the twentieth century.

At first glimpse ATS Tyres, a steel-framed industrial unit with tarmac car park set back from Grove Street, is probably the last place one might expect to come across a ghost story but, as we have discovered during our meanderings across the Vale, sometimes the most unlikely places can play host to odd mysteries. This tale dates back to the late 1970s and was told to me by Peter, who was at that time the manager of the premises and lived in one of the bungalows which stood off to one side of the site.

The building is a fairly standard tyre and exhaust centre with large metal doors facing onto a parking-area-cum-courtyard. One day two customers were standing just outside the sliding doors, next to a heap of tyres, when Peter, who stood just inside the building, noticed a young girl walk past the entrance, at a distance of around ten feet, and then on past the pile. Intrigued, he peered around the two men but could see no trace of her. Peter had only managed to catch such a fleeting glimpse of the girl that he was unable to describe her clearly, but he commented that she looked for all the world like any other teenager, dressed in jeans and anorak. He found this seemingly unremarkable incident memorable because there was literally nowhere the mysterious girl could have gone.

Clearly this seemingly innocuous incident played on his mind because from that point on, whenever Peter worked at one particular workbench inside the building, he often had the sense of being watched by a person or persons unknown, even though he never actually saw anything to confirm his suspicions. Peter stressed that he never felt at all worried by the unseen presence, just slightly unnerved by the attention. When Peter's sister Jane came to visit the bungalow she sometimes heard her name called from outside (often others would hear the voice calling too), but the yard was always empty.

Inside the shed, along the walls, were long tyre racks, consisting of two parallel bars with individual tyres wedged between them. These racks held the day-to-day stock for ATS. Often tyres would spontaneously jump from the rack (even though they were wedged in so hard that they could normally only be removed with a firm tug) and roll down the aisle to land at the feet of one of the men working nearby. No-one ever saw a tyre actually jump from the rack as this only ever occurred when there was no-one present in the main building. Each of the three men working at ATS experienced this phenomenon at various times over a period of years and they seem to have become almost blasé about the succession of strange events occurring around them.

As if to add a little excitement to the situation, one evening, at about 5.30pm, just as it was starting to get really dark, one of the mechanics was standing beside the main doors looking down the slope towards the road when all of a sudden, Peter's

German Shepherd, which had been inside the workshop, shot past him in a state of terror. Any questions about what had inspired such distress in the poor animal were soon answered as it was almost immediately followed by a soft drink can which sailed out of the semi-dark interior and clattered onto the tarmac in front of the building. Needless to say, a check of the shed revealed that no-one was inside. While most of the human employees shrugged the incident off as just another prank, the poor dog felt otherwise and afterwards resolutely refused to enter the outer yard after dark.

Eventually, the ghost became so familiar around the site that the men started to call her Matilda and became quite fond of her; in fact she became something of a mascot to them all. Only the poor German Shepherd seemed to be unhappy at the ghostly presence and often seemed ill at ease, as if disturbed by something no-one else could ever see.

The family were understandably curious about this mysterious girl who was apparently haunting their home and business and started to make some enquiries of their friends and neighbours. To their surprise, many other people seemed to be aware of 'Matilda' and they began to piece together a story that might help to explain the haunting.

Next to the ATS site there was once a small chapel, The Chapel of the Good Shepherd, which, along with its small graveyard, was lost during redevelopment of the area in the 1980s. At the other end of Grove Street, at the site of what is now a car showroom, stood a house called The Elms where there lived a young girl called Amanda who, according to the various accounts they collected, was said to have died in the house and presumably been buried at the Chapel.[27] Recent reports say that Amanda now walks from the site of

---

[27] One lady in the town reported seeing the ghost of a young girl standing beside the old chapel when she herself was a child over half a century ago, which may add weight to this story.

the old chapel down to the showroom (presumably pausing occasionally to cause a stir at ATS) and has been observed by a number of witnesses, all of whom describe her as being very ordinary and dressed in trousers and a jacket rather like a duffel-coat. A dyed-in-the-wool cynic might ask how a girl who looks so ordinary should come to be identified as a ghost of course, and why a girl who died so long ago is now dressed in modern clothes. I would suggest that this is a purported haunting which would benefit from a few more confirmed sightings before we can draw any firm conclusions.

Until not-so-very long ago, Olivers shoe shop stood on the southern side of the town square with upper windows looking out at the (literally) finely chiselled profile of Lord Wantage adorning the statue of King Alfred. Downstairs was a modern shop floor with a small storage area and a rear staircase leading to a rather old-fashioned unused space on the upper level. When Sue, who told me the story, began working at the shop around 30 years ago, it seemed to be a friendly place, but this was hardly the experience of Jane, a new manageress, who started there some 15 years later. The original shop owners had been content to operate entirely on the ground floor, but the new management determined that having an entire floor of wasted space was uneconomical and decided to use the upper story as a stock room, so the whole floor was cleaned up, tidied, redecorated and racking installed.

It was immediately after this renovation work that Jane began to notice some odd things occurring. The first sign that anything unusual was happening will be quite familiar to us by now – the frequent sound of loud footsteps from the upper floors when Jane was alone

in the shop in the evening. Possibly this could be put down to simple nervousness, after all a woman alone in a shop at night has every entitlement to be apprehensive, but as time passed she became increasingly convinced that her movements were being watched by some unseen presence. This too could be construed as simple anxiety but then things took a turn for the worse and one evening, while she was working on the sales floor, Jane felt a shoe fly past her head, hitting the opposite wall with a dull thump. Given that no-one else was present at the time Jane promptly fled the premises. Thereafter she insisted her husband was present whenever she had to stay late in order to lock up the shop in the evening.

The poltergeist, if that is indeed what it was, was not content with simply throwing shoes. In what might be starting to seem a fairly consistent pattern, it soon became destructive and one morning a number of glass jars from a shelf above the sink in the gents' toilet on the first floor were found smashed on the floor. Naturally there was no sign that anyone had gained entry to the shop. In this case, unlike the Didcot PetFare haunting, no-one seems to have even considered calling the police; given their lack of success in previous incidents of this sort there was probably little that they could have done anyway.

Eventually, just as with the hauntings at Long Wittenham and Didcot, Jane decided to ask for spiritual assistance and a medium was called to perform a 'cleansing'. Strangely, according to my contacts, despite the noises coming from upstairs the ceremony was conducted entirely on the ground floor, although at the end of the proceedings the building was still declared 'clean'. Unlike the neat cut-off to the phenomena in the Didcot case this seems to have had little effect; the noises and 'atmosphere' continued to plague her and eventually Jane was forced to quit her job.

So what were the causes of this particular outbreak of

paranormal activity? I have to stress that this story comes at second-hand and so details are sketchy, but one possible explanation is, as we have seen before, the simple act of opening up the top floor of the building. As the stories from Long Wittenham and Blewbury show, there are numerous cases of hauntings being sparked off through the simple action of demolishing a wall or reopening a sealed door, so this is a distinct possibility. There is, however, another possible cause. Another woman who worked at the shop became severely ill whilst simultaneously undergoing a rather unpleasant divorce. Sadly she died of her illness but, rather than being cremated and having her ashes scattered in accordance with her wishes, her estranged husband arranged for her to be buried in the local cemetery. Was it a coincidence that the hauntings started shortly after her death? Jane, at least, never thought so.

The dental surgery in Portway was, until 50 years or so ago, the town residence of a local doctor. This eminent gentleman was engaged to be married to a young lady who also, and presumably somewhat scandalously, lived at the house. Unfortunately, almost at the last minute he deserted her and ran off with another girl. His original fiancée was so overcome with grief that she either hanged herself in one of the downstairs rooms of the building or, in an alternative version of the story, threw herself into a well built into the property.

Many years after this tragedy the house was converted to a dental surgery but the story continued to play a part in the life of the building. The tragic suicide victim would occasionally be glimpsed in the flat above the 'work' part of the surgery, invariably dressed in old-fashioned dark clothes and long skirt. Contrary to our previous experience, following the conversion of the upper floor to further dental examination rooms these visits ceased.

Until, that is, 4 April 2000. Fiona, the dental hygienist

at the surgery, arrived for work one morning, took off her coat and turned around just in time to catch a glimpse of a woman dressed in dark clothing with a long black skirt. The apparition vanished almost as soon as she was noticed, but Fiona commented that she felt no sense of menace emanating from the figure and was not in the slightest bit unnerved by her appearance (Fiona has also experienced occasional visits from Mr Ryan, the late dentist at the practice, so she is perhaps unusually relaxed about such things!)[28] One further point of interest about this sighting is that the room in which Fiona works has a well hidden beneath its floor; given that a well features in one version of the suicide story it would be interesting to speculate as to whether the date of the apparition's appearance was as significant as its location.

The Priory in Wantage is a beautiful old building with a history stretching back many years. Originally built some time before 1534 when the first documentary evidence of the building occurs, it was first held by the Priors of Bec in France (although it was never actually inhabited by a prior despite its name) before passing into secular hands. At various times the Priory functioned as a minor manorial property and a boy's school before settling down to a genteel retirement as a family home. The most famous inhabitant of the house was the moral philosopher the Reverend (later Bishop) Butler, who later became personal chaplain to Queen Caroline, the wife of King George II.

The Miller family, who lived in the house for 30 years, were always quite reconciled, perhaps even proud, to have a ghost, especially one as gentle as theirs. Their first inkling of another presence in the house had come when Mrs Kathleen Miller felt what she presumed to be an animal brush against her legs

---

28 Who would have thought a dental hygienist could get into so many paranormal scrapes?

in the kitchen one day. Assuming that it was the family dog she turned around only to find the animal asleep on a chair in another room. Shortly afterwards the family began to notice that one of the doors in the kitchen, a door which had warped so badly that it was very difficult to open by hand, would inexplicably open itself when no-one was around. Equally mysteriously, the lid of the family piano began to slam itself shut when nobody was present in the room.

Following on from this initial contact the resident ghost began to become more and more tactile. One of the family daughters felt an unseen hand stroke her arm, an occurrence that became commonplace within the household. But, strangely, only the dark-haired ladies of the house. Clearly this phantom was a person of particular tastes. In fact the groping ghost seemed to take a particular interest in women with dark hair and eyes. A female locum from the nearby doctor's surgery once lodged at the house and on the first day she arrived Mr John Miller was down in the cellar with a local builder, looking at some maintenance work that needed doing. As the locum (an attractive young lady by all accounts, with dark hair and dark eyes) knocked at the front door a heavy oaken door to the side of the cellar, a door that had been sealed for as long as the Millers had owned the house, swung open of its own accord, as if someone was in a hurry to get past the two men. 'Our locum has arrived,' commented Mr Miller, 'I bet she has dark hair.'

The family had a theory to explain this mysterious presence. During the Napoleonic War era the houses opposite the Priory were used to imprison French soldiers. Their explanation is that one of these soldiers fell in love with a serving maid but was eventually repatriated to France after 1815 (this date is significant, not just because of the Battle of Waterloo but also because this date was found scratched into the glass of one of the upstairs windows). According to the Millers' charming

 explanation, the soldier made his way back from France to claim his love, only to discover that she had married someone else in his absence. Presumably, after his death his spirit returned to a place where he had once hoped to know happiness.

As is so often the case, there may be an alternative explanation to this particular haunting. Local history records that one of the Napoleonic prisoners was found dead in the nearby Letcombe Brook under mysterious circumstances one night, so it is also possible that it is his ghost at the house. The Millers were certain that the ghost was French because of the discovery of an old sol coin dating to the time of George II found during renovation work some years ago, but there have been other Frenchmen in and around the house over the years. During the time the Priory was a boys' school it proudly advertised that 'French is taught by a native of Paris' (doubtless some poor refugee from the war who had gravitated to Wantage for unknown reasons) so perhaps it is this personage who was responsible for both coin and haunting.

Following the departure of first the daughters and then Mrs Miller herself from the house, the ghost has been rather quiet of late. It would be nice to think that the gentle ghost of the Priory is still in residence and it will just take a visit from a dark lady to arouse his passions once more.

The Parish Register in Wantage records what was at the time seen as a marvel, but which we today would consider a sombre medical tragedy:

> September 1598. A strange miracle! The eighth day were buried 2 male children growing together from the breast to

the navells, having all their right members each of them, being the children of John Russell and Elizabeth his wife.

There are no other details given, nor are we told whether the unfortunate mother survived what must have been a difficult birth. There are no memorials in the church to these unknown conjoined twins, but there is one notable whose mortal remains can be located in Wantage Church: Ivo Fitzwarren. Fitzwarren was the father-in-law of Dick Whittington of Lord Mayor of London and subsequent pantomime fame and, without being too specific about the exact location of his memorial, if you stand gazing at the altar, he's behind you...

Back in September 1971 an uncultivated field on the edge of the newly built Stockham Park housing estate was the site of a fascinating, and entirely bizarre, monster panic. The story first made the news when an anonymous but concerned parent phoned the police one weekend complaining that children playing in and around the field had been terrified by a creature described as 'eight feet tall, off-white in colour with furry skin, large eyes a foot apart and with horns and a pointed beard.' Two boys told police that they had been chased by the monster and one of them, 14-year-old Michael Nicholls from East Challow, drew a picture to illustrate what they had seen. To their credit, the police did not dismiss this fantastic tale out of hand and two policemen using car headlights and torches combed the field and surrounding area for traces of the creature. Perhaps unsurprisingly, they found nothing.

Earlier that morning, a Mr Herbert Halstead of Stockham Park had reported being startled by something on a grass bank beside the Denchworth Road as he drove to work at around 5.30 am:

> The headlights of my car picked out a big white head which appeared to have two large eyes. As I drove nearer the head appeared to move back and then disappeared. I'm certain it wasn't a cow or other animal but didn't stay around to find out!

Later that same day, an 18-year-old girl described seeing a large hairy figure entering woods beside the old Wilts and Berks Canal between Stockham and Grove. Linda Milne of East Challow said:

> I'm not the type to imagine things. It was very tall and had broad shoulders. It moved very quickly through the woods. Don't ask me what it was – I was very frightened.

After these reports had appeared in the local *Wantage Herald* paper the story spread – children were said to be afraid to play outside and parents were understandably concerned that there might be something behind the monster story. Of course, no-one was sure exactly what that 'something' might be. One mother claimed that her 13-year-old son came home in a distressed state saying he had seen the monster. 'I can't believe there is such a thing roaming around but I can't disbelieve my son,' she said. *The Herald* sent a reporter and photographer to search the area but they found nothing that might confirm the existence of the monster. Reporter Alan Cousins commented:

> The wood where the creature was reported to have been seen moving quickly is covered in thick brambles. It would be impossible for anything to move quickly without leaving traces. It is almost certain that a furry or hairy object or animal would have its coat torn by the brambles.

They also searched the fields where the children had reported their sighting, but to no avail.

In an interview broadcast on Radio Oxford a few days later, the two Challow boys elaborated on their previous tale by describing how, after they had been spotted by the creature, it had raced towards them and they had pelted it with stones before fleeing. Hoping to slow it down, they clambered over a gate as they fled, but the monster easily jumped the same gate in its pursuit. Luckily the boys eventually managed to either outpace the creature or lose it in the woods and shortly afterwards they watched in amazement as a disc-shaped UFO took off from a nearby field, presumably carrying the creature away.

Interestingly, these monster encounters coincided with a cluster of well-reported UFO sightings around Banbury, though whether these reports were known to any of the monster witnesses is open to conjecture. Connection or not, some weeks later Michael Prewett and Richard Colborne of the Surrey Investigation Group on Aerial Phenomena interviewed children who had claimed to have seen the monster and the British UFO Research Organisation also showed an interest in the goings-on at Wantage.

Sadly the story seems to have been lost to memory after this and there are few people who still remember the incident. As a boy in 1971 I can certainly confirm that it was much discussed at the time, but I would disagree with *The Herald*'s assertion that children were too traumatised to go out to play; I was often part of one of many search parties comprising local children all combing the area for the monster. It is probably for the best that our parents never discovered what we were doing.

There were, of course, many theories as to the identity of the creature. Alien visitors in silver discs may have been top of the agenda for passing UFOlogists, but more down-to-earth commentators favoured a simple hoaxer dressed in a fur coat and mask, though no suspect ever came to light. If this was the correct explanation then evidently some aspects of the descriptions given to the police and press were much exaggerated, especially the monster's height. Also, don't forget that the two reporters declared that no-one could have moved through the heavily overgrown woodland without leaving some trace, so if it was a hoaxer he or she would have had to have been an excellent woodsman. Taking these factors into consideration I am unsure how much weight to give to the claim by two local men named Keith and Richard that they started the whole affair, with one balancing on the shoulders of the other while disguised by a long coat. Chasing teenagers, leaping gates and moving through undergrowth seem impossible feats for the precariously balanced pair, but even such an uncomfortable explanation seems more plausible than an unknown monster terrorising the outskirts of a small town.

At this point I have another coincidence to bring to your attention: a few years later, in 1977 to be precise, a seven-feet-tall hairy creature with red staring eyes was seen near Wantage and its appearance terrorised the Stiles family, who lived on the outskirts of town at the time. Was this the same creature? I think it highly unlikely, since this sighting took place in Wantage, New Jersey...

Given the ability of our local monster to move unhindered through undergrowth and vanish into thin air, could it really be possible that this was some sort of supernatural visitation? The idea does seem unlikely but compare and contrast with the following account from an area nearby, which took place 30 years earlier.

This story was told by Mrs Jan Giles and happened when she was a child out with her sister one evening, on an errand in Newbury Street for their parents. Having completed their appointed tasks she recalled that they 'dawdled along, taking a peep at this and that and having a good giggle as children do.' Realising it was getting dark, the girls decided to head home from town along Ickleton Road towards their house, Ham Lodge, which was located beside the road turning to Letcombe. Their route took them past King Alfred's School and down the slope towards Letcombe Brook and it was on this part of the road that their encounter began:

> As we hurried down the hill my sister happened to glance over her shoulder and then, looking a bit pale, whispered, 'There's someone following us.

Both girls promptly broke into a run.

> Glancing back after a time we were horrified to see that the figure was exactly the same distance away and there was no sound of footsteps. In sheer desperation I gasped to my sister, 'Let's walk very slowly so he will have to pass us.' This we did, huddled together for protection. Taking a quick peep we found, to our further consternation, that the figure was still exactly the same distance from us and completely silent. From then on we alternated between fast and slow with the same results each time. The position of the figure was precise in that it never varied one inch.

Finally, and doubtless with a huge sense of relief, the girls came within sight of their house but, on looking back for the figure, they found the road completely empty and the figure vanished, even though there was nowhere anyone could easily (and silently) have left the road. Thankful to have shaken off their odd pursuer, they approached their front path only to be suddenly confronted by the shadowy stalker. Paralysed with fear, they watched the figure glide across the road in a crouching posture and vanish through a brick wall. 'Glide is not the right word really,' observed Mrs Giles, 'this figure seemed to amble on all fours like an ape.'

On hearing their story, the girls' father came out to

investigate. He found nothing out of the ordinary but he did tell the girls that he too had encountered the mysterious phantom. In his account a shadowy figure joined him at the bridge over the Brook and remained menacingly beside him until he reached Ham Lodge. Fearing he was about to be attacked, he attempted to strike the figure with his fist. Imagine his horror when his arm passed right through the apparition, which immediately vanished into thin air...

Apart from a shared air of unreality and an approximate geographical proximity there is actually very little to link these two stories. I am not aware of any subsequent reports of either of these sinister visions, but even so it is always worth keeping an eye out for crouching spectres and eight-foot monsters should you find yourself heading westwards out of Wantage.

Ardington

A common myth in the Middle Ages (although variants of the theme date back to the early Christian era) was that in times of famine a mother pelican would pierce her own breast with her sharp beak and allow her young chicks to feed on her own blood. The religious imagery is clear and the legend is illustrated in a charming carving on a corbel in the porch at Ardington Church; the same fable is illustrated in a carving on one of the misericords at Wantage.[29]

Next time you find yourself strolling through Ardington think kindly on the memory of poor Martha Warman from Hendred who was, somewhat scandalously, out walking near Ardington with two young men in June 1832 when a bolt of lightning struck from a stormy sky, killing her instantly. One of the witnesses described how the 'electric fluid' leapt onto the metal wire forming the structure of her bonnet and then passed through her body, tearing her stockings and totally destroying her boots. Her two young gentlemen companions were thrown to the ground but were otherwise unhurt. Needless to say, her fate was blamed on her immodest behaviour (what the young men had to say about this is not recorded), and a memorial seat, known locally as Martha Warman's Bench, was placed at the spot where she died. It was still in place in the early years of the twentieth century and was often used to illustrate to local girls the perils of straying from the straight and narrow.

---

29 Misericords are wide lips on flip-up seats in a church. They date back to the time when much of a church service involved standing, something that was clearly not possible for the elderly or infirm who would therefore take advantage of the relief offered by these small shelves: a similar arrangement of stone benches around the church wall is often said to be the origin of the phrase 'the weakest to the wall'.

Ginge

Ginge Manor, the family seat of the Viscounts Astor, was constructed in the early seventeenth century and much extended in the hundred or so years thereafter. For much of its history it was content to be an unremarkable country pile, but in the early years of the twentieth century it acquired a reputation locally as a haunted house, though very little actual haunting seems to have taken place. Details are sketchy but the ghost was popularly believed to be a man named Tubb, who was murdered by his brother and his body dumped down a shaft under the cellar. This same cellar was used as a place of punishment, a subterranean naughty-step if you will, for unruly servant boys at the manor and many was the young lad who was released from the dark telling tales of unearthly noises coming up from below the floor. One serving woman whose duties habitually took her down into the cellar to draw beer would often flee back upstairs on hearing ghostly footsteps in the blackness. One night Lord Ernle, who held the Lordship at the time, was reported to have dreamt of two men sitting round a large oak table in a stone flagged kitchen. He described one as a huge burly chap and the other thin and wiry. They were arguing furiously about something and his Lordship felt sure that one was on the verge of murdering the other. Unfortunately, just as a possible clue to the identity of the spirit said to haunt the house was about to be revealed… he woke up!

This is not the only ghost story from the village, as there is also a curious sighting associated with a sadly unspecified barn in Ginge, dating back to the 1940s or 1950s. One darkish night a lady farmer went out to close up this barn and was astonished to find it full of helmeted and armoured Puritan soldiers. As they moved she was further astounded to notice that they all seemed to be missing the lower part of their legs from the shins down. I have no further information about this spectral company, but the fact that the barn floor was some twelve inches lower during the Civil War might serve to confirm the veracity of the tale and explain the soldiers' missing feet.

Curiously, there is an almost identical story from nearby East Hendred. In this case we have the name of the witness, a lady who died in 1946 and who was known as Old Mrs Chatterton, who is said to have seen a number of Roundheads without feet in her house, Barn End. Documents show that some of Cromwell's men did sleep there after the battle of Newbury and Mrs Chatterton is said to have later discovered that the floor had been raised in the years since the soldiers' sleepover. Are these two entirely independent cases of pared-down parliamentarians or has the story at some point been transposed from one location to the other (clearly a distinct possibility given the proximity of the two locations)? Unless the footloose soldiers decide to make another appearance it is unlikely we will ever know.

Ghost stories are all very well but Ginge has much more to offer. In particular the village once hosted a highly unusual industry, one which is rarely mentioned in these unenlightened times but which was at one time a very popular topic of discussion locally: the Ginge Treacle Mines. No-one seems to know when or where this local myth originated but it was certainly in circulation in the 1960s and 1970s, especially amongst the children of the area, encouraged no doubt by slightly teasing parents and less-credulous friends. What most people fail to realise is that this is far from being entirely fanciful, even

though treacle mines are, if you will pardon the expression, more than usually unusual folkloric locations. Nationally there are numerous examples of treacle *wells*, the best-known of which is the St Margaret's Treacle Well at Binsey, made famous by Lewis Carroll in *Alice's Adventures in Wonderland*, but considerably fewer equally celebrated *mines*. The nearest to Ginge are located at Bisham and Tilehurst, but there are a few other examples scattered across the country from Sussex to Scotland.

A possible explanation for the name, one which is especially associated with the treacle mines in Tadley, Hampshire, is that during the Civil War, parliamentarian soldiers buried barrels of valuable molasses on the outskirts of the town, and these barrels later leaked, allowing the contents to seep to the surface. As we have noted, there was a strong parliamentarian presence in this area but, even so, this seems to be stretching the bounds of credulity. An even more unlikely development of this idea is that syrup or treacle tins were used as ad-hoc savings accounts and filled with coins or other valuables and buried; subsequent treacle miners were criminals who dug up other people's secret stashes. I have a suspicion that anyone who discovered that their life savings had been dug up and stolen would have a few choice names for the thief but that treacle-miner would not be among them!

The more usual explanation given for the naming of treacle wells is that the word 'treacle' as used here derives from the old French word *triacle,* meaning an antidote to venomous bites, and one can only assume that a similar derivation applies to treacle mines. In similar vein, *treacle-water* was a mixture of various herbs suspended in liquid, a concoction which was said to be a powerful cure-all. The alchemist Paracelsus prescribed *Treacle of Mummy* for the same purpose. This is not just a British belief by the way – the Persian *tiryak* or *Treacle of Baghdad* was also said to be a sure-fire antidote to poison.

The implication is that treacle wells (and mines) were in some way associated with healing but, for this to be applicable for Ginge, it must, like Binsey, have had some sort of reputation as a healing well in the past.

The Binsey Treacle Well has a stone surround designed to make it easier for supplicants to approach and draw water from the well, whereas, in stark contrast, the Ginge Brook currently rises largely unnoticed before running away equally unremarked. This was not always the case, however; Eleanor Hayden, writing around 1902, was told that at least one or two generations before that, the spring had once been marked by a 'nuck' or hollow, where the chalk rock retreated in a rude semicircle forming a pool. According to one aged local this water must have been warmer in previous times: 'It steamed like a furnace it did, a' all the water quimpled an' b'iled somethen cur'ous' – although he may just have been visiting on a frosty morning since hot springs do seem to be an unlikely amenity to find along the edge of the Downs.

This *whirllypool* as it was then known was certainly appreciated for its health-giving properties at one time, since the same character described how many people came back again and again, staying at a 'House of Mercy', which stood near the pool. Hardly modern medicine of course, but if the water *was* warm it might have been of some use in easing aches and pains at least; alternatively, it may have been drunk as at Cheltenham or Buxton. The health-giving pool was eventually remodelled and planted up with watercress (much to the distress of Miss Hayden), but interestingly Leslie Tubb,[30] who was the last commercial tender of the watercress beds, reported that the water from the spring was constant in temperature being cool in summer and 'pleasantly warm in winter', so it might just be possible that multi-seasonal bathing

---

30 I wonder if he was related to the battling brothers at Ginge Manor?

was indeed the treatment of choice. How sad that Ginge never attained the status of a spa town like Bath. In any case, even the watercress pool seems to have fallen into disuse at some point in the mid-nineteenth century, becoming overgrown and unkempt.

So, nothing now remains of a place which, in the minds of numerous children at least, would have been the highlight of a trip to Ginge, real treacle or not. It seems that, even in folkloric terms, Britain is becoming more and more post-industrial and it would be a shame if the memory of the mines were to be lost forever. There are a few Treacle Mine Hotels and Inns across the country in locations associated with putative treacle mining – are there any intrepid entrepreneurs out there in the Vale who might be persuaded to follow suit in Ginge?

Lockinge

There is a very brief anecdote, reported in the *Daily Telegraph* no less, as told by the nephew of Robert Loyd-Lindsay, Lord Wantage, of a strange vision he witnessed while visiting his uncle for dinner. George Holford, a Scots Guardsman who at one point served as equerry to the Duke of Clarence and was later knighted, never specifically dated his tale but we can infer that it took place some time during the early 1880s. Captain Holford's account tells us that he was walking towards Lockinge House when he came to the crossroads of the Oxford to Newbury and Wantage to Wallingford roads. Before him he saw two men struggling, one man stretched out on the ground and the other poised above him stabbing down with a knife. Captain Holford dashed forward in an attempt to intervene and swung his walking stick at the aggressor but was horrified to see it pass right through the struggling figure; the combatants then vanished to thin air and he found himself alone.

Needless to say, when he arrived for dinner his tale was greeted with more than a little scepticism, but when Lord Wantage mentioned the story to a tenant some time later the farmer informed him that a murder had indeed taken place at that very spot and that it had been considered haunted ever since.

From our point of view it is a shame that the two figures are not described in any detail, as this account bears a startling similarity to the struggle of the two brothers as dreamt by Lord Astor just down the road at Ginge Manor.

Hendred

Locals in East Hendred will tell you that Allin's Lane is perhaps haunted and that a ghost may occasionally be glimpsed at the sixteenth-century Kings Manor in the centre of the village, but it is the more western of the two Hendreds which can boast the best-documented and most shocking apparition. As you approach Wantage along the A417 (from the haunted crossroads at Rowstock in fact) you will find the Hare Public House on the right hand side of the road, just after Hendred dip. If you are of a mood you might stop for a drink or a meal; if not your journey will take you on past Lockinge and Ardington to the left and on to Wantage and beyond. However, one evening in 1964 two women making this very same trip had an encounter that they would rather have avoided.

Mrs Prior and her sister, both in their late twenties and living in Blewbury, were heading into Wantage for an evening class just before Christmas when they met their ghost. Mrs Prior takes up the story:

> We were a little late leaving home at around 7.15pm and as we were approaching the Hare a figure like a man dashed out in front of my car from the direction of the cottages to the left. I braked instantly because I thought I was going to kill him; I expected a collision but we felt nothing. I couldn't possibly have avoided hitting him. I prepared myself for the bump but nothing happened.

Both women in the car had seen the figure and both looked back expecting the worst, but could see nothing except the disappearing tail lights of a car which had passed them immediately after the phantom accident.

After the incident the sisters continued on to their evening class, shaken but otherwise none the worse for the experience. Could the headlights of the approaching car have caused some optical illusion which they interpreted as a running man in the darkness, or could this possibly have been a real man who narrowly avoided death on his way to the pub? In fact an elderly man had been killed at that very spot three years before so this may, just possibly, have been a ghostly replay of that tragic event. Sadly, despite the story appearing in the paper, the driver of the other car never came forward to report seeing anything amiss so there is no way to verify what the two young women saw that night.

Road phantoms are a fairly well documented part of paranormal folklore – there are almost identical cases recorded fairly locally, at High Wycombe in 1936 and Gloucester in 1996 to name but two – but the Hendred figure is the only example I know of in the Vale. I had assumed that the story told by Mrs Prior was a unique sighting for this location until I heard about the experience of Richard, who was driving the same route sometime in the early 1990s when he too had a collision with a strange figure dashing across the road. He was so shaken by the experience that he immediately drove to Wantage Police Station and reported the 'accident' even though no trace of a body could be found after the collision.

This second incident throws a whole new light on this ghost sighting. Rather than just being an interesting one-off event, it is possible that we may now be looking at a recurrent haunting, which opens up the possibility that another driver could experience a similar traumatic episode at some time in the future. So, if you are driving past West Hendred late at night, make sure to pay particular attention to the road ahead.

Scutchamer Knob

Hard beside the Ridgeway, up beyond the Hendreds, stands a lonely burial mound which, considering its remoteness, is not only known by a bewildering variety of names but also has a considerable array of stories to account for its origins. According to one telling many, many years ago, back in the dawn of history the Devil (for reasons known only to his infernal self) decided to dig a ditch across Berkshire and Oxfordshire. The ditch he dug ran along the space between the prehistoric tracks of Ridgeway and the Icknield Way and even today remnants can still be seen in the form of Grim's Ditch. Near Chuckhamsley he paused in his work to clean the earth off his spade and the clod of earth that remained has been known since as Chuckhamsley Knob. Other names for this landmark have included Cuckhamsley, Cuckhamslow, Cuchinslow, Suchamere, Sotchamfly, Scotsmans and, more usually today, Scutchamer Knob. Two of these names derive from alternative theories for the barrow's existence; in one story it marks the grave of local soldiers killed after a battle with the Scots, in another it marks the burial spot of one Captain Scutchamer who was killed in the Civil War.

Historical accuracy aside, this name must have more force than any other for it is the one featured on modern OS maps. The more prosaic academic community insists that the Knob is a Bronze age burial mound, although its present croissant shape is of a more modern derivation, for the mound was severely damaged by crude excavations in 1842 (plus an attempt to use the soil from the mound as fertiliser!) and then reduced in height during the Second World War so as to present less of a danger to aircraft using local airfields.

The Knob seems to have been used as a *gemot* or moot point, a sort of local meeting place, parliament and legal court, during Saxon times. One of the Saxon names for the site was *Cwicchelmeshlaew* meaning 'the law of Cwichelm' – Cwichelm being a local chief of the *Gewissae* (pronounced Yoo-iss-eye) tribe, probably some time around the seventh century AD, two centuries before the birth of King Alfred. He was also the son of King Cynegils, whom you may remember as the eventual patron of St Birinus. Is the violent nature of Saxon justice reflected in the nearby Kilman Knoll and Bury Down? Certainly the mound has known violence in the past, for in 1006 an invading army of Danes were passing through the Vale, casually sacking Wallingford on their way, when legend has it that they were given a prophecy that they would never need to take a ship from England again if they camped at Cwichelm's Law. Assuming that this meant that their eventual conquest was assured they hastened to comply but, as is so often the case with such auguries, they were sadly mistaken; the Saxons fell upon the invaders as they slept and slaughtered them to a man. The Anglo-Saxon Chronicle wryly comments: 'They then went home by another way.'

There is a fragment of fairy lore associated with Scutchamer Knob that tells of how a local farmer was working in the fields nearby when his plough hit a rock, badly deforming the ploughshare. Unable to proceed with his work he was forced to walk back down the hill to fetch tools to make repairs, presumably partaking of some lunch and a drink during the break, and then returned some time later to the field by the Knob. It was at this point that he discovered that some kind benefactor had taken pity on him and straightened his plough blade; indeed, it had been left sharper than before.

The obvious implication of this tale is that some fey being took the time to assist the man for reasons of their own; possibly a simple desire to help or possibly just pure caprice. This explanation ties in nicely with the proximity of Scutchamer Knob, because prehistoric monuments were often associated with fairy folk in the popular imagination and were seen as 'fairy mounds' within which whole communities of the Seelie Court would dwell. There is only one problem with this interpretation and that is that the touch of cold iron was anathema to any of the fairy blood; in fact its mere presence was sufficient to make any of the elven kind uncomfortable. It seems likely that the Good Samaritan in this tale must have been one of the more earthen spirits, perhaps a dwarf or hobgoblin, who are usually depicted as being more malevolent (or at least mischievous) but who are unharmed by iron and steel and who were said to occasionally aid mortals should the whim take them. There was a type of dwarfish fairy found in Devon known as a *Derrick*, which had something of an evil reputation for leading travellers astray in the south-west, but which could also be found on the Berkshire Downs, where they were said to be much more helpful. Perhaps one of this little-known tribe went to the aid of the farmer in this story.

There is just one more legend associated with Scutchamer Knob which is worth the telling. This tale relates how one enterprising local attempted to dig into the barrow in search of buried treasure.[31] In this case the response of the  fairy inhabitants was considerably more direct and a massive thunderstorm sprang up, frightening him away. Note how the idea that anyone who searches for gold in burial mounds is doomed to failure is echoed in the similar story from Wittenham Clumps.

---

31 Perhaps he had also heard tell of golden coffins buried hereabouts.

Larger than life

Born in 1714, John Elwes (né Meggott) was a miser among misers and, quite unusually (for often the truly mean grow uniquely from an otherwise normal family tree), he came from a line of those similarly inclined. His father, Robert Meggot, was a respected brewer from London and his grandfather was Sir George Meggot, MP for Southwark; his mother, Amy Elwes, was of more noble birth being the granddaughter of Sir Gervase Elwes, 1st Baronet and MP for Suffolk. John was only four years old when his father died and he was the main beneficiary of the estate; in the will his mother was left the sum of £100,000 (a huge fortune in those days) but reputedly starved to death because she was too mean to spend any of it. (*Her* mother, the Lady Isabella, was also well-known for her parsimony, but not to such a life-threatening extent.) On the death of his mother, the young man inherited the family mansion Marcham Park, west of Abingdon (now Denman College, the Women's Institute adult education facility), which his father, clearly paying no heed to the financial caution of the distaff side of the family, had bought only a year before his death.

John's uncle was another notorious miser, Sir Harvey Elwes, 2nd Baronet, of Stoke, a man who famously refused to spend more than £10 on himself annually and who clearly encouraged the family tendency for thrift in his nephew whenever he had cause to visit. As Drew puts it in *Lives and Portraits of Curious and Odd Characters*:

> There they would sit ... with a single stick upon the fire and with one glass of wine occasionally betwixt them, inveighing against the extravagance of the times; and when evening shut in they would immediately retire to rest as going to bed saved candle light.

In order to curry favour with his uncle, John changed his name to Elwes, a gesture which bore fruit when he eventually inherited another quarter of a million pounds in 1763.

Even all this additional wealth did not encourage him to a more lavish lifestyle. He became MP for Berkshire but spent the princely sum of eighteen pence in conducting his election: fortunately politics was driven far more by patronage than popularity in those days. Although Berkshire was his constituency he much preferred to stay at his house in Suffolk, because while travelling to Berkshire by coach would cost a whole *fourpence,* he could get to Suffolk for just *twopence-halfpenny*. Naturally, as an MP he regularly had to visit London but he eventually took to avoiding paying for his trip at all, travelling on an old worn-out nag, choosing routes which avoided toll roads and insisting on sleeping out in the open rather than frequenting any of the inns along the way. Although he owned numerous properties in London, he preferred to stay in a rotting, glassless pile in Marylebone attended by a single old woman as servant. This nearly led to his death, for later in his life he fell ill in one of these tumbledown properties and no-one could find him. He was only located when his nephew, Colonel Timms, heard from a pot boy who recalled seeing an 'old beggar' go into a stable at one of Elwes's houses and lock the door behind him. Timms contacted the constables, who broke in and found Elwes in bed with a fever – the old woman was discovered frozen to death in another room. Many of his houses were in a similar parlous state of disrepair and on one occasion Col. Timms, who was staying with Elwes at the time, reported having spent an uncomfortable rainy night moving his rough bed about the room in a vain attempt to find a spot where the roof above him did not leak.

For all his personal parsimony, Elwes was an easy target for those who came to him offering to increase his wealth. He invested, if that is anywhere near the right word, in a number of schemes such as non-existent properties in the United States and bonds issued by noblemen with no capital to their names. Luckily he had no head for figures, for had he realised that these get-rich-quick schemes had cost him anything up to £150,000, the shock would probably have killed him on the spot.

Elwes took to wearing rags until they almost rotted from his body and at one point found an old beggar's cast-off wig in a hedge, wearing it proudly thereafter. In fact his demeanour was so miserable that passers-by would sometimes press pennies charitably into his hand. His frugal lifestyle eventually took its toll and he was one day found dead in bed, wearing his usual threadbare clothes and tattered shoes.

Despite these personal foibles he was an honest and generous politician, often lending huge sums of money (which were rarely recovered) to friends and financing major building and improvement projects in London. He (somehow) mixed in high society despite his lack of sartorial care and was highly regarded as a thinker. He refused to pay for John and George, his illegitimate sons, to go to school, on the grounds that 'putting things into people's heads, was taking money out of their pockets', but when he died in 1789 he left them half a million pounds! Presumably, they had to pay someone else to count it. If you are looking for something more to mark the passing of a man of such contradictions then it is worth noting that Charles Dickens cited John Elwes as being the inspiration for Ebenezer Scrooge in *A Christmas Carol*.

In 1781, just a few years before John Elwes met his cold and miserable end, another notable character by the name of Morgan Jones became curate of the village of Blewbury and set about creating a reputation for mean-spiritedness to rival that of his more illustrious contemporary. It is said that 'Blewbury Jones', as he became known, lived in the village for 42 years and for all that time always wore the same hat and coat. This coat, he patched himself, until little of the original cloth remained and when the hat finally became too ragged to wear he was only too happy to purloin a replacement from a scarecrow he passed in a field near Upton. He rarely lit a fire, even in the depths of the coldest winter, and even then would collect fallen branches rather than pay for firewood.

Of course even misers have to eat and Jones, being particularly fond of bacon, managed to turn the process of procuring his meat to his advantage. He would buy his bacon from a farmer who lived nearby but would make one trip to arrange the purchase (and stay for tea and supper while he did so), another trip to collect the meat (two more free meals) and then, finally and doubtless most painfully, would pay another visit to actually hand over the money to the farmer (although another two meals would doubtless take a sizable chunk out of any profit the farmer might have hoped to make). Like Elwes, Parson Jones would also retire early, both to seek the relative warmth of his bed and to avoid the need for expensive candles. From an income of fifty pounds a year his expenses are thought to have been as little as two shillings and sixpence a week, which meant that on his death he was the proud possessor of over £18,000, a significant fortune for a country parson. Apparently his famous coat was kept in a display case for a while before finally being consigned to the scrap heap, although I have no idea whether this was in celebration of his life or as a dire warning of the dangers of his lifestyle.

Should this talk of the miserable and miserly depress you I will, by way of contrast, just mention a contemporary gentleman, one Mr Tiptaft of Sutton Courtenay, who lived humbly, gave almost all his property away to charitable causes and yet single-handedly funded the building of a new chapel in Abingdon.[32] On hearing of his generosity a friend insisted on giving him £800 with which to support himself; Tiptaft only agreed to take the money on the proviso he could give half of it away. His friend agreed and Tiptaft gave away £400... and then the *other* £400! He died entirely penniless but doubtless considerably happier than either of our previous two characters.

Little is actually known about the next gentleman in this section; I do not even know his first name, only that he was usually referred to in respectful tones as 'Warlock Manning'. Manning was a Cunning Man – one of the very last of the breed – during the Victorian era and seems to have been something of a local celebrity who was sought out for advice and assistance on a wide range of matters. He may well have lived in the Vale at some point[33] because contemporary sources tell of a man from Marsh Gibbon, a village near Bicester, who walked all the way to Abingdon to consult Manning about a £5 note which he had lost in suspicious circumstances and to ask for his help in recovering his losses. Now, even though £5 was a considerable sum in those days (this incident took place in January 1841), a round trip of 40 miles in the depths of winter speaks volumes for Manning's reputation, even if we do not know if his assistance resulted in the return of the missing cash.

---

32 Finally, someone we could legitimately call a Valedictorian...

33 He could usually be found in the Bicester area.

While Warlock Manning could offer advice it seems that his words of wisdom were not always followed to the letter and so his cures were not universally successful. In one story, told in 1897 by an old lady called Jinny Bigerstaff, there lived near Chipping Norton in the late 1850s an old woman named Dolly Henderson who was renowned locally as a witch, and not a nice one at that. One day a neighbour of Dolly's named Anne Hulver had the temerity to argue with her and, as a result, old Dolly secretly cursed the poor woman, who subsequently became seriously ill. Hulver was sick for a long time and when medical treatments seemed unable to help she began to suspect that she was the victim of malign magic. In desperation she visited Manning, who advised her that on her way home she would meet the woman who had caused her illness, but that she was not to speak to her or say anything to anyone about her; if she followed these instructions to the letter she would be cured. Alas, Anne Hulver was clearly unable to hold her tongue and she told some friends working in the fields what Manning had said and thus her cure was ineffectual – in fact her condition worsened until she was said to have become almost skeletally thin and very near to death. Despite Manning's lack of success on this occasion there is still a happy ending to the story, because at about the same time as Anne Hulver was having her problems a young local boy was also bewitched by old Dolly. On discovering this, his brother threw a thorn stick at the old woman, which tore her arm and made it bleed a great deal. Anne Hulver and the boy then both miraculously recovered but the old witch died, much to the delight of the rest of the village. (Note how this cure exactly matches that in the Abingdon witches case; one can only wonder why Manning did not suggest it himself.)

Mostly, as might be expected from his reputation, Manning was rather more successful. To the north of Faringdon near Radcot a tall wooden construction known as Old Man's Bridge crosses the Thames. This was built in the 1890s and replaced an earlier footbridge, which, it is said, was named in honour of Manning after he visited the area and performed a singular service for the locals. It seems that when Manning was passing through the village of Bampton, the inhabitants of nearby

Clanfield took the opportunity to contact him about a matter of some urgency. At that time various prominent members of the community in Clanfield had fallen into some sort of disagreement; certainly a significant proportion of the village had taken one side or the other and recriminations and harsh words were widespread, causing major disruption to normal village life. Something had to be done and the arrival of Manning must have seemed providential to say the least.

After being appraised of the situation, Manning announced that the names of everyone involved in the feud should be engraved onto pieces of wood and, at the stroke of midnight, all were to be thrown off Old Man's Bridge into the river in a spiritually cleansing version of the game of pooh-sticks. As the wood was swept away by the current the pieces would intermingle and, in a rather neat piece of sympathetic magic, so would peace be restored to Clanfield. Whether the magic was genuinely effective or whether it was just a clever piece of theatre, the plan clearly worked and normal relations were quickly restored.

Not all of our local characters are to be found beyond living memory – some seem far more 'modern' to our contemporary gaze. Take, for example, writer and composer Gerald Hugh Tyrwhitt-Wilson who was born in 1883 and, with his naval officer father away at sea for long periods, was raised by his mother and grandmother. It seems he railed against their traditional Victorian values from a young age. It was as a child that his enquiring mind and impetuous nature first manifested itself: on hearing that a dog could be taught to swim by throwing it into the water he wondered whether a dog could be taught to fly if thrown from an upstairs window... Contemporary accounts report that the experiment was not a success though the dog was, luckily, unharmed.

Tyrwhitt-Wilson was educated at Eton and spent a brief spell in the diplomatic service before, on the death of his uncle in 1918, the young man suddenly found himself the 14th Baron Berners, a role that enabled him to express his personal eccentricities without having to worry about the cost, either financial or reputational. The new Lord Berners was a talented composer, artist, writer and friend of many of the artists and literati of the day; Nancy Mitford actually based Lord Merlin in her

Pursuit of Love on Berners, though Virginia Woolf unkindly referred to him as a 'round, fat little man'.

With money in the bank Berners quickly purchased Faringdon House, which his family had up until that point been renting, and soon gained a reputation for living a lavish and eccentric lifestyle. He kept doves and had them dyed in many colours, using only the most harmless vegetable dyes of course, (a practice which is still followed today) although he found painting his cows too onerous a task to complete. This fascination with animals extended to all aspects of his life: his earliest musical composition, *Le Poisson d'Or*, tells the sad tale of a goldfish endlessly circling its lonely bowl. He gave all his beloved pet whippets diamond collars and at one point he purchased a pet giraffe, which was allowed to wander the grounds as it wished. On discovering that poet and neighbour John Betjeman and his wife Penelope had a magnificent Arab stallion called Moti, Berners invited it to afternoon tea in the drawing room of Faringdon House (although, to be fair, he did graciously include the owners in the invitation). In contrast to the welcome he gave this particular horse, he was less tolerant of other animal visitors and the Faringdon estate was dotted with signs that read 'Trespassers will be prosecuted, dogs shot, cats whipped'.

Berners loved his Rolls-Royce and had a small clavichord (sadly, not a grand piano as some stories would have tell) fitted in the vehicle so that he could play undisturbed, and would happily use the car as a reading room when he wanted to escape the clamour of his own social events. While this eccentric Lord loved his car he disliked train travel, especially having to share a carriage with strangers. In order to encourage anyone who had the temerity to join him to depart as quickly as possible, he regularly carried a rectal thermometer in a jacket pocket and would quite publicly produce it and very ostentatiously check his temperature at five-minute intervals until he had achieved his objective of driving his fellow travellers away.

Another of his affectations involved serving monochromatic meals; as the composer Stravinsky once observed after a visit, 'If Berners's mood was pink, lunch might consist of beet soup, lobster, tomatoes and strawberries.' Berners was undoubtedly delighted by the further creative culinary opportunities offered when Stravinsky's wife joined in the spirit of the game and shared her recipe for bright blue mayonnaise. In dress Berners was always formal, even wearing a three-piece suit when painting, but he did not let this get in the way of a good joke; one evening when entertaining the Marchesa Casati he spent the whole of dinner resplendent in formal attire – accompanied by a large false nose.

When he was 50, Berners fell in love with 20-year-old Robert Vernon Heber-Percy (nicknamed 'the Mad Boy') who quickly became his constant companion. As a birthday present for Robert, Berners had a 100-foot-high folly constructed atop the fortuitously named Folly Hill even though, by his own admission, the young man would have much preferred a horse. The tower was often referred to by locals as 'Lord Berners' monstrous erection', doubtless to his secret delight. It is also a folly in the truest sense; Berners himself commented, 'The great point of the tower is that it is entirely useless' although, perhaps sensing one potential use, he did have a notice placed on the tower stating 'Members of the public committing suicide from this tower do so at their own risk.'

Berners died in 1950 and his personally composed epitaph reads:

> Here lies Lord Berners
> One of the learners
> His great love of learning
> May earn him a burning
> But praise to the lord
> He seldom was bored

A line from one of his notebooks is more succinct: 'Mistrust a man who never has an occasional flash of silliness.'

Lord Berners left his estate to Robert Herber-Percy who, in turn, left the folly to a charitable trust and it is now regularly open to the public on selected Sundays during the summer months.

Something rather different for our final person: a genuine local showbusiness celebrity and, at last you may say, a woman. A London advertising bill from the early nineteenth century tells us a great deal about one of the most physically remarkable specimens that Wantage has ever produced:

The Greatest Wonder of the Age

Now exhibiting at 194, Strand, opposite St Clement's Church and near the Crown and Anchor, from 10–9 daily, the wonderful woman, Mrs E. Farmer of Wantage, Berkshire. The highest authorities in physiological science have pronounced her to be absolutely the largest woman in existence, and assuredly the most gigantic lady ever known in any age or country. Forty-three years of age. Weighs 42 stone or 338 lbs. Size round the waist, 58 inches; round the shoulders, 72 inches; round the arms, 32 inches. Mrs Farmer is in perfect health, active, and is the mother of six children. Her health and activity have astonished the leading medical men of the day. She is considered by them the greatest physiological phenomenon of the day. Mrs Farmer is well known among the private families of Berkshire. Admission, sixpence.

I have been able to trace no more information about Mrs Farmer but she was clearly a remarkable woman in many ways and, after the spirit of the times, obviously found a highly lucrative way to feed her six children.

Charney Bassett

No-one is sure what the fourteenth-century monk Robert of Glastonbury had done to incur the displeasure of the Abbot of Abingdon, but whatever it was had been serious enough for him to be banished from the abbey and sent to what is now Charney Manor for an extended period of penitence and prayer. The manor was originally constructed as a grange for the abbey in the thirteenth century, so was a logical place to send a disgraced brother for a period of penance and reflection. Had he been able to use this time to make his peace with his Maker, then perhaps all would have been well, but Robert died shortly after his arrival with his unknown sins remaining unforgiven, and his guilty spirit seems to have felt unable to depart this world after his demise.

Charney Manor is now a conference centre and many of the staff working there over the years have encountered his unquiet shade as the brown-robed figure drifts quietly about his mysterious business. Perhaps it is Robert who is the cause of the bangings and creakings which can sometimes be heard in the manor late at night when everyone should be safely asleep or, then again, perhaps these are the perfectly mundane sounds one might expect from any building of this age.

Unlike many of his more reticent brethren, Robert is not afraid to make himself known to the living as one delegate discovered in 1976. Seating herself in the first-floor solar, originally a private room set aside for the local lord to receive visitors, the woman was somewhat surprised when a figure in a brown monk's habit with the cowl pulled down to hide his face approached her and asked her to move to a different chair. Unaware of his possible supernatural nature she complied but became puzzled, and probably somewhat annoyed, when the figure left the room rather than sitting down on the newly vacated seat. At the time she had been unaware of the story of Robert of Glastonbury, but when she realised that she may have spoken to a ghost she reported the matter to members of the centre staff. Many were sceptical about her encounter, but not the cook, who told her that a number of visitors had reported seeing the hooded figure over the years and that their descriptions matched hers exactly. For my own part I cannot  help but wonder what sort of accent a fourteenth-century monk might have: it seems a shame no-one thought to ask.

Two years later, the cook at the manor received a letter from the same woman delegate with an interesting update on the story. In the letter she described how she had been at a prayer meeting in Harlow, Essex, when she noticed that a figure in a brown habit had silently entered the room, knelt down and spent 30 minutes in silent prayer before leaving, still without having said a word. Could this, she wondered, be Robert of Glastonbury joining her for a last prayer before finally moving on to take his rest?

At first glance it might seem that the witnesses' report of a brown colour for Robert's habit is a mistake in this story, because Abingdon Abbey was a Benedictine house and the Order of Benedict traditionally wear black robes, brown being more usually associated with Carmelites or Franciscan friars. It is worth remembering though that the Benedictine black robes only came into common usage several centuries after Robert's time and the original monastic rule simply specified, among other items, 'a cowl [robe] (thick and woolly for winter, thin or worn for summer)' and added that

> The monks should not complain about the colour or the coarseness of any of these things, but be content with what can be found in the district where they live.

The implication here is that fourteenth-century monks would probably have worn clothing made from whatever cloth was available locally, probably dirty-brown homespun wool in this case.

In truth, it is difficult to say whether Robert has ceased his haunting of Charney Manor or not, as the building is home to other ghosts of, dare I say, very similar habits. Villagers have long reported processions of monks moving around the manor gardens or behind the church next door. Another monk, this one known as William, has been observed in the chapel adjoining the solar. His actual identity is unknown, but he is so named because one woman saw him while visiting the chapel and was apparently moved to go to the lectern and open the sixteenth-century bible which rested there. She placed her finger randomly onto the page, found that she was pointing at the name William in the text, and the name has stuck ever since. While I would not wish to question the veracity of this account I am almost certain that the name William is not to be found in any of the books of the Bible. Perhaps the name cropped up in an annotation or perhaps the page fell open to I Thessalonians 5:18: 'In every thing give thanks: for this is the Will of God.'

Even aside from the ecclesiastical elements of the manor hauntings, there is certainly something more than natural about the area of the solar itself. As an illustration of this, consider the occasion some years ago when a professional soprano singer performed a recital in the solar in front of a packed audience of conference delegates. The day after the concert, a number of these guests were standing in the room below the solar when they heard her lilting tones once more coming from upstairs and, assuming that she was either practicing or performing again for another group, they stood enraptured until the singing finished. Shortly afterwards the singer made an appearance and was greeted with a smattering of applause. Puzzled, she asked what she had done to merit such congratulations and on being told that her second performance had been just as wonderful as the first, her audience were doubly surprised when she revealed that she had been in her room packing all morning and had been nowhere near the solar since the previous day's concert. No-one had recorded her recital at the time so where had the sound of the second performance come from?

Even today, the solar continues to offer mysteries to those who choose to visit the manor hoping for a little calming contemplation. Take Len, for example, who was there not long ago and seated himself to one side of the solar to await the arrival of the rest of his party for a discussion. In the quiet of the room he became aware of a rustling or cracking sound coming from what seemed like the inside of the wall behind his head. At first he suspected a mouse or some other small animal had somehow found its way into the fabric of the building and thought little of it until the sound started to become irksome, so he moved further down the row of seats to a place the other side of one of the deeply recessed windows. No sooner had he taken this new place than the sounds started again from immediately behind him. Annoyed, he moved to the other side of the room and seated himself there, only for the rustling to begin from behind his new position. He spent the next few minutes nervously pacing up and down until his fellow group members finally put in an appearance. Despite them trying all the chairs, the noises did not reappear.

To end our brief survey of Charney Manor there is an interesting snippet of local legend, which tells of how the stones above the gate posts of the manor leave their settled positions and run around the walls of the grounds when they hear the church bells strike midnight, although (in a clever twist which prevents the story ever being verified) never if they are being watched. A slightly more relaxed alternative to this belief says that the stones simply swap places at the stroke of twelve. In an odd combination of the stories of church and manor, Maud Ody (in *The Length of the Road*) refers to an unattested story of a headless woman who dashes around the church walls at the midnight hour.[34] She also mentions tales of a secret tunnel running from the manor back to the abbey at Abingdon; clearly never a realistic possibility, not only because of the distance but because of the low-lying, waterlogged nature of the land.

The tympanum above the altar of Charney Bassett Church just next door to the manor bears the unusual design of a human figure being lifted into the air by two dragon-like creatures (though this attribution is somewhat questionable given that the creatures seem to have fish-like tails).[35] The local explanation is that this carving represents Alexander the Great being lifted up to glimpse the edge of the world, but an alternative explanation is that it relates to lines from Psalm XLIV:

18   Our heart is not turned back, neither have our steps declined from thy way;
19   Though thou hast sore broken us in the place of dragons, and covered us with the shadow of death.

---

34   Charney is clearly the place to be if you like a lively night-life.
35   Pevsner identifies them as gryphons, part eagle and part lion.

As our trip along the Michael and Mary lines demonstrated, dragons are not actually an unusual motif in the area: there are examples carved into the stonework at Faringdon and onto the ironwork on the main door; Uffington has two dragons as does North Moreton (one of these has a human head) while the lectern at East Hendred has three; the pulpit at West Hanney is decorated with a dragon, as is that at Long Wittenham, although the church here can also boast a capital emblazoned with two dragons consuming a human head. It is possible, though admittedly unlikely, that all this draconian iconography is linked to associations with the St George legends around the White Horse.

Goosey

Until the dissolution of the monasteries by Henry VIII the monks of Abingdon Abbey had what has quaintly been referred to as a cheese farm in the village of Goosey, the main building of which is now known as Abbey Farm, and there is said to be an underground passageway leading from the cellars here to the nearby thirteenth-century church. While this might seem to be nothing more than a romantic local legend, some locals say that inside one of the houses between the farm and the church the singing of the choir during services can he heard far more clearly in one of the rooms which faces *away* from the church than any of the rooms which face towards it. Is the sound travelling along this long-forgotten tunnel?

Because Goosey originally had no church of its own, all burials had to take place at nearby Stanford-in-the-Vale and until very recently there was a 'corpse path' across the village green, along which funeral processions would wind their dolorous way. Sadly, the stones which laid out this pathway were removed in the last century.

Fyfield

This story, undated and purportedly from Fyfield, is something of a puzzle and not just for its alarming content. Fyfield has an architecturally idiosyncratic, mostly fourteenth-century church (the age is specifically mentioned in the original account) dedicated to St Nicholas, with an interesting octagonal tower, gothic porch and reputed haunted underground tunnel. It is also surrounded by a quiet graveyard and it was to this graveyard one sunny afternoon that a lady, identified only as Mrs Grace, came to visit the grave of a relative. As she stood before the headstone she slowly began to feel what she described as a 'disturbing presence'. At first she saw nothing that might have caused this odd sensation, but after a short while she became aware of the figure of a woman floating near the church doorway. The figure seemed to be wearing a dark dress and head covering and, as Mrs Grace watched her, suddenly moved behind a large gravestone. The figure did not reappear. Mrs Grace thought little of this odd apparition beyond an understandable mild curiosity, concluded her visit and left the churchyard and the village.

Six months later, so the story continues, Mrs Grace was enjoying a walk on a hillside overlooking the church when she happened to glance upwards and saw the same dark-clad figure waving to her from the top of the hill. Gathering her courage she climbed towards it, noticing as she did so that it seemed semi-transparent and had a 'weird hypnotic look about it'. Suddenly, she was seized by the conviction that the figure meant her no well and she was horrified to discover that she had lost control of her body and was being forced to do the bidding of this weird apparition. The figure beckoned and, finding that she was unable to resist its summons, she began to climb the hill towards it. At this point Mrs Grace realised that she was actually walking towards a precipice on

the eastern side of the hill and that the figure was somehow hovering in mid air just beyond the edge! Just as she came to this realisation the church bells rang out, the ghostly figure fluttered its hands (in dismay?) and faded from sight. Mrs Grace came to her senses and discovered that another few steps and she would have walked right over the edge and fallen to certain injury and possible death.

From a folkloric point of view, there is a direct correlation here with traditional tales of fairies and demons similarly banished by the sound of church bells. Caxton mentions the belief in his edition of *The Golden Legend* from 1483, though Scot, in *The Discoverie of Witchcraft* from 1584, pours scorn on the use of bells as a deterrent: 'They run to bells ... as though spirits could be fraied awaie with such externall toies,' he writes dismissively. Not everyone was this rational of course; bells were also rung to ward off storms and eclipses and, just across the river from the Vale, there is a legend that snakes and serpents cannot abide the sound of the bells of Dorchester Abbey and thus none are ever found in the town.[36]

The odd thing about this Fyfield story (assuming that you don't consider malevolent mesmeric manifestations to be quite odd enough) is that there are no significant hills near the village – so where could the second episode have taken place? There are some raised areas of ground but none with a suitably dramatic drop to match Mrs Grace's description. Not only that, but as a cursory visit will reveal, there are no gravestones large enough to hide the figure of a woman anywhere near the doorway to the church. Rather than dismiss the account

---

[36] A lovely story which entirely fails to take into account the fact that snakes are totally deaf.

as being entirely fictional, could it be possible that it actually happened in a *different* Fyfield in another part of the country and has been accidentally relocated to Oxfordshire at some point?

There is another village of Fyfield in Hampshire (coincidentally, this too has a church dedicated to St Nicholas) but this church, dating as it does from the twelfth century, does not fit the story so well. Of course the Oxfordshire Fyfield church has, in common with every old building, parts dating to other centuries, so attempting to locate the story by architectural period is always going to be problematic but, in any case, the Hampshire Fyfield is not overlooked by any high ground either.

There is another Fyfield near Marlborough (St Nicholas again...), set amongst the rolling Fyfield Downs, hardly flat but in no way the dangerously hilly landscape with precipitous drops which the story suggests, and yet another in Essex. This last Church of St Nicholas may be a more likely location for the tale, as it too dates primarily from the fourteenth century and has a renowned peal of six bells which are rung regularly, but, alas, once again, there are no significant hills nearby.

So, all in all, the origin of this story remains something of an unsolved mystery. Irrespective of the accuracy of the narrator's account, it is uncertain which, if any, of the Fyfields was the original site of the tale and how (if not the one actually referred to in the story) it became attached to the Oxfordshire Fyfield. I will leave it to the reader to wonder how many of the tales contained within this volume might be subjected to this sort of analysis by future authors.

And, just as an aside, I wonder why *all* of the four Fyfield churches in the country are dedicated to St Nicholas? I think we should be told.

There is another, more widely attested, haunting at Fyfield: The White Hart Inn. The White Hart dates back to 1444 and was originally a poor house, providing succour for the impoverished of the parish, but its resident ghost is said to be 200 years younger and is something of a laughing cavalier, occasionally playing pranks in the kitchen and moving small items around, to the dismay of the staff trying to prepare meals. More often though, he can be sensed as a passing presence or a shadow glimpsed out of the corner of the eye. Luckily the staff and regulars seem quite proud to be able to share their pub with one of its earlier customers.

Tubney

Tubney is more a group of cottages scattered along the road and across the landscape than a traditional nuclear village and its primary point of interest to us is the Tubney Tree, a massive wych elm over six hundred years old, which stands beside the Oxford road at the boundary between Tubney and Fyfield. Estimates of the size of this tree vary but its circumference is usually given as at least 36 ft (11 m) and is sometimes quoted as 45 ft (13 m). The tree served the local community as a meeting place and impromptu market as well as being used as a gathering place for the May Day dancing. Alas, the size and location of the tree meant that it was also an ideal hiding place for highwaymen awaiting the Oxford stagecoach and the location began to acquire something of a dangerous reputation amongst the coachmen of the eighteenth century. In later times, once lawlessness in the Vale had receded, the elm once more regained its romantic image to such an extent that Matthew Arnold mentions it in his poem 'The Scholar-Gypsy':

Maidens, who from the distant hamlets come
To dance around the Fyfield elm in May...

Some of the local people used to claim that witches would dance around the tree at midnight, but by the twentieth century, even before the coming of Dutch elm disease, the tree had badly decayed. It can still be seen today but it is now little more than a dead shell with an identifying plaque. Since it no longer graces the roadside with its spreading greenery, May Day revels are no longer held beneath its cool shade. I can't comment on what the witches are doing now though.

Longworth

Had he not decided to return as a ghost, Sir Henry Marten could easily have featured as one of our celebrated local eccentrics; certainly the idea of a leading Puritan gentleman with a taste for some decidedly ungodly lifestyle choices makes for an odd combination. Sir Henry was MP for Berkshire in both the Short and Long Parliaments before the Civil War and was later imprisoned for two weeks in the Tower of London for treason. He was a prominent political agitator rather than a soldier, although he did pledge the not inconsiderable sum of £1,200 to raise a regiment of horse for the parliamentarian cause and take part in the struggle directly while he was Governor of Aylesbury (although, according to contemporary sources, he does seem to have been as much motivated by the chance of plunder as by military ambition).

He is most famous for his part in the trial and execution of King Charles I (his is one of the shakier signatures on the king's death warrant) but he was also a prominent Leveller and deeply distrusted Oliver Cromwell, whom he considered nothing but a dictator. Given his political and religious leanings it is surprising to learn that although he married twice he also had numerous mistresses, staying loyal to one, a woman called Mary Ward (his 'Lady of Delight'), for over thirty years. He may well have had Marten's Hall Farm especially built for her so as to have her near to hand. He was also renowned as a gambler and heavy drinker. Before the war, the antiquarian John Aubrey, the man who first extensively documented both Avebury and Stonehenge, claimed that 'He was a great lover of pretty girles, to whom he was so liberall that he spent the greatest part of his estate.' Certainly, despite his extensive wealth he accumulated enormous debts by managing to spend over £1,000 a year on good living. Aubrey also relates how it happened that Henry was in Hyde parke one time when His Majesty was there, goeing to see a race. The king espied him and says aloud, 'Let that ugly rascall be gonne out of the park, that whore master.

Clearly, even at that point, he had made enemies of important people; perhaps it was this incident that drove him to seek so strongly for the abolition of the monarchy.

Following the Restoration it is surprising that Marten was not executed; he did however spend the rest of his life in various prisons (often accompanied by the long-suffering Mary Ward), finally dying in Chepstow in 1680. His ghost is sometimes glimpsed at his (occasional) home at Longworth Manor: some commentators have suggested that he is seeking to atone for his dissolute life although one source jokingly suggests he may be looking for the key to the wine cellar! Whatever the reason for returning to Longworth his lively spirit has, sadly, not been seen in recent times.

Should you pass through the village, take the time to study the sign for the Blue Boar pub, which bears images of a white boar and a white rose, representing the symbols of Richard III, on a pennant above the more obvious blue boar motif. The blue boar was the personal badge of the De Vere family, who were the Earls of Oxford, and folklore says that when King Richard III was killed at the Battle of Bosworth in 1485, all White Boar pubs were quickly repainted as Blue Boars in accordance with the sudden change of political and royal power. The pennant on the sign is a simple reminder of this turbulent time in English history.

By the early years of the twentieth century, Longworth Lodge had long been considered haunted and it was, for this reason, left deserted and avoided by all right-thinking persons in the area. All *right-thinking* persons perhaps, but it was common supposition in his home village of Coleshill that Robert Polebrook was far from being a person of that sort; indeed, many of his neighbours considered that he had made certain, unspecified, agreements with the Devil himself. Polebrook was an elderly man, an ex-cowherd who had retired from his life of labour and now supported himself in his old age through various shady deals and nefarious practices, so it was with covetous eyes and very little fear that he approached Longworth Lodge one moonless night, probably sometime at the very end of the nineteenth century. Forcing the door, he surveyed the dusty parlour until his gaze fell upon a small three-legged table, which he felt would suit his own cottage perfectly. Scooping up the table, he made to leave with his prize. Unfortunately, his plans were about to encounter some difficulty as once he had left the cottage, the table began to display a life of its own, thrashing and twisting in his hands in an attempt to escape from his larcenous grasp.

A strange battle now ensued with the small table leaping about, lunging at Polebrook, beating him about the head and forcing him to the ground. In league with the Devil or not, Polebrook was clearly going to have no luck with his thievery that night. After some hours of unsuccessfully trying to subdue the truculent table,[37] Polebrook finally admitted defeat and decided to return the fiendish furniture to its rightful home, although, even with that decision made, the table struggled constantly against his attempts to move it back inside. At last, as dawn was breaking, he managed to settle it back into the parlour and peace was restored.

Whether the table resented the attempted theft or whether it was more generally ensorcelled is an open question – certainly there were tales of its independent behaviour even prior to Polebrook's visit. Apparently the table had been observed

---

37 And how often do you get to read that?

moving itself around in whichever room it was placed, although in these earlier stories it could actually be taken outside and was perfectly placid until it came near water, at which point the violent behaviour it displayed with Polebrook would assert itself. The local explanation for this behaviour blamed a witch at nearby Duxford for possessing or bewitching the table in some way, an almost logical piece of reasoning since water was said to reject witches (hence witch-swimming in trials) – they were also sometimes believed to be unable to cross running water. One can only wonder whether the table eventually made its way to an antique shop, across dry land presumably, and now resides in someone's front room, stirring itself occasionally in memory of past notorieties…

Hinton Waldrist

Henry Bolingbroke, fourth son of John of Gaunt (the uncle and staunch supporter of the boy-king Richard II) was aged only 14 in 1381 when he married the beautiful and cultured Marie de Bohun, who was deemed one of the most eligible heiresses in England having inherited the Manor at Hinton Waldrist from her father William de Bohun, Earl of Hereford. The couple promptly decamped to his estates in Lincolnshire and set about the business of starting a family. Marie was aged only 12.

The following year Marie gave birth to her first child, which tragically died soon afterwards, causing her mother to (belatedly) complain about the young age at which she had been married and forced into bearing children. Consequently Marie returned to the family seat at Hinton Waldrist, then something of a draughty old pile rather than the Elizabethan manor house which now graces the village, for two years until she was deemed to be of suitable child-bearing age, at which point she resumed her married life.

The couple's subsequent attempts to produce an heir were rather more blessed. Their next child went on to become Henry V, hero of Agincourt; other sons became the Dukes of Clarence, Bedford and Gloucester. Humphrey, Duke of Gloucester, was a renowned scholar and it was he who supported the Bodleian in Oxford and gave his name to one of the most spectacular parts of the old library buildings. The couple also had two daughters, Blanche and Philippa, and the whole family would often spend time at Marie's family estates at Hinton.

Marie died in 1394 and it is her ghost, clad in a red velvet gown, which is thought to return to the location, if not the original building, of the home she loved in life. Members of the Loder-Symonds family, who owned the house up until the middle of the twentieth century,[38] often reported encountering this lady in red in the upstairs rooms of the manor. Nicholas Davenport, a subsequent owner, was awoken one night by footsteps in a hallway and came out of his room to find that one of the lamps had been switched on by someone or something in the otherwise deserted house. A visiting RAF officer called Christopher Clarkson once opened the door from the library to find a ghostly girl in red velvet sitting at a table in the music room in broad daylight: despite recognising her instantly as a ghost he described her as appearing very 'substantial'. She appeared to be gazing out of the window looking towards the location of the old castle. Perhaps she was reflecting on happier times or perhaps she was contemplating the vagaries of fate that led her warrior son Henry to become a king, whilst her scholarly son Humphrey met his end in a lonely prison cell, a victim of the Wars of the Roses.

Another story associated with Hinton Waldrist tells of some trouble at the funeral of one of the Ladies Loder-Symonds in the early 1900s. One of the local farm labourers at the time related how, as the funeral cortege, consisting of a wheeled bier pulled by a pair of horses, was about to leave the manor to take her body for burial, the horses shied and refused to move. A local witch was summoned from Duxford and she advised: 'Them horses won't pull her. You must get two milk-white martens.'[39] I assume that this advice was followed and that the funeral was able to proceed (unless of course two descendants of Sir Henry were somehow summoned to help), but the brief anecdote ends there so we cannot be sure. Presumably, this is the very same Duxford witch who had cast the spell on

---

38 John Loder bought the Manor from Henry Marten of Longworth in 1658 when the latter's financial problems had become particularly acute.

39 Martens, or more properly freemartens, are infertile heifers (always the female half of mixed-sex twin calves).

the table in Longworth which caused Robert Polebrook such problems; perhaps we should see her in a better light after this incident (or at least speculate on her propensity for sly puns aimed at the local gentry) and wonder whether her witching of that table was actually meant to deter theft from the cottage rather than simply being a mischievous trick.

Buckland

Buckland House was originally planned by John Wood the Elder but the design was substantially altered by his son, John Wood the Younger, who built the Royal Crescent in Bath, and the house was finally completed in 1759. Architectural historian Nikolaus Pevsner described it as 'the most splendid Georgian house in the County' and it was at one time used as a Hall (an independent college) of Oxford University before returning to private ownership. It is said that the ghost of a mysterious white lady haunts the house, but no-one seems to know the story behind her appearances, nor has anyone encountered her for some time.

One of the farmhouses (sadly, now demolished) at Lower Newton just outside Buckland was originally held by Abingdon Abbey and used as a base to collect tithes from the village. By 1922 ownership had passed to Sir Leo Page, who described the experience of sharing his home with the ghost of an old woman who would appear sporadically to various members of the family. His daughter Emily not only saw the old lady but also heard her moving around upstairs. While the property no longer exists, many of the stones from the original structure were reused in other buildings, so perhaps the old lady may yet reappear elsewhere in years to come.

Pusey

We often think of English history in black and white, in terms of heroic local defenders and evil foreign usurpers, but of course not everything in history is quite so clear-cut. The Romans, who originally arrived with Julius Caesar in 55 BC and stayed after the Emperor Claudius returned in force in AD 43, were later assimilated to become the Romano-British who, led by the heroic figure known to us as King Arthur, fought against the invading Anglo-Saxons. The Anglo-Saxons themselves subsequently gave us our own local hero in the figure of King Alfred. The Anglo-Saxon kingdoms then fought an intricate series of skirmishes with various of their closely related Scandinavian brethren, before the Norman Conquest in 1066 allowed another group of Northmen who had settled in northern France to take the throne. In amongst this patchwork of shifting population and power we can find the charming story of the Pusey Horn, which is set during one of the internecine dynastic struggles of the later years of a united Angle-land, some 50 years before the coming of the Normans.

In the Anglo-Saxon world kingship was not based on the principle of hereditary primogeniture used today and the Witan, a sort of cross between a parliament and a council of ministers, was actually able to elect the king, albeit from a fairly limited pool of suitable claimants. While this supposedly meant that the most able candidates reached the top job, it also ensured that politics played an important role in the royal succession. And, in those times, politics and military action were often hard to tell apart.

As an example of this, consider the state of the country at the turn of the first millennium. Aethelred 'the Unready',[40] who was then king, was unsuccessfully attempting to stem the

---

[40] The translation of his unofficial title is actually 'the un-raed', meaning ill-advised.

tide of Danish invaders into the islands. In 1002 he married Emma, the daughter of Richard I Duke of Normandy, in an attempt to bring allies to his aid and at the same time ordered the killing of many male Danes in England to prevent them joining a possible invading army – something which later became known as the St Brice's Day Massacre.

Possibly enraged by the slaughter of so many of their kin the Danes invaded anyway, led initially by Swein Forkbeard and, after his death, by his son Cnut, more usually known as Canute. According to the legend, at this point in the campaign Canute had marshalled his troops at Cherbury Camp, a ringed fortress near Charney Bassett, while the local forces, under King Aethelred, were amassed at their stronghold of Uffington Castle. The Saxons decided to make a surprise attack and left Uffington in force, but a local shepherd boy by the name of William Pusey, who was sympathetic to the Danes, spotted the approaching army and blew his horn as a warning, thus alerting the unprepared Danes and preventing a massacre. Although battle was joined the Danes were, on this occasion at least, driven back and defeated. So great was the bloodshed that the local stream is still known as 'the Gore' in commemoration of the battle.

In the longer term Canute came out on top. He eventually became king of not only the whole of England but of Denmark and Norway as well. He did not, however, forget the bravery and support of a shepherd boy in the Vale and, on attaining the throne, Pusey is said to have been rewarded with a commission in the King's army and all the land within the reach of the sound of his horn. The instrument itself was richly decorated and inscribed with the words, 'I kynge knowde gave Wyllyam Pecote thys horne to holde by thy land' and was then gifted to Pusey (note the name is different on the engraving) as a token of his new status.

So, is the story true? Well, clearly not in all its details but it is certainly possible to visit the Victoria and Albert Museum in London and view the undoubtedly real Pusey Horn.

Stanford-in-the-Vale

According to the Rev. George Maine, writing in *A Berkshire Village*, there are six church bells in the church at Stanford and each was rung three times on a Sunday morning to announce the death of any man or boy in the parish. The number three naturally represented the Trinity; women and girls, 'to mark their inferiority'[41] were allowed only two tolls of the bells. This old custom is actually quite widespread and derives from the old tradition of ringing a 'passing bell', otherwise known as a 'knell', at the death bed of a dying person, the idea being that those hearing the bell would then offer up prayers for the soul of the unfortunate person as they passed away.

The churchyard itself is said to be haunted by a grey lady who has been seen intermittently over the years. She is supposed to move at great speed as if trying to avoid being seen, but as to why she is to be found in Stanford no-one can say. Maine dismisses a local belief that a graveyard is always haunted by the last person to be buried there and in this case he is undoubtedly correct, since the girl has clearly witnessed many a committal and refused to give way to another spirit.

Stanford-in-the-Vale may seem an unlikely location for a Close Encounter of the Third Kind but, as one family from Gloucestershire discovered in 1978, it isn't just the mid-west of the USA which can lay claim to alien abduction stories. In fact, this particular episode not only made national headlines but also led to the writing of an entire book documenting the investigations into the family's experiences.

It was an ordinary night's travel for John and Gloria, along with their children Natasha and Tanya, aged five and three respectively, and John's sister Frances, as they returned home to Gloucestershire along the A417 through Stanford-in-the-Vale. It was late in the evening on 19 June when they departed

---

41 A direct quote, not a personal opinion!

the village and headed towards Faringdon, by their estimate probably around 10.15 pm. As they drove westwards the family noticed that a very bright light had appeared in the sky in front of them and seemed to be maintaining a fixed distance from the car. John joked that it might be a UFO and they dismissed the object for a while but, becoming increasingly uneasy, John pulled over to the side of the road to see if they could hear any noises associated with the light that might help them work out what it was. So far so unexceptional, but their account of what happened next was far from ordinary.

As John climbed out of the car, a second light, this time red, appeared and the original white light seemed to swell in size, eventually resolving itself into a huge lenticular UFO, which proceeded to hover over the car. At the same time the full moon, which had been clearly visible in the sky up until that moment, suddenly vanished. Noticing that John seemed to be in a daze, Gloria shouted out that the UFO looked as if it was about to land and that they should get away as quickly as possible. On hearing this John snapped out of his trance, leapt back into the car and drove off towards Faringdon at top speed. The family later commented that as they drove this stretch of road they had the strangest sense that something was, in some indefinable way, not quite right. When they reached Faringdon the family noticed that it seemed strangely quiet for around 10.30 in the evening, but they continued their journey home and doubtless felt much relieved to arrive safely. John phoned RAF Brize Norton to report their UFO sighting, but as he checked the time he belatedly realised that it was actually past midnight and consequently much later than he expected: at some point during their trip they had managed to mislay an entire hour.

Over the next few days the entire group started to develop odd rashes on the skin and John had a very vivid dream about the earlier encounter, which this time included meeting the UFO pilots and being taken inside the spacecraft and examined. After he shared details of this nightmare Frances and Natasha both had similar dreams themselves and the family decided that they needed to contact a UFO group for help, at which point UFO researcher Frank Johnson enters the picture. He put them in contact with a therapist who used hypnotic regression on the older members of the family to extract the 'true' version of what had happened.

The version of the story recovered under hypnosis is very much more impressive than even the close encounter the family originally described. In the new and improved account pieced together from individual hypnosis sessions, Johnson detailed how the family had left the car and entered a beam of light which had whisked them all aboard a UFO crewed by seemingly human aliens, dressed in the now traditional skin-tight spacesuits with tight hoods. These UFOnauts claimed to be representatives of the Janos people, whose home planet had been destroyed by bombardment from space when one of their planet's moons had broken up and who were now cruising around the solar system looking for a new planet to call home. After the obligatory (but thankfully friendly) examination, the family were given memory-erasing drinks and returned to their car.

UFO stories are always highly controversial and rouse considerable passions from both sides of the argument, so I don't intend to over-analyse this incident, but I will just caution that hypnotic regressions are a very unreliable way of recovering details of past events, especially from imaginative subjects. It is almost a cliché to blame UFO sightings on astronomical phenomena but the planet Venus was certainly shining very brightly in the western sky that evening in 1978, which could easily explain the white light which paced the car, although how to explain the rest of their tale (and what happened to that missing hour) is an entirely different matter. Much of the story told by the family bears a striking resemblance to standard contactee and science-fiction imagery from the decades preceding the incident. For example, a picture of a lenticular spaceship shining a beam of light downwards features prominently on the promotional poster of the 1955 film *This Island Earth,* a film which also features silver-suited humanoid aliens looking to colonise Earth: one of the iconic scenes in the film features the alien planet being bombarded by meteorites from space. Coincidence? I don't know, but I am puzzled as to where those Janos people and their space fleet could possibly have got to. We should certainly have seen them by now. Whatever did the family say to them to stop them landing here? Whatever the truth is about this weird incident, if you are ever passing through Stanford-in-the-Vale late at night, keep watching the skies!

Hatford and Baulking

On 17 March 1628 an unknown East Anglian MP by the name of Oliver Cromwell first took his seat in the Houses of Parliament and thus England took its first steps towards civil war.[42] Of course no-one could have foreseen this in advance and, to the best of my knowledge, no-one reported any signs and portents before the Civil War began but, had they been looking, events in the Vale a few weeks later might well have been seen in that light.

I will let a manuscript from the British Library entitled, 'Looke Up and See Wonders; a miraculous Apparition in the Ayre lately seen in Barkeshire at Bawlkin Greene, neere Hatford, 9th April, 1628.' tell the tale:

> The foure great quarter masters of the world (the foure elements) have bin in civill warre, one against another. ... The fires of Heaven have gone beyond their bounds. The Aire is the shop of Thunder and Lightning–many windows hath God set open in Heaven, to shewe what artillery hee has lying there, and many of our kings have trembled when they were shown unto them. With feare and trembling, casting our eyes up to Heaven, let us now behold him bending his fist onely, as he lately did to the terrour and affrightment of all the inhabitants dwelling within a Towne in the County of Barkshire.

---

42 The Act of Union with Scotland was not enacted until 1707.

The name of the Town is Hatford, some 8 miles from Oxford. Over this Towne upon Wensday being the ninth of this instant moneth of April, 1628; about five of the clocke in the afternoon, this miraculous, prodigious, and fearfull handyworke of God was presented. The weather was warme, and without any great shewe of distemperature; only the skye waxed by degrees a little gloomy, yet not so darkened but that the Sunne still and anon by the power of the brightnesse, brake through the thicke clouds. A gentle gale of wind then blowing from betweene the West and North-west, in an instant was heard first a hideous rumbling in the Ayre, and presently after followed a strange and fearefull peal of Thunder, running up and downe these parts of the Country, but it strake with the loudest violence, and more furious tearing of the Ayre, about a place called the White Horse Hill, than in any other. The whole order of this thunder carried a kind of Majesticall state with it, for it maintayned (to the affrighted Beholders seeming) the fashion of a fought Battaile. It began thus: First, for an onset, went off one great cannon as it were of thunder alone, like a warning peece to the rest that were to follow. Then a little while after was heard a second; and so by degrees a third, untill the number of 20 were discharged (or thereabouts) in very good order, though in very great terror. In some little distance of time after this was audibly heard the sound of a Drum beating a Retreate. Amongst all these angry peales shott off from Heaven, this begat a wonderful admiration, that at the end of the report of every cracke, or cannon thundering, a hissing noyse made way through the Ayre, not unlike the flying of bullets from the mouthes of great Ordnance; and by the judgment of all the' terror-striken witnesses they were Thunder-bolts. For one of them was seene by many people to fall at a place called Bawlkin Greene, being a mile and a half from Hatford; which Thunder-bolt was by one Mistris Greene caused to be digged up out of the ground, she being an eye witnesse, amongst many other of the manner of the falling. The form of the Stone is three-square, and picked in the end; in colour outwardly blackish, somewhat like iron: crusted over with that blacknesse about the thicknesse of a shilling. Within it is a sort of a gray colour mixed with some kind of minerall, shining like small peeces of glasse. This stone brake in the fal: the whole peece is in weight nineteen pound and a halfe. The greater peece that fell off weigheth five pound, which with other small peeces being put together, maketh foure and twenty pound and better. It is in the countrey credibly reported that some other Thunder stones have bin found in other places. But for certainty there was one taken up at Letcombe, and is now in the custody of the Shriefe.

A local man, John Hoskins, also witnessed the event and wrote to his son-in-law in London describing the same skyfall:

On Wednesday before Easter, being the ninth of April, about six of the clock, in the afternoon, there was such a noise in the air, and after such a strange manner, as the oldest man alive never heard the like. And it began as followeth: First, as it were, one piece of ordnance went off alone. Then, after that, a little distance, two more, and then they went as thick as ever I heard a volley of shot in all my life; and after that, as it were the sound of a drum, to the amazement of me, your mother, and a hundred more besides; yet this is not all; but as it is reported, there fell divers stones, but two is certain in our knowledge. The one fell at Chalows, half a mile off, and the other at Barking five miles off. Your mother was at the place where one of them fell knee-deep, till it came at the very rock, and when it came at the hard rock it broke, and being weighed, all the pieces together, six & twenty pounds. The other that was taken up in the other place weighed half a tod, 14 pound.

The thunderstones were, as we are well aware today of course, meteorites, possibly from the Gamma Virginid meteor shower which peaks at around that date each year.[43] There are numerous videos online of the Chelyabinsk meteor which exploded over Russia in February 2013, all of which give some feel for how the seventeenth-century inhabitants of the Vale must have felt on witnessing their own exploding fireballs. From the descriptions of the fragments which hit the ground, the initial chunk of rock must have been of considerable size and it is little wonder that it inspired religious awe and terror in those who saw it flashing across the sky. It is interesting to speculate as to how many of the events we currently consider as marvellous as this 'Apparition in the Ayre' (some of which you can find in this very volume of course) will seem just as interesting, but in no way inexplicable, in another four centuries' time.

---

43 Which means that the various stones which fell in 1628 may once have been part of the excitingly-named Comet BD44.

Uffington

The church of St Mary in Uffington is a magnificent early Gothic construction, affectionately known as the Cathedral of the Vale, both because of its size and because of the exceptional quality of its workmanship. The current building, erected on the site of an earlier church in around 1250, is slightly eccentric in architectural terms, with a splendid octagonal central tower and some oddly flattened arches in the west wall, which had to be rebuilt after the Civil War. The tower was originally topped by an impressive steeple but this was 'beat down by a tempas wind, thunder and liten December 2nd day 1740', as one contemporary witness noted in the margin of the family Bible. The mechanism of an old clock which was built in 1701 is on display in the church but the clock suffered, in the eyes of the local people anyway, one major flaw, which is recorded in a rhyme which may be found next to the clock:

> Oh Uffington – poor people,
> Got a Church without a steeple,
> But, what is more, to its disgrace,
> Got a clock without a face.

It is interesting to note that the village of East Ilsley, which sits up on the Downs towards Newbury, has a similar rhyme to Uffington except that this one starts 'Sleepy Ilsley, drunken people'. In what seems a slightly unfair disparity, East Hendred and West Hagbourne both have faceless clocks and steeple-less churches but have to suffer no derogatory ditties highlighting the fact or disparaging the villagers.

There are no great historical ghost stories associated with St Mary's but I was told this personal tale by a lady called Marie. It dates back to the 1980s at a time when her brother Jack, who lived in New Zealand, had been involved in a car accident and was lying critically ill in hospital in Christchurch. Despite the seriousness of her brother's condition, Marie could not afford to fly out to visit his bedside and so was forced to stay at home in Uffington and worry. While not being particularly religious, when the stress became overwhelming she began to take comfort in brief visits to St Mary's where she would just sit quietly, hoping and praying for her brother's recovery.

Days and then a week passed and as no good news came from overseas her worries obviously increased. One afternoon she was sitting in the church when she heard footsteps approach from the back of the church and someone sat quietly down behind her. Marie did not turn around but said that she felt comforted by the presence of someone else in the building. To her surprise the figure behind her suddenly spoke, saying, 'Don't worry, everything will be all right' – a sentiment she found so moving that she immediately burst into tears. After a few moments she dried her eyes and turned to speak to her comforter only to find that she was the only person present in the church. Marie is certain that, even crying as she was, she would have heard someone leaving, so what had happened to the consoling stranger? Had she missed her comforter leaving, had this been a spiritual or supernatural encounter of some kind or simply some sort of auditory hallucination brought on by the stresses of her situation? Marie could never quite decide for herself but the following day news arrived that her brother had finally recovered consciousness.

It's a plant!

It is odd to think that the very existence of the carved figure known as the Green Man had been almost entirely forgotten until Lady Raglan drew attention to the carvings in her 1939 *Folklore* article, 'The Green Man in Church Architecture'. Usually though by no means exclusively found in churches, Green Men are carved into the stonework as a decorative feature and consist of a combination of human (or humanoid) face along with leaves or sprouting branches. Green Men can be found in churches and abbeys, as well as in secular buildings, all over the country and they are well represented in the Vale and surrounding areas.

Green Men come in a number of varieties, generally differentiated by the way the face sprouts greenery, but the two main types are the *Foliate Head*, where the hair, or sometimes the entire face, is actually composed of leaves and other plant material, and the *Disgorging Head*, where the face is more human but with greenery emerging from the mouth and possibly also ears, nose and so on. There is a nice example of the former type at St Mary's Church in Ashbury as well as a splendid specimen at Ardington, while the wonderful Norman Romanesque arched doorway at Charney Bassett has a whole series of disgorging heads vomiting leaves engraved into the tympanum.

R. and H. Carter, again writing in *Folklore* in 1967, identified the additional *Jack in the Green* type, a normal face peering through a gap in an apparent curtain of greenery, but I am not aware of any carving of this type in the Vale. Obviously, there are variations in all these versions of the Green Man and some show characteristics of more than one type.

Carvings of Green Men seem to have started to appear as features in church decoration around the twelfth century (St James's at Hanney has one of the earliest examples locally) and the custom persisted for three hundred years before falling out of fashion and then undergoing a modern revival in the nineteenth century. No-one is entirely sure what the Green Man represents, always assuming that they are something more than a running joke planted in churches by generations of mischievous masons, but there are a number of theories which seek to explain his background.

The most obvious suggestion is that the Green Man is a reference to a pre-Christian woodland deity or fertility spirit, or perhaps the Wild Man of the Woods, the northern European equivalent of the fauns in classical mythology. Certainly, there are classical antecedents and Green Men heads appear in both Greek and Roman architecture, but these are always of the Foliate Head variety and never disgorge leaves. An alternative, or possibly parallel, hypothesis suggests that the influences behind the Green Men came along the Silk Road from India, since disgorging heads are a common motif in that part of the world.

As well as human heads there are also a number of animal and hybrid carvings in the Vale: Sutton Courtenay has one in the likeness of a cat, Woolstone a lion and Sparsholt a fantastic pair of foliate female felines flanking a more traditional Green Man figure.[44] While Green Men are relatively common, Green Women are much less so and so the examples to be found at Sparsholt are especially interesting.

If you are interested in seeking out more of these remarkable figures then Oxfordshire has a Green Man Trail highlighting known examples, but doubtless many more carvings have gone unnoticed and unremarked in odd corners of local churches; who is to say how many more are hidden away in a shadowy corner just awaiting rediscovery?

---

44 Additionally, Wantage Church can claim a disgorging lion head carved into one of the wooden misericords.

East Challow

In their history of the village *Ceawa's Burial Mound,* Hazel and Clive Brown note that an old map drawn by cartographer John Rocque in 1761 has an intriguing feature halfway between Challow and Wantage in a field near to the present Challow Cricket Ground. This map shows the presence of an 'obelisk' where none exists today. This mysterious standing stone is at the end of what the mapmaker marks as a 'long vistow' (vista) and was described by the 1883 *Kelly's Directory* as 'an obelisk placed at the end of an avenue stretching to Circourt in the parish of Denchworth'. *Kelly's* further noted that 'some of the stones, it is said, may be seen in a paved pathway east of the church'. Since the stone is not given a specific name, it seems unlikely to have been erected as a monument of any kind (at least within the living memory of those at the time the map was drawn), so could it have been a prehistoric standing stone that has now been destroyed? Do the stones described in *Kelly's Directory* refer to a paved path towards the obelisk or more of a ceremonial avenue such as can be seen today at Avebury?

The obelisk was still standing in 1896 (it is shown in the Ordnance Survey map of that year) along with a number of other marked stones in the same area, which could either be related to the obelisk or merely boundary markers. By 1912, and up until 1946, just two stones remained – still aligned towards Denchworth. If there ever was an avenue of stones approaching the obelisk it seems likely that they were a major obstacle to cultivation and so would have been cleared from the fields and reused, making it entirely possible that the Denchworth pathway does indeed contain these relics.

Part of the path followed by this 'long vistow' is now a trackway but, with suitable apologies to the village of Denchworth, not one that leads to anywhere especially visually noteworthy as seen from Challow. However, there are tales of a presence haunting the attic of the Fox Inn at Denchworth and if we extend the line onwards it reaches Charney Bassett and its collection of ghosts, so there may be some tenuous connection to a ghost path here. Perhaps though, we need to look even further back – both in time and in this book – and consider that we have seen similar avenues before at Drayton, Abingdon and beyond. There are some faint but intriguing crop marks in the area and excavation may provide further clues but, despite the start of this putative avenue being up on the hillside rather than down in the Vale proper, perhaps, just perhaps, we are actually looking at traces of a previously unrecognised prehistoric feature; not a cursus certainly, but possibly something equally curious.

Presumably unconnected to the mysterious stone (though who can say?), there have been occasional reports of an armoured man, assumed to be one of the invading Danes, who has been spotted riding along some of the lanes surrounding East Challow; bear this in mind and make your own comparisons as we move a little further south.

Letcombe Regis and Letcombe Bassett

Nestling in a coombe below the Downs just outside Wantage are the Letcombe villages, which are said to take their name from an incident during a fierce battle between the Saxons and the Danes. According to this etymology, during the height of the battle blood began to pour down the hillside from the scene of the fiercest fighting and the locals shouted encouragement to the Saxon army, crying 'let it come'. Given this lurid tale it may be surprising to learn that it is Roman soldiers, not those from either of the sides involved in the fighting many centuries later, who are said to haunt the Ridgeway above the village.

Both Letcombes feature in the Domesday Book: Regis, as the name suggests, being the property of the King and Bassett being owned originally by Robert Doyley and later passing to Richard Bassett, whose name remains with the village. Letcombe Regis was once the site of the Dow Agricultural Laboratory, a sprawling research facility centred around an old manor house, now a retirement community. This most recent of the three manors built in the village was erected in Georgian times and has had a chequered history over the years. One previous owner supposedly had nude statues erected around an ornamental lake; this so displeased a subsequent lady Victorian owner that she had all the statues uprooted and thrown into the water to be lost in the mud. However, it is the presence of a grey lady in the building that makes it particularly fascinating.

No-one seems quite sure how long the lady had walked the halls of the manor, but she always made her presence felt, both to the lab workers who stayed after dark and to the security staff who patrolled the scenic site throughout the night.

Some years ago Bob,[45] one of the night staff, described some of the strange things he had faced:

> I have never seen the ghostly lady but I have had the lights put out on me. This was around four or five years ago when I was walking around in the early hours of the morning. I put the lights on to do my rounds and halfway around they just went off; as I came back around again they suddenly came back on. It's not just the lights either. A couple of weeks ago I had two new batteries in my torch and I was walking around at the back of the house when my torch went off. As soon as I came round the front it came back on and when I went around to the back it went off again. I can't explain it.

The story behind this gentle ghost is a tragic one, for she is generally thought to have been a young bride who found herself unwanted and alone on her wedding night and threw herself, still in her bridal gown, into the deepest part of the lake, where she drowned. Despite the sadness of her tale, no-one seemed unduly bothered by the Grey Lady and she was generally described as friendly or harmless.

Another correspondent also told me this story with an interesting twist. In his version, the young girl was actually an unwanted bride who was pushed into the deepest part of the lake by her far-from-gallant husband. After her tragic murder a solitary swan took to frequenting the pool. Could this have been a manifestation of the young girl returning to the spot where she met her untimely death?

Moving farther along the road from the Vale and up the side of the rising Downs, we come to the daughter village of Letcombe Bassett. Here is Arabella's Cottage, featured by Thomas Hardy in *Jude the Obscure*; here too are the watercress

---

[45] The same Bob who described his experiences at Crown Cork and Seal: clearly, some people just have the knack of encountering the paranormal.

beds which supplied produce picked at midnight to the morning markets in London. Between the two villages the road runs alongside the Letcombe Brook with meadows to the side and the Downs as a backdrop to the scene. Back in the summer of 1914 the farmer who owned the fields on the uphill side of this road began to tell his family stories of meetings with a mysterious figure he would pass on misty mornings as he brought his cows to be milked – a curious figure in antique armour mounted upon a horse. The farmer was never intimidated by this apparition and seems to  have viewed the figure as something of a comforting presence, someone with whom to share the dawn quiet, almost a friend perhaps, but one morning in early August of that year the farmer's family noticed a change in his demeanour when he came in from his early morning rendezvous. Reluctantly the farmer described a change in the armoured figure's behaviour; unprecedentedly, he had actually crossed over the brook and his crossing had been immediately followed by the sound – *though not the sight* – of many more horses splashing through the shallow water, which quickly became churned up and muddy from the passage of so many spectral hooves.

The family were understandably excited by this vision but not, perhaps, for the reason we might expect. They were, in fact, aware that the armoured warrior and his unseen troop were viewed as a presentiment of war and had been reported behaving in exactly the same way just before the Boer War; there were also local legends telling of a similar appearance at the beginning of the extended period of conflict in Napoleonic times. For reference the First World War formally started at the end of July 1914... By 1939 the farm had invested in an automated milking facility and the farmer no longer had to rise so early to gather his herd for milking, which perhaps explains why the horsemen had not been noted at the time of the Second World War; might the company have made other unseen crossings in more recent times of conflict?

As if to deliberately confuse the issue, some local people tell a variant of this story in which the armoured knight patrols the upper reaches of the village and perhaps as far as the Ridgeway on a white horse. This story may be associated with the presence of Segsbury Castle, the largest and most impressive of the local hillforts strung along the Ridgeway above the Vale, which lies just above Letcombe. There is also a link to the previous tale – locals say that if this warrior ever moves far enough down from the heights to pass the village shop, another war is inevitable.

Even more interestingly, the all these stories become fused together in one piece of folklore, which tells of how the grey lady from the manor sometimes haunts the road upwards from Letcombe Regis, and the knight sometimes advances down towards from Letcombe Bassett. If they ever meet it will mean that some unspecified disaster is about to befall the realm.

As if armoured horsemen were not enough, there have also been numerous sightings of a woman (perhaps that should be a *Lady*) on a white horse in the same area. Michael Toepfer met her one night in the 1980s while camping with friends near a track known as Shelly's Lane. It was around 2.30 in the morning and he had just stepped outside the tent to answer a call of nature when he saw a rider on a white horse approaching along the track. As the figure drew nearer he realised that it was a woman and, although he thought it odd that anyone should be out riding at that time of night, Michael politely called out a greeting. Rather than reply, the horsewoman simply stopped in front of him, gazed at him silently for a moment and then swung around and rode off towards Letcombe Regis, all without uttering a sound. Puzzled, Michael returned to his bed but when the friends emerged the next morning and looked for hoof prints there were none to be found.[46]

---

46 Although it seems an unlikely link, it is tempting to wonder whether any of these tales of uncanny horsemen are related to the sightings on the Downs above Chilton.

Childrey

On the Downs above Childrey is a curious depression in the land known as the Devil's Punchbowl. Most sites with this name have a well-defined story of why the Devil decided to scoop out the soil (usually to drop on someone he didn't like), but in the case of the Childrey Punchbowl there is no universally accepted version of the story. Instead it is usually subsumed into the myth of the Devil digging Grim's Ditch, my favourite version telling how, on tiring half-way through his task, Old Nick sat down for a rest and the indentation his rear left behind is the Punchbowl. In reality the Punchbowl is in itself rather interesting, being the remains of ancient flint mines worked by local peoples back in Neolithic times.

The manor at Childrey, properly called Rampanes Manor, was the home of a branch of the Fettiplace family, landowners who were part of an aristocratic triumvirate so rich that a local saying went:

> The Tracys, the Lacys and the Fettiplaces
> Own all the manors, the parks and the chases.

The house is reputed to have a tunnel running from the cellars to the village church; whether this is actually true or not is unclear but there is certainly a bricked-up entrance to a tunnel that could conceivably run in that direction, though no-one has explored it in living memory. While the existence of such a tunnel may be in doubt it is certain that Rampanes Manor had a firmly established ghost, one who often used to frighten the serving maids by his sudden appearances. This apparition, who would appear on horseback wearing Jacobean clothes, was supposed to have hidden a stash of coins in the vicinity but then died before he was able to retrieve his treasure. His vain post-mortem attempts to reclaim his money were said to be the reason for his appearances. One of the previous owners of the house discovered a hoard of Jacobean coins (now held at Reading Museum) in the 1930s while alterations were being made to the property; perhaps the removal of this treasure trove finally persuaded the ghost that it was time to pass on, because he has not been seen since.

Just down the road, an unseen presence used to visit Jenny, who lived in one of the many pretty cottages in the village. This ghost could hardly be described as malevolent, since the only activity Jenny ever noticed was that a door would mysteriously open when she sat in the front room reading. She seems to have been entirely blasé about these occasional intrusions, usually turning around and commenting 'I'm reading', although this attitude might also have been partly due to a certain degree of scepticism about the nature of the phenomenon. 'It could just have been passing traffic' was her laconic comment. Other members of her family were rather less sanguine about the ghost and became decidedly uneasy about visiting the property, despite the placidity of the possible phantom. In any case Jenny and the unknown spirit continued to share the house quite happily: perhaps her unseen lodger was a book-lover or maybe it just wanted a little company.

Sparsholt

Derek often strolled from his house on the outskirts of Sparsholt along the dark lanes of the village towards the warm welcome offered by the village pub, the Star Inn. Normally his ten-minute walk was entirely uneventful, close encounter with the occasional car notwithstanding, but on one autumn night some years ago things went a little differently.

At first the stranger leaning against the wall by the roadside seemed entirely ordinary, if somewhat oddly dressed in long dark coat and wide-brimmed hat pulled well down to completely conceal his face. Nor did the two large dogs at the stranger's side seem particularly unusual, although their size, which seemed somewhat excessive even for German Shepherds, gave Derek some slight concern. It was as he drew level with the man in the hat that Derek started to become worried by the palpable aura of presence and menace exuded by the figure, who did nothing but turn his head and watch as Derek passed hastily by. On glancing back a moment later Derek was startled to realise that the figure no longer occupied his position beside the road, although there was no obvious place he could have hidden himself, especially with two enormous dogs.

It was only after a soothing pint that Derek began to wonder if this unnerving encounter had been more than simply two strangers passing in the road and his suspicions were raised further when some time later he learned the tale of Odin the Wanderer. The Norse god Odin was renowned for his habit of travelling the world incognito, paying visits to mortals and often rewarding them for particular acts of kindness or generosity. Odin is usually depicted with a pair of companions: either a brace of ravens known as Huginn and Muninn (Thought and Memory) or, more importantly for us, two wolves named Freki (alternatively Gifr) and Geri; all three names meaning 'ravenous' or 'greedy'. The god, who tends to be easily recognisable due to only having one eye, disguises himself with a large hat pulled down to cover his face (remember his alias of Grimir from Grim's Ditch?). With a long history of invaders and settlers of both Danish and Saxon extraction, it would not be surprising if a Norse god felt at home in the area: could Derek have had an unwitting encounter with the Wanderer himself?

The poet John Betjeman, who lived in Uffington for many years, had an odd experience one night in the 1950s as he was returning home from a party with his daughter Candida. Candida was driving and they had just reached the beautiful stretch of road between Sparsholt and Kingston Lisle, which is spanned by an avenue of tall beech trees, when Betjeman suddenly started in his seat and shouted 'Stop!' After what must have been something of a sudden halt his daughter was amazed to see him climb from the car and announce that he was going to open the gate in the fence that ran across the road. Needless to say, nothing could be found blocking the highway, nor could the bewildered poet understand what had caused his sudden panicked sighting of this ghostly gateway as he climbed back into the vehicle. Was this simply the effects of an evening's indulgence or had he had a vision or waking dream, one invisible to his daughter, of a gate that had, at some point, crossed the path that the road now followed? Betjeman firmly believed in his own spirituality and described other paranormal phenomena during his life, including reportedly coming face to face with what seemed to be a troop of Roman soldiers near White Horse Hill, so it is possible that he was particularly sensitive to impressions of the past. I will, as usual, leave readers to draw their own conclusions as to the reality of the phantom fencing which interrupted their journey that night.

Kingston Lisle

A little further along the road, just beside a row of cottages near the village of Kingston Lisle, sits a curiously shaped stone. Around four feet tall and roughly cylindrical in shape, this is the Blowing Stone, with which, it is said, King Alfred summoned his army to fight the Danes at the Battle of Ashdown in 871, hence its sometime alternative name of King Alfred's Bugle Horn. The Blowing Stone is weatherworn and riddled with holes, many of which pierce the rock entirely. One of these towards the top has been worn smooth by generations of visitors attempting to sound Alfred's Horn, which I am assured sounds an eerie and mournful tone and which can be heard for a considerable distance (presumably much to the discomfort of the residents of the cottage next door). Unfortunately I have never been able to sound the stone so I cannot personally verify this observation; this is a pity because there is an additional coda to the story, which says that anyone who can make a sound loud enough to be heard at the White Horse is entitled to be King of England. I'm told the technique is to put the stone and your lips together and blow...

Just as a historical note: the exact location of the Battle of Ashdown has never been determined (despite the presence of Ashdown House and a village called Ashbury near the stone offering some hints). The battle is known to have taken place on a hill topped with a single ash tree but beyond that detail there is no clue to the location of this crucial engagement. Furthermore, it was actually Alfred's brother King Ethelred who, as king, was in overall command at the battle but Alfred, tired of waiting for pre-attack prayers to finish, led his personal coterie against the Danes in advance of the rest of the force. He was most of the way towards carrying the day before the rest of the Saxon army joined the fray and so Ashdown has always been seen as his victory.

The cottage where the stone was originally placed used to be the Blowing Stone Inn in the early 1800s and the local landlord, who had clearly mastered the art, would demonstrate the sound of the stone to customers. The sound could supposedly be heard as far away as Faringdon (in which case why he never became king remains an enduring mystery). The various holes in the stone were generally kept plugged with wooden pegs but visiting couples would remove the pegs and blow into the stone to ensure good luck.

One other notable location in the area is Black Jack Spring, one of the many sources of water emanating from the chalk reservoir of the downlands above the Vale. Although I have been unable to find any treacle-based folklore associated with the spring, its water was much valued in previous times for its healing powers and was especially prized as a cure for eye problems.[47]

And, to leave the village on a darkly comic historical note, it seems that at least one of the earlier residents of Kingston Lisle valued hard cash much more highly than propriety and was prepared to hound his debtors to their deaths and beyond. There is an entry in the Parish Register which records how a solemn funeral procession leaving the village for a burial at Sparsholt was halted on its way by an aggrieved creditor of the deceased, who refused to step aside until the balance of an outstanding debt was repaid. A standoff ensued, with the creditor aggressively blocking the path and holding up the entire funeral cortege, leaving the dead man's family little choice but to return to their homes and come back with enough money to clear the account. Only after the transaction was satisfactorily concluded did he step aside and allow the

---

47 The spring has been totally forgotten today, which seems a little short-sighted.

burial to proceed as planned. I hope that the value of the money he collected made up for what I can only assume were weeks of awkward silences whenever he walked into the Blowing Stone Inn.

Ashdown House

Up on the Downs beyond Kingston Lisle sits Ashdown Park and House, built in 1662 as a hunting lodge and retreat for Elizabeth, Queen of Bohemia, sister of Charles I and (possible) lover of the Earl of Craven. At the time of construction, plague was a recurring problem throughout the country and, because medical opinion at the time held that disease was transmitted by bad odours in the air, his Lordship is said to have insisted that all the doors should have four-inch gaps at the bottom to ensure a constant flow of healthy breezes throughout the house: undoubtedly healthy, but possibly a little chilly given the exposed location of the property. Whether the tunnel, which was said to run from the house to the hamlet of Russley over a mile away, was part of this design for healthy living is not on record: in any case, as might be expected, no trace of this mysterious passageway can be found today.

Healthy air or not, Elizabeth did not live long enough to enjoy Ashdown House and, lending some weight to the arguments for her close relations with Lord Craven, left a number of paintings to him in her will, many of which can still be found in the house. Once he eventually moved into the house Craven certainly seems to have made the most of his new playground; the upper floor contained an enormous ballroom which he used to host extravagant entertainments and parties; the wine cellar had a greater floor area than the above-ground footprint of the house. Craven was notorious as a fashionable dandy and entertained the Royal Family on many occasions, as well as keeping numerous mistresses (as many as four at any one time), but at some point the pleasure from his party lifestyle seems to have palled and he started to become increasingly depressed. The socialising stopped and, although Lord Craven continued to dress in his increasingly outdated and more and more threadbare finery, he eventually became such a shadow of his former self that he became known locally as the Ragged Dandy.[48]

Following his death, his spirit was said to have been unwilling to leave this world and his ghost was frequently seen both at the house and the barn. He also gained a reputation for patrolling the roads of the estate, dressed in his trademark patched and faded clothes and always walking down the centre of the path, willing to step aside for no man. One brave local who met this wandering wraith followed him up to Ashdown House, whereupon the ghost promptly let himself into the parlour and settled down to warm himself before the heat of an unseen fire. His shade has also been seen through the windows of the ballroom performing a stately pavanne, often in conversation with an invisible partner upon his arm. One night some local men climbed up to the roof and peered inside to see Lord Craven seated at a long table and lit by the light of unseen candles, seeming for all the world to be entertaining guests and making frequent toasts to his invisible company.

There may well also be another unknown presence in the house. Novelist and volunteer guide Nicola Cornick was photographing the house one evening when she noticed the silhouetted figure of a woman gazing from one of the upstairs windows. On another occasion she described how, while out looking for bats with a group of visitors to Ashdown Park, she looked back from the grounds towards the locked and deserted house to see a soft golden light like candle- or lamplight shining behind one of the windows on the first floor. As the party watched, the light moved upwards, presumably climbing the staircase onto the next floor and the shadow of a woman became visible through another window. However, a further shock was in store for the group, because

---

48 It seems that he never entirely abandoned his former interests because some sources say that he died at Ashdown after being struck about the head during a tavern brawl in 1669.

as they approached the house the light faded away to reveal that all the windows were closed and shuttered. How could they have seen the light shining and moving about when all the windows were completely covered? This was evidently a most unusual apparition consisting of both a spectral figure and an ethereal house visible at the same time. Not so much a haunted as a *haunting* house perhaps.

Some of the phenomena encountered at Ashdown are of a more physical nature. Following repair work on the roof, a hatch on the uppermost level of the staircase has been observed to open of its own accord; similarly the main door to the house has been observed to swing itself open to the astonishment of tour parties climbing the entry steps. I will merely reiterate my comments on the wind-swept location of the property at this point...

As if the events in the house itself were not enough, it seems as if the stables of the estate are frequented by the ghost of a groom who hanged himself from the rafters in Victorian times. Whether this ghost is associated with the childish cries that sometimes drift from the surrounding woods is unknown. Equally mysterious is the lady in seventeenth-century dress who was encountered by a visitor to the house recently. The ghostly lady was clearly aware of her surroundings as she looked directly at the visitor and commented: 'I'm so glad you're back.' I wonder whom she thought she was addressing?

Ashbury

And, at last, a possible hint towards explaining those stories about knights and coffins on the Ridgeway. P. H. Ditchfield notes that a local man from the village told a visiting antiquarian about a long-held tradition that a knight in golden armour was buried underneath one of the numerous barrows in the vicinity. Seizing the moment, the enterprising visitor promptly assembled a team of willing workmen and proceeded, in the most professional way of course, to demolish the mound, eventually unearthing the body of an ancient chieftain wearing a gold (or at least bronze) breastplate.

Ashbury Church is reputed to have been built within a long-abandoned circle of sarsen stones and some can still be seen on the west side of churchyard. Similar stones in a field near to Ashdown House, known locally as the Grey Wethers, are supposed to be sheep petrified by the wizard Merlin, hence they are sometimes also called druid stones.

Idstone

Trip the Daisy House in Idstone was once a pub held by landlord Alexander Horsburgh, a noted dog breeder in the district. A picture of his most famous hound, Trip the Daisy herself, used to hang in the house with an accompanying rhyme:

> A dog am I as you may see,
> There can no harm be found in me.
> My master he confines me here
> To tell you that he sells good beer.

It was said that the quality of the artwork was so exceptional and the dog so famous that a number of passers-by asked to buy the painting. While Horsburgh's beer may have been as good as the rhyme attested the same cannot be said for his integrity, because in each case the travellers were allowed to purchase, doubtless at considerable cost, this supposedly unique piece of art only for it to be immediately replaced with another copy ready for the next unsuspecting punter. Obviously a classic case of a sucker being sold a pup...

Another of those occasional visitors from other skies passed by Idstone in February 1985, or so one UFO report would have us believe. Two people, one a pilot and thus generally assumed to be a reliable witness, were driving near the village when they spotted an orange oval light in the sky. Understandably intrigued, they pulled over and stopped to take a better look at this unusual phenomenon. The pilot later said that the object was not any type of aircraft that she could recognise, but added that it was impossible to estimate either the size of the object or its distance because the sky was clear and there were no clouds to use as points of reference.

And, on the subject of flying objects, in this case perfectly identified, it was widely believed that bees were able to

understand human speech and consequently took a lively interest in local affairs. This meant that beekeepers would often rush off to tell the hive any news from the district in the belief that happy and well-informed bees were more likely to produce well. Hives were sometimes draped in black after a death in the village and would be solemnly informed of the death of the king or local squire. On a more cheerful note they would also get to hear news of forthcoming weddings:

Bees, Bees, there's joy in the house,
For a maid has promised to wed!

This 'telling the bees' was quite a widespread practice, but one old lady who lived near Idstone in the late nineteenth century took it one step further, firmly believing that her bees sang psalms at night when everyone was asleep. Perhaps she had visited Charney Bassett at some point because, as with the story of the churchyard stones there, the bees would not sing if even a single person was awake to hear them. Presumably if anyone came within hearing they just hummed the tune.

Bishopstone

As we proceed further westwards to Bishopstone we actually leave the comforting borders of Oxfordshire behind and nervously enter the county of Wiltshire. We need not fear that things will be too different; Bishopstone is another village that used to reside in Old North Berkshire until the 1974 upheaval. Once a haunt of highwaymen and ne'er do wells who were said to conceal their ill-gotten gains in the tombs in the local churchyard, Bishopstone does have a far more heartening snippet of local folklore, which relates how many years ago a man of the village found himself lost and cold atop the Downs when night fell. Unable to see his hand before his face and reconciling himself to an uncomfortably chilly night outside, he was delighted to suddenly hear the sound of the bells of the village church drifting across the countryside and was able to follow the welcoming peal back home to safety. It was said that for many years following that day the church bells were rung between eight and nine each evening to similarly guide home any villager who might be wandering forlornly in the dark hills above Bishopstone.[49]

---

49 'Curfew bells' were common throughout England so it seems likely that the 'lost shepherd' explanation is only part of the story of the Bishopstone bells – though this particular story has its own appeal.

Hinton Parva

You will, I trust, forgive one further excursion to the very fringes of Swindon and the village of Little Hinton or, more properly in its latinate form which emerged in the seventeenth century, Hinton Parva. In former times the hills surrounding the hamlet were thought to be the haunt of witches and other, even less savoury, supernatural creatures, who would capture horses turned out at night to pasture and ride them up hill and down dale throughout the dark hours until the owners found sweating and shivering animals when they came to reclaim them at daylight. The Downs hereabouts are scattered with pits, some of which are certainly of prehistoric origin, but which also served in more recent times as foundations for primitive huts. In these hovels lived the poorest of the poor of the area, the last of whom, old Mary Clargo, was widely reputed to be a witch, a reputation which was shared by many of her clan as we shall see.

Following the Dissolution of the Monasteries under Henry VIII, the Hinton family took possession of what shortly thereafter became Earlscourt Manor from the Priory of St Swithun. Alas, the monks who had been so cruelly evicted left with a prayer, or perhaps a curse, that the house should thereafter be forever haunted. As if in fulfilment of this curse, local people noticed that owls would constantly roost in and peer down from the gables of the property and soon decided that they were the restless spirits of the dispossessed clerics returning to the scene of their casting out into the wilderness.

These eerie visitors were clearly eager to witness the progress of their malediction and they were not to be disappointed; the house would regularly be filled with shrieks and ghastly cries, chains would rattle at midnight, unexplained breezes would prowl the darkened corridors and the oddly specific sound of rolling cheeses would be heard across the boards

of the bedroom floors. All attempts to propitiate the spirits behind these terrifying phenomena – prayer, pilgrimage, benefactions to the church and even the sprinkling of holy water throughout the house – failed to have any effect, so it was clear that more drastic measures were required. Consequently a plea went out to the *weirds*, who lived on the fringes of the village; doubtless the antecedents of Mary Clargo and most certainly sharing her uncanny reputation.

And so it was that seven hooded and cowled figures arrived at the manor with the avowed intention of cleansing it of its malignant and excitable spirits.[50] This Secretive Seven set up base in a small, windowless, cupboard-like room deep within the house, laid out a protective circle in chalk upon the floor and from within its defensive perimeter began to chant out a ceremony of binding while, according to witness accounts, the spirits haunting the building screeched and howled impotently outside. The spell seemed to have some effect as the small sprites infesting the room gradually coalesced into a human-like figure which, when asked why it was haunting the manor, proceeded to elaborate a long list of grievances and hurts, foremost of which was the eviction of the monks from Earlscourt. Deciding that the best course of action was to chain the spirit or spirits to the room in which they stood, the Seven spoke the words that they hoped would end the haunting, declaring that the ghost should be 'laid for a thousand years tomorrow'. Unfortunately, their choice of phrasing proved to

---

50 It is interesting to compare the number of mystery visitors in this tale with the groups of eleven which we encountered further east at Moreton and Long Wittenham.

be their downfall and the moment they stepped triumphantly from their sheltering circle a crash of thunder made them realise that not all had gone as planned. In this case it seems that the Devil was most literally in the detail and the entity that they had considered bound for a millennium had taken advantage of the fact that its confinement did not start until 'tomorrow' to turn the binding upon its foes. In a flash the Seven disappeared and only their dark ghosts remained to gibber and scratch futilely at the walls of their prison.

After this catastrophic failure the accursed room was locked and barred, though this did not in any way help; in fact the ghostly monks seem to have completely revised their tactics because ghostly noises were replaced by white faces peering in  through windows and odd were-lights in and around the house, as well as, in a decidedly odd turn, a beautiful young woman who would drift ethereally through the gardens after dark. As the stress caused by these phenomena mounted, a brave, or possibly foolhardy, servant girl ventured to open up the sealed chamber and was horrified to witness seven hooded figures gathered around an equally insubstantial fire burning brightly in the fireplace. In shock she fainted completely away to be discovered by the farmer's wife in a cold and empty room, though a room with fresh ash in the fireplace...

For a while the haunting continued: locks would refuse to open; milk would jump inexplicably from the pails in which it was stored; doors would refuse to close and the farm animals began to give birth to still-born young. As a climax to these events a funeral bier accompanied by seven tall figures would be glimpsed in the lane approaching the manor and the beautiful drifting maid was replaced by an old hag who could be observed floating across one of the local ponds mounted on a black calf. Some brave locals once approached her saying, 'Mother, you be late gwain whoam' to which she replied 'I've heard un crack; I've heard un crack' and then vanished before their very eyes.

Of course no haunting can keep up such a flow of ghostly occurrences indefinitely and life in Hinton gradually returned to normal. The sealed chamber became known as Taffy's Room and eventually its contingent of trapped exorcists were forgotten. But perhaps, just perhaps, a trace of the haunting still lingers around Earlscourt, for a century ago a visitor to the manor was both surprised and shocked to wake during the night to discover a white face, framed by an old-fashioned hood, peering in through the window...

The rolling hills hereabouts, from these Wiltshire borders and back to the fields on both sides of the White Horse itself, have been host to a wonderful range of crop circles over the years, laid out with elegant precision in the oilseed rape or gently waving corn. Musician-turned-researcher Reg Presley of the Troggs made much of the fact that 75 per cent of all crop circles in the UK fell within a triangle bounded by the three towns of Warminster, Wantage and Winchester; the three representing, according to his explanation, *War*, *Want* and *Win*. Whatever the symbolism behind the patterns they range from simple, or indeed decorated, circles through geometrical and curled snake glyphs to the frankly bizarre alien face which appeared in 2011. A quick online search will reveal a huge variety of these beautiful *agriglyphs*, as well as an equally impressive selection of possible explanations: whirlwinds or mysterious weather vortices for those of a scientific bent; alien visitors for UFOlogists; mysterious messages from Mother Earth for those of a more mystical nature; helicopter downdraughts or microwave radiation for technology buffs;

torch-wielding men with ropes and wooden boards for the terminally mundane. My favourite, and for me by far the most convincing explanation to date, suggests that the patterns may be created accidentally by hedgehogs, presumably in large numbers, crushing crops during frenzied mating activity. Or possibly I suppose just two outsized or hyperactive hedgehogs. There have been no reports of anyone stumbling across animals involved in this kind of creative coitus but, as always, if you do happen to be the first, please get in touch.

The White Horse

And so (finally you may say) on to the Uffington complex itself. The Uffington carving, 374 ft (110 m) long and famously featured in Hughes's *The Scouring of the White Horse*, was created by the removal of a layer of turf from the hillside and infilling the resulting bare area with dazzling chalk. It is not actually a very realistic likeness of a horse at all but, as if that were not bad enough, it was not even part of the parish of Uffington until 1776; prior to that date it had technically been the 'off-white horse-like shape of Woolstone'.[51] Of course these are minor quibbles considering its amazing longevity. It has maintained its presence on the hillside thanks to regular scouring by local people, mostly organised by whatever local gentry held Uffington and the surrounding area and often accompanied by a Whitsuntide fair and other festivities – usually in Uffington Castle atop the hill. The first mention of such a scouring was by local diarist and author Thomas Baskerville, who visited the site in the 1670s and commented that 'some that dwell hereabout have an obligation upon their lands to repair and cleanse this landmark'. These were often well-attended affairs: in 1780 a reported 30,000 people joined in the celebrations and the fair accompanying the 1843 scouring included an appearance of Wombwell's Menagerie, a travelling zoo. Regular scourings are now organised by the National Trust and members of the public can sign up to join in on a rota basis.

There is little doubt that the basic outline of the Horse has changed considerably since it was originally cut, and work by the Oxford Archaeological Unit has established that at the very least the outline has become considerably slimmer over the years, something which may explain its unusual contours (although the writer Guy Underwood speculated that a more

---

51 To be fair, the current name *is* catchier.

realistic outline of a horse could still be perceived using dowsing rods).

Demonstrating both the antiquity of the scouring tradition and the changes in the shape of the carving, a correspondent to the *Reading Mercury* in 1789 wrote:

> The White Horse, on the side of the Downs in the White Horse Vale, has been lately recut, so that at a distance of three or four miles it is perhaps one of the most lively representations of an elegant shaped horse, except that the horse's back ... is rather too long, otherwise it is now one of the best delineations of that animal [I] ever beheld.

Conversely, by 1896 Augustus John Cuthbert Hare was describing it as 'far more like a weasel than a horse'. Historically, the oddly elongated shape and disjointed limbs are reflected in equine imagery from across Europe on coins minted far apart in space and time, by Philip of Macedon in the east and the ancient Celts of northern Europe to the west, so modern complaints that it is not a literal representation carry little actual weight. Clearly, artistic license was far more liberally applied when the Uffington carving was cut and only the modern Wiltshire hill carvings were actually meant to *look* like horses!

Antiquarian John Aubrey attributed the original carving of the monument to the invading Saxon leaders Hengist and Horsa, whereas local folklore has two explanations for the cutting of the figure: the first is that it was cut as a victory celebration by King Alfred after the Battle of Ashdown; the second is that it was cut by grateful locals to commemorate St George's defeat of the dragon after the slaying which took place nearby.

There is an old Berkshire ballad which holds to the first theory and runs:

A was made a lang, lang time ago,
Wi' a good dale of labour and pains,
By Alfred the Great, when he spoiled their consate[52],
And scaddle[53] they warshird[54] the Danes.

In the St George version of the legend, the shape cut into the chalk, if not representative of the knight's mount, is of course a dragon, although given the ambiguity of the (current) shape of the Horse there have been numerous other attempts to redefine it as various other types of animal. Writing to the *Veterinary Record* in 2010, retired vet Olaf Swarbrick expounded the theory that the figure might represent a wolfhound and, in an even more fanciful notion, children's author Paula Broderick claimed that the 'horse' had originally been a unicorn and that the horn was removed during the Middle Ages by over-zealous religious leaders. The shape of the Horse's head is decidedly odd, and possibly birdlike, leading to scholarly speculation that it may be representative of the 'hen-headed steed' associated with the Celtic goddess Ceridwen: academic arguments about age, shape and derivation may have been more restricted in scope than public discussions but have obviously been no less lively over the years.

Of all the theories proposed to explain the carving, my personal favourite is that the White Horse may actually be a representation of one of the last of the dinosaurs which had somehow managed to survive the 65 million years since the extinction of most of the rest of its kin. If this idea is correct should we be celebrating the epic combat between St George and the Dinosaur? Fossil remains have certainly been

---

52 Conceit

53 Scuppered

54 Rogues, rascals. Apparently. Personally I suspect a rather less restrained translation might be in order.

uncovered all around the area but it seems unlikely that any of them are quite that recent. Although... Take a look at a picture of the White Horse taken from the air and turn it 180 degrees so that it is upside down. From this angle it certainly looks very like a Pteranodon, a flying reptile from the age of the dinosaurs, and it is true that the carving is difficult to observe properly from the ground and is best seen from the air... Even stranger is the theory, voiced in *Country Life* magazine in the 1920s by H J Massingham, that the figure is supposed to represent an ichthyosaurus, a fossil *fish-like* reptile, even though a plesiosaur would be more logical from the shape (perhaps this is what he really meant?). Why such a carving would appear on a hillside miles from the sea is anyone's guess, although I suppose it is just remotely possible that the unearthing of a suitable fossil many years ago might have provided the initial inspiration.

In case you are wondering at the actual age (or at least the most recent and scientifically accurate assessment of the age) of the Horse, then you may be pleased to know that using the technique of Optical Stimulated Luminescence Dating (which measures how long the stone beneath the horse has been hidden from sunlight) David Miles and Simon Palmer of the Oxford Archaeological Unit determined in 1995 a date in the late Bronze or early Iron Age as being the most likely time for the first carving of the monument – somewhere around three thousand years ago give or take a couple of centuries. Of course that doesn't tell us what it was originally meant to represent so, in that sense at least, all bets are still on.

One further mystery: was there once another carving, now lost, which used to sit alongside the main figure? Ralph de Diceto, the author of *De mirabilibus Britanniae,* a catalogue of the thirty-five most amazing wonders of Britain written around 1100, wrote of:

The White Horse *with its foal*.⁵⁵ It is wondrous that it was so made in the figure of a horse that, while the whole place where that image of a horse is grassy beyond measure, grass never grows over the shape of the horse, but the ground to the extent of the horse is always exposed.

No other writer ever mentions this elusive foal, so was this nothing more than a literary allusion? Was the writer referring to a now vanished second carving (could the white spot atop Dragon Hill once have resembled a horse perhaps?) or is this just a mistranslation from an ancient source?

There is currently a discreet line of fencing to stop visitors from tramping all over the figure but there has long been a local tradition pre-dating such protection which holds that anyone who stands on the eye and turns around three times while making a wish will have that wish granted within a year. There is a modern tradition that visitors who do this will incur the eternal enmity of both English Heritage and the National Trust.

The landscape around the White Horse is impressive in its own right. Below the carving lies a winding valley, carved from the chalk by melting ice from departing glaciers after the last Ice Age, and known as The Manger because it is said that the White Horse lifts itself from the hillside and descends into the valley to feed on certain moonlit nights. (A variation on this theme holds that the thirsty Horse goes to drink at the Woolstone Wells springs.) There is a curious snippet of Arthurian legend (odd in that there are no other real links with King Arthur in the immediate area) which holds that should King Arthur ever awake from his slumbers and return to save the realm then the Horse will dance atop Dragon Hill in celebration. Incidentally, The Manger was the location of

---

55 My emphasis.

Old Berkshire's own cheese rolling races during the periodic scourings of the chalk figure. The rippling hillside to the west of The Manger is known as the Giant's Stairs and if you are very lucky it is possible to find one spot on the hillside about a quarter of a mile away from the figure which acts as a natural whispering gallery, allowing conversations to be held with someone standing beside the Horse.

On the hill above the White Horse lies the hillfort known as Uffington Castle and, a little below that, a Neolithic long barrow. Nearby there is a round barrow, which was first excavated in 1857 and then again in 1993. The second dig unearthed a buried copy of the 1831 book *Demonology and Witchcraft*, by Sir Walter Scott. In red ink on the inside of the front cover someone had drawn a pentacle and written the words 'Demon de Uffing'. The soil was settled around the book so it was assumed to have been in the ground for some years; corrosion from the chalky soil tended to support this conclusion. It seems unlikely that one of the original archaeological team would have left such an odd souvenir, so who can have crept up to the barrow and buried such an incongruous item? And why?

In the valley below the horse, the natural mound of Dragon Hill presents an unusual spectacle because, whereas the sides are completely covered in grass, there is a spot directly atop the mound where nothing will grow, whatever the season. The usual explanation for this phenomenon is that during the epic killing of a marauding dragon, St George spilled its blood at that exact spot, thereby sterilising it for evermore. Alternatively, the mound is also supposed to have been raised over the corpse of the slain beast, hence its name.

Wayland's Smithy

In the mythology of the Saxons who brought his story from the continent, Wayland is a supernaturally skilled smith, the son of Wade who apprenticed him to the dwarves so that he might learn the arts of metalwork. Wayland is kidnapped by the unscrupulous King Nidud, who is eager to make use of his talents, and then maimed to prevent his escape. In revenge he kills the King's sons and makes cups from their skulls before assaulting their sister and escaping by magical flight, finally settling back down to a life of metalwork in an underground cave, hence the logical association with the long barrow. Additionally, in the original legend Wayland owned a horse called Skemming, described as 'the best of all horses'; perhaps the proximity of the White Horse is another reason that the barrow became linked to his legend.

Apart from starring in his own story, Wayland gets a mention in the epic Anglo-Saxon poem Beowulf ('That is the legacy of Ilraeda, the work of Weland') and features in some French legends, under the name of Galand, as the weapon-maker who forged the sword Joyeuse for the Emperor Charlemagne. An English translation of the fourteenth-century story *Romance of Horn* tells us all we need to know about the quality of Wayland's work: 'of all swords it is king, and Weyland it wrought.' Unsurprisingly perhaps, he is even credited with forging the sword Excalibur in some versions of the Arthurian legend. Curiously, or perhaps logically, his name defines his trade because in Icelandic the word *voelund* simply means a smith.

Wayland's association with the long barrow was obviously significant to the various peoples who lived around the Smithy, because there are a smattering of other sites scattered around which also refer to his story. Between the White Horse and the Smithy lies Hardwell Camp, which was originally known as Tilsburh, or Til's Castle, Til being one of the brothers of

Wayland. Similarly, Beahild Barrow, also nearby, refers to Wayland's sister and Wittich's Hill, near Hardwell Wood a mile or so from the barrow, may commemorate Wayland's son, Wittich.

Walter Scott tells the most popular version of the legend of Wayland the Smith in Kenilworth:

> You must tie your horse to that upright stone that has a ring in it and whistle three times and lay down your money on a flat stone and then sit down among the bushes and not look for ten minutes. Then you will hear the hammer clink. Then say your prayers and you will find your money gone and your horse shod.

Local folklore tends to prefer that you leave your horse and money overnight. Such was the power of this belief that in the nineteenth century local children would frequent the area in order to purloin the pennies left by hopeful travellers and even dig into the mound in an attempt to find Wayland's stash of coins, which is why, archaeologists believe, that they have singularly failed to find any coins associated with the monument during their excavations.

There is a local legend which says that once every one hundred years, presumably after eating its fill at The Manger, the White Horse calls at Wayland's Smithy in order to be shod by the smith. There is another tale told locally which describes a mysterious stranger dressed in a large hat and leather apron who entered the White Horse Inn at Woolstone one night and ordered a drink. No sooner had he started to sup his ale the sound of a horn was heard outside and the stranger downed his beer at a gulp and rushed away at top speed. Curious as to the reason for the horn and his hasty departure, everyone else in the pub rushed outside only to be assaulted by the deafening sound of horses' hooves overhead. Gazing up towards the slopes of the Downs above the village they were astonished to see that the figure of the White Horse was missing from the hillside. The Horse later reappeared in its usual place, presumably having been reshod by Wayland, the stranger at the inn. Since this story dates from sometime during the 1920s we may be due for another walkabout at some point in the not too distant future: I am hopeful that satellite imagery will be able to capture the event for posterity.

In archaeological terms Wayland's Smithy is actually made up of two successive Neolithic long barrows, built one atop the other some five and a half thousand years ago. Fourteen skeletons were found inside the earlier structure and another eight in the later extension. The site was substantially excavated and repaired in 1963 but, during an earlier excavation in 1919, what were thought to be two Iron Age currency bars were unearthed and greeted with a great deal of excitement. Sadly, after further examination these turned out to be rusted hinges of much more recent origin.

Other items allegedly recovered from the barrow are genuinely far more interesting. In March 1939 an unusual object was exhibited at a meeting of the Folklore Society – a carved disc-shaped piece of human bone inscribed with seven sets of marks, possibly some sort of runes, on its surface. This item, probably discovered by Gerald Gardner, who had done some digging around the site in 1932, was described as a 'witches moon-dial'; the seven runic carvings were said to represent what witches call the 'seven hours of dread'. With a stick through the centre hole acting as handle and gnomon (the part that casts the shadow), it could indeed have functioned as a nocturnal version of a sundial. In addition to this artefact, a cunning woman named Mary Chalmers who lived at (probably) South Moreton and died in 1810, was supposed to have owned a skull which had been dug up from Wayland's Smithy. She was said to use it in her magic, mostly curing sheep and cows for local people. It is interesting to discover evidence of an ongoing tradition of wise women in Moreton: hopefully Chalmers's fortune-tellings were a little less opaque than those of her successor.

While only a couple of chambers are accessible to visitors at the tomb there is a persistent belief that a tunnel runs from somewhere deeper inside the barrow all the way to Ashbury Coombes about a mile away up towards the Downs. In Victorian times local shepherds would strike their crooks on the ground and claim to be able to hear a hollow echo from the subterranean passage. There is variant of this story which has the tunnel running towards the White Horse.

Another, lesser-known, legend from the site refers to the time Wayland decided to employ the services of an assistant, a local country boy (or, in some versions, a young imp) by the name of Flibbertigibbet. One day Wayland discovered that he had exhausted his supply of nails and sent his errand boy down into the Vale to arrange the purchase of more. Like most young boys sent off to run errands on a sunny afternoon Flibbertigibbet did not take his task too seriously and stopped frequently along the way to search for birds' nests in the hedgerows. After two hours of waiting and with work in the form of a local horse waiting to be shod, Wayland became irate; in fact his legendary temper began to smoulder. Casting his gaze around the Vale spread out below him he spotted his errant apprentice with his arm deep within a hawthorn bush, searching no doubt for eggs. This sight so infuriated the smith that he picked up his anvil stone and hurled it in the direction of the wayward boy. Thanks to the smith's incredible strength the stone flew a full two miles, but even this prodigious feat was only just sufficient. The rock came crashing to the ground, grazing the boy's heel and doubtless causing considerable consternation. Flibbertigibbet immediately burst into tears and belatedly ran off towards the nearest village to collect the nails. Locals who witnessed the event immediately christened the place Snivelling Corner and the anvil stone can be seen at the spot near Ashbury to this very day, as can the indentation caused as it landed on the heel of the indolent Flibbertigibbet.

There is a ghost story of a more orthodox sort associated with the Ridgeway near Wayland's Smithy, which concerns a hiker who camped nearby sometime in the early years of the twentieth century. During the night he was wakened by a great uproar which sounded as if a large number of men and horses were either making or breaking camp. When he awoke the following morning the traveller remembered the night-time commotion and resolved to investigate. Working on the assumption that, since he had not noticed them before making his own camp they must have been setting up during the night, he went over to where he had heard the noises, expecting to see a sizable group of men camped out. To his surprise not only was there no-one in evidence at all but, even though the grass was damp with morning dew, there was not the slightest sign to indicate that anyone had ever been there during the night. Mystified as to what might have happened he mentioned his experience later to a local man who matter-of-factly commented, 'It would be them Romans you heard.'

Longcot

Until the nineteenth century the village of Longcot boasted a magnificent maypole which was permanently erected on the village green. Alas, it was coveted by any number of neighbouring villages and was one night spirited away by a group of young men from nearby Ashbury, who promptly erected it outside the Crown Inn, doubtless celebrating their escapade with a number of well-earned pints of ale. Possibly too many, for it was shortly thereafter purloined by a group of men from Uffington who were equally unable to hold on to their ill-gotten gains, promptly losing it to a gang from Lambourn. The affair then escalated dangerously with the Uffington crowd attacking the Lambourn men with pails of boiling water to drive them away and reclaim the maypole. The Rev. Watts, parish priest of Uffington, was so horrified by this violence and lawlessness (and possibly also keen to find an excuse to remove an obviously pagan relic from the neighbourhood) that he insisted the pole be chopped up and given away as firewood to the poor of the parish. Regrettably, Longcot did not replace the maypole.

There are a few anecdotal ghost stories linked to the village. Plomers, a large cottage on the village green, is haunted by the ghost of a young girl who appears in the garden wearing a white dress (although both her identity and the reason for her appearance are unknown) and a young man in a house which must remain unidentified once experienced a strange procession of lights parading through one of the upstairs bedrooms. Another property was haunted for a while by the mysterious and plaintive cries of a non-existent baby. There is also an old farmhouse at the edge of the village which rang to the sounds of mysterious crashes and clanking whenever family members climbed the stairs; sometimes they would also be overtaken by a rushing of strangely warm air which would pass them and move into one of the bedrooms. On one occasion the farmer's wife, who was alone in the house at the time, awoke in the middle of the night to find the figure of a man standing at the foot of her bed. Terrified, she immediately burrowed her head under the bedding but when, after some time, she summoned up enough courage to peer out and take a peep at the mysterious intruder the room was empty. Again, there is no indication that any explanation for these strange occurrences was ever discovered.

And, before we leave Longcot, here is something to salve the hurt of all those still smarting from the revelations about the death knells rung in Stanford-in-the-Vale: in Longcot it was traditional to sound the church bell twice to mark the death of a local woman but only once for a man.

Watchfield

Watchfield is blessed with a rare remnant of an ancient sacred shrine, namely Maiden's Well, a site thought to have been used by young women or girls as the location for some purification or fertility ceremonies in times past. It is not just the girls of the distant past who had cause to remember their visits to the well though, as one lady who was a young girl in the 1920s can confirm.

Miss Morse and her sisters lived at the Old School Cottage in Watchfield and would make a trip to a farm in Shrivenham each day to fetch milk for the family. Late one wintry afternoon the girls were coming back home with their purchase when they saw a misty white figure, seemingly clutching an old-fashioned oil lamp in each hand, standing beside Maiden's Well. Although they were all too frightened to approach the figure they did manage to muster enough courage to watch it for a while from a distance until, under their collective gaze, it slowly began to fade away. When they described their experience some time later, a number of other people in the village admitted that they too had seen exactly the same apparition. The explanation the villagers gave to explain the haunting was that the figure was the ghost of a man named Jefferies who used to work on the Squire's Barn premises and who had drowned himself in a pond by Squirrel Copse some years before. It is interesting to note that the 1881 census of Watchfield does list an Emily Jefferies as a widow, so there may be some truth to the suicide story at the very least, although whether this relates to the ghost is, of course, entirely speculative.

While the villagers of Hanney may have squabbled over the location of their church, some contemporary accounts dating from the latter half of the eighteenth century suggest that the inhabitants of Watchfield may have stolen theirs entirely away. At this time the old village chapel had fallen into some disrepair and the parishioners were unwilling to expend a great deal of time and effort on any kind of restoration project. Consequently, according to the story, it was quietly dismantled, literally stone by stone, in 1788 and carted away to be sold as building material around the village: to salve the collective conscience the proceeds of this dubious business were used to pay the wages of a new schoolmistress. Some sources add that the wily churchwardens continued to send glowing reports about the state of the chapel for twenty-two years before the deception was uncovered. An unconfirmed corollary to this tale tells of how divine retribution struck down the duplicitous wardens who had been behind this sacrilegious act; each died a violent death, with one being found with a broken neck having fallen from a bridge and another being struck by lightning in broad daylight in a hayfield. Sadly for the tale there is a note on the official Chapel Visitation ledger from 1788 which records that 'The Chapel has been taken down by order', although some of the proceeds of the sale of the old stones were indeed used to fund local Sunday Schools. A replacement chapel was not built until 1857.

Shrivenham

Before the days of reliable weather forecasting, locals at Shrivenham had a sure-fire way of predicting the forthcoming day's weather by gazing towards White Horse Hill and reciting:

> When the mist goes up the hill,
> Then the rain runs down the drill.

Do feel free to compare the efficacy of this forecast with the prognostications of the Met Office today: I suspect that the ditty will be as accurate as anything they predict.

In a similar vein I doubt that the climate locally has changed enough over the years to render the following lines invalid:

> Rain afore seven, dry afore 'leven;
> 'Tween one and two, see what the day'll do.

Bird behaviour is presumably equally unchanged:

> In summer if the blackbirds are piping and the thrushes
>   are silent,
> Look for two or three days' bad weather.

While the sayings above may have been adequate for purely local, short-term planning, I am not sure the following adage was ever such a reliable long-term predictor:

> If it rains on Easter Day
> Plenty of grass but not much hay

although the idea of using leaf size as a measure of how far the season has progressed makes a certain amount of sense:

> When the leaf of a mulberry tree is as big as a mouse's ear
> No fear of frost 'til next autumn.

It might seem that local people were obsessed with the weather (much like everyone today in fact) but understanding the weather is an important skill for an agricultural community. Not every belief was quite so practical, however, and some would seem downright outlandish today. For example, the common houseleek, a fleshy-leaved plant traditionally sacred to the gods Jupiter and Thor (according to one's preferred mythology), was thought to be a sure-fire defence against lightning when planted on the roof of a house. Jupiter is associated with thunderbolts and Thor is the God of Thunder so the association is quite sensible within its own frame of reference. Many old cottages in the Vale have a covering of these low, spiky plants hidden away in the thatch and householders would take great care to maintain these precious protective plantings.

Some of the folk-beliefs of the Vale may give the impression of being slightly eccentric but, when set against the odd behaviour of some of the monarchs of the time, they start to seem much more prosaic. Take for example the following story, which could easily come from a fairy tale. In the year 1188 King Henry II granted an estate in Shrivenham to Reynold le Fouwer, who held the responsible job of maintaining the fire in the king's bedchamber. This is not especially noteworthy in itself and the manor quickly became known as Fowersmill after its owner and is probably the area known as Friar's Mill today. What makes this behest noteworthy is that his descendants were only allowed to retain their estates on the proviso that whenever the king passed over the bridge at Fowersmill they must appear before him clutching two white hens and exclaim: 'Behold, Sire, these two white capons which you shall have another time but not now.'

Highworth

Squire Crowdy of Highworth was another of those local characters who was something of an eccentric in life and something of a nuisance in death. Crowdy had high personal standards – if he ever felt that he had failed to live up to his individual moral code he would parade himself through the streets of the town with a halter about his neck and a rope trailing on the ground as a penance for his transgressions. It seems that after his death Squire Crowdy continued to suffer the pangs of guilt over some undisclosed misdemeanour because his ghost could often be seen, bedecked as in life with halter and rope, wandering the town after dark and no doubt upsetting late-night strollers no end. When not bemoaning past sins, his ghost would relax by personally pulling a spectral cart noisily up and down the approach to the house; not, I suspect, a sight to inspire terror but certainly an inconvenience to anyone attempting to sleep.

Eventually, a decision was reached: the ghost must be laid to rest and consequently the local vicar, bailiff and other notables of the parish warily approached the house one night and attempted to exorcise the disruptive spirit. This did not prove to be an easy task because Crowdy, even in spirit form, was clearly set in his ways and refused to submit to any higher authority. In the end a compromise was reached between parson and phantom and the squire agreed to be laid to rest, as long as it was within a barrel of cider. The interested parties all trooped down to the cellar, opened a large barrel of apple juice, performed the ceremony and hastily resealed the

barrel (presumably before Crowdy realised that he was headed for a decidedly non-alcoholic afterlife). Just to make doubly sure that the shade was well and truly gone, local masons were then summoned and the doorway to the cellar was bricked up. Apparently Crowdy was satisfied with the apple juice (or perhaps it simply fermented with the passage of time) because his visitations ceased from that point onwards. Of course, somewhere in the cellars of Highworth House there still lies a barrel and a ghost and who knows what may happen if the two ever see the light of day again?

The King and Queen Inn at Highworth was once a coaching inn but, critically from the point of view of the account that follows, it stands next door to what was once a monastery and is supposed to have a tunnel running from the basement across to St Michael's Church nearby. The monastic connection may well account for the apparition of a hooded monk who has been seen by numerous customers over the years and heard moving around upstairs above the bar. One customer reported following what seemed to be a perfectly normal figure from the bar towards the gents' toilets only to watch the figure unexpectedly vanish. More dramatically still, a previous pub landlord was clearing up one night after closing time when he heard his two German Shepherd dogs outside in the courtyard start to howl. When he went out to investigate the noise he found them crouching down, rigid with fright, with their hackles raised. He looked in the direction they were staring and saw the figure of a monk move away and disappear through a wall. As soon as the shape had disappeared the dogs started to behave as if they had never been disturbed at all; doubtless the landlord was rather less sanguine about the experience.

The accepted back-story to the haunting is that the phantom monk fell in love, broke his vows of chastity and was consequently put to death, but it is interesting to note that none of the witnesses ever seem to see quite the same figure.

The varying accounts describe a figure either of normal height or abnormally small as well as either walking normally or bent over as if the ghost was a hunchback. Could there be more than one monk at the King and Queen? As for the footsteps from upstairs, it seems that the building was used as a courtroom and the sounds may perhaps be a replay of some wretched individual plodding miserably from his imprisonment towards an unfavourable judgement from the court.

Just to confuse the picture a little more, one figure has also been seen outside the pub and another 'hunched grey or white form' was observed in a field next door (presumably before the town expanded considerably). Furthermore, many years ago a local farmer's wife who had just moved into a house in the nearby Westrop area of the town was troubled by an unpleasant 'atmosphere' in her new home, particularly in the stables. Eventually she was told the tale of how the previous owner of the property had returned home one evening and had ridden into the stables to unsaddle his horse. Something clearly spooked the animal because, despite it being described as almost exhausted, it suddenly reared up and threw him to the ground, breaking his neck and killing him instantly. In the same stables two workmen reported an encounter with a cowled figure; could this be related to the ghost at the King and Queen or is it another spirit from the same monastic community? It is interesting to note that there is a road called Coffin Close in the area, which is alleged to be so named because the dead were left there overnight while awaiting burial.

Whatever the truth about the hauntings in and around the King and Queen, one wily landlord made the most of the story by taking out an insurance policy against any of his customers dying of shock after encountering anything supernatural. Luckily he was never forced to make a claim but the publicity doubtless did wonders for his trade.

The Christmas 1959 edition of the *London Illustrated News* reported that a blank-featured ghost was haunting St Michael's Church at Highworth (just across the road from the King and Queen) and that the figure had been seen by the verger 'as recently as 1938'. Another eyewitness who ran into the disturbing apparition said that

> instead of having an ordinary face the figure had a featureless grey blank, though where the eyes should have been were sunken dark shadows.

Highworth may even have had its own witch in former times; at least that was what local people dubbed Peggy Tawnley, who was accustomed to go about dressed in a man's black jacket with big green buttons worn over a blue gown and topped by an old-fashioned bonnet. Perhaps it was her sartorial strangeness or perhaps it was due to some oddity of character, for she was most definitely a regular at church, but Peggy was widely believed to be half-man, half-woman and a witch to boot. Any odd phenomena in the area would eventually be laid at her door but it was the reported manner of her disappearance from the town that lent credence to such beliefs. It so happened that one Saturday night Peggy met a local man on the road into Highworth and, according to his testimony, fixed him with a steely gaze, attempting to bring him under her influence. Luckily for him he was able to resist and hurried on into town, only to discover that Peggy had somehow managed to overtake him and was now on her hands and knees scrubbing her doorstep as if nothing untoward had ever happened. Doubtless feeling somewhat aggrieved he rushed forward to deliver her a stern kick but Peggy simply curled herself into a ball, rolled smoothly away down the hill and was never seen again!

Coleshill

Local tradition says that Coleshill is named after Old King Cole, he of the nursery rhyme, who was reputed to live at Cole's Pits. Sadly, no exact time is given for his period of residence.

Legend has it that deep within the bowels of Coleshill House, hidden away somewhere in the basements of the (now lost) building, there was a secret chamber and sealed within it lay the embalmed body of a young girl. Furthermore, it was thought that the fortunes of the house and those who owned it were intrinsically bound up with this enigmatic mummy, for should it ever be removed from the property financial disaster would strike and the house would pass to new owners. A somewhat more recent, and perhaps politically correct, version of the tale downgraded the embalmed body to a mere waxen doll although, as four women once on trial at Abingdon discovered, even wax figures can be potent symbols if uncovered at the right place and time. Mind you, this was no ordinary doll as it was said to walk the deserted corridors of the house at night, doubtless to the consternation of anyone unfortunate enough to encounter it during its nocturnal peregrinations. Another legend describes how nine spectral cats would appear seated in niches in the entrance hallway of the house should any evil events threaten the family. Whether the tale of the cats is directly related to that of the sealed chamber, and whether they would simply appear as a warning or were somehow empowered to offer assistance in a crisis, is unclear.

During the Second World War Coleshill House was the headquarters of the highly secretive GHQ Auxiliary, the British Resistance Organisation which would have undertaken sabotage attacks and other resistance activities in the case of invasion. After the war the house was bought by a member of the Thomas Cook travel company family; a few years later in 1952, just as documents were being prepared to hand it over to the National Trust, a major fire destroyed the entire building. The grounds of the house are indeed now owned by the National Trust, so clearly this was simultaneously a financial disaster and a change of ownership. It would be interesting to know whether the spectral cats appeared before the fire but, if they did, it seems obvious that they were not able to offer much in the way of fire-fighting assistance. Despite pleas from many local and national luminaries (including John Betjeman) funds were not made available for rebuilding and the remaining shell of Coleshill House was eventually demolished. The outline of the building is now marked out by a low box hedge.

Many years ago, or so the story goes, a ploughman was working at his trade in a field down beside the River Cole when one of his horses suddenly stumbled as one of her forelegs disappeared into a hole which had suddenly appeared beneath her hooves. On examination it was discovered that she had fallen into an ancient, long-buried stone coffin which had been lying just below the surface of the field. Within this ancient casket were nothing but dust and bones and a small urn of coins so, in accordance with the customs of the day, the bailiff of the farm claimed the coins for himself and left the unfortunate ploughman with nothing but the bones for his trouble. And possibly something else, for after the ploughman took the bones home (whether for reburial or whether as a gruesome souvenir is not stated) his home was assailed by mysterious spectral groanings and other terrifying sounds to such an extent that the poor man was

forced to flee his cottage. As if this were not enough to warn the local farmhands that they had stumbled upon something they should have left well alone, it proved impossible to move the stone coffin from the field, even with a team of the strongest horses in the area pulling in unison. Farm workers in those days were clearly able to recognise a no-win situation when they saw one and the bones were quickly returned to the coffin; this was hastily reburied after which the nocturnal noisiness immediately ceased. Doubtless everyone concerned did their best to forget the whole incident; everyone that is but the bailiff, who presumably thereafter went about his business richer to the tune of one urn of ancient coins.

Buscot

Never mind the splendours of Buscot Park (built in 1779 and managed by the National Trust) or the lovely Buscot Manor (built in 1692 and now a bed and breakfast guest house), to find a ghost at Buscot we need to follow the Thames Path from Buscot Lock, past the wartime concrete bunker, until we reach a large bay in the river which marks the position of a deep hollow in the river bed. This is known as Bloomer's Hole, although no-one can say for certain how it came by this name. There are however two possible explanations, either of which might possibly be true. The first claims that the name commemorates a wagon driver named Bloomer who drove his horse and cart into the river at this point and was never seen again. His ghost, complete with phantom cart, is said to haunt the spot. The second version of the legend claims that the pool is named after a local rector, the Reverend Bloomer who shocked his parishioners by skinny-dipping in the river at the spot that now bears his name. I don't believe he has been claimed to come back as a ghost however, which is, on reflection, perhaps just as well.

Customs and Exercise

Many of the old traditions and country customs have withered away in the Vale, but it is surprising how many time-honoured events are still practiced, or have at least been revived in comparatively recent times. Many of the seasonal events in the Vale could be found anywhere in the country – who didn't celebrate Christmas after all? – but there are enough interesting local variations to warrant a closer look.

Shrove Tuesday, the last chance before the start of Lent to party and use up all the good things in the cupboard before they have to be avoided for the next forty days – Pancake Day in modern parlance – offers the first opportunity to look at some Vale-specific celebrations. In times past, the day was more than just a pretext for some culinary excess, it was also an excuse for local children to get out and about begging for pennies around their village, usually accompanied by a song or rhyme along the lines of this traditional chant:

> Snick-snock the pan's hot,
> We be come a-shrovin',
> Plaze to gie us zummat,
> Summat's better 'n nothin',
> A bit o' bread, a bit o' chaze,
> A bit o' apple dumplin' plaze.

It was a particular custom in Hendred, said to date back to the sixteenth century, for village children to troop to the door of Hendred House en masse and beg for buns on Shrove Tuesday, something which, in the nineteenth century at least, they repeated on Maundy Thursday, waving rattles and shouting, 'Money, flour, bacon or eggs!'

Modern equivalents of pre-Lent entertainments are the pancake races which are sometimes held locally. Shrivenham held lively pancake races in the 1970s and the event is still a popular annual event in Wallingford. Blewbury once held pancake races but nowadays has moved its celebrations and now holds annual Easter egg-rolling competitions instead.

After the universal celebrations of Easter, on the second Tuesday after Easter Sunday to be precise, came Hocktide, a time of mixed blessing for the local peasantry because while it was a significant holiday it was also one of the 'term days' when rents had to be paid. The nearby town of Hungerford still holds an annual fair known as the Hocktide Court and claims the term 'Hocktide' derives from the German *hoch*, meaning a high-day. This was disputed by local folklorist Alfred Williams who suggested a link to the Saxon custom of Hocking, a celebration of the death of the Danish King Hardicanute in 1042, which led to the end of Danish rule in England. The festival is still celebrated today as 'Tutti Men' tour the town collecting pennies (although these are no longer heated and thrown to small children). They are also entitled to claim a kiss from every lady commoner of the town;[56] in return the ladies receive an orange handed out by accompanying 'Orangemen'. In the past the occasion was accompanied by comical plays stage-managed by a group of local worthies known as Aldermen of the Hocker Bench; all that remains of this particular aspect of the tradition today is a street in the town called Hocker Bench.

May Day was another occasion for celebration, heralding as it does the return of the warm weather after the (almost certainly disappointing) English spring, and May Day 'revells' in Wantage are first noted in churchwardens' accounts as long ago as 1565, though no details are given on what form these celebrations took. We can perhaps get a clue from accounts which relate how children wearing garlands of flowers and carrying a similarly decorated doll would parade from house to house through the villages of Aston Upthorpe and Aston Tirrold begging (do we see a pattern emerging here?) and singing:

---

56 As opposed to a kiss from each of the commoner ladies...

On the first of May, sooty bud day,
Give me a penny and send me away.

In nineteenth-century Childrey, May Day was also known as Garlantin Day. A garlanded doll on a stand made from two hoops and decorated with ribbons was carried around the village preceded by a Jack in the Green figure – a man with a blacked face and draped in green ribbon and leaves. The Jack in the Green is a common feature of May Day ceremonies all across the country, but this seems to be the only documented example from the Vale.

Ginge children would gather on the village bridge similarly attired, but simply sang rather than indulging in any begging activities. In an even more public-spirited display, children from Long Wittenham would give their garlands away to the older people of the parish whereas, you will not be surprised to hear, the acquisitive children from Hendred were out and about from early morning each May Day singing and scrounging pennies. Perhaps we should not be so hard on these poor children as a local saying sums up the relative poverty of the village: 'No-one ever took a fortune out of East Hendred!'[57]

Most villages would have had maypoles up until a few hundred years ago, usually cut and erected especially for the occasion rather than a permanent feature as at Longcot, and we have already mentioned the Fyfield elm and its attraction for 'maidens from distant hamlets'. May Day dancing was, hardly surprisingly, strongly condemned by the puritans and banned by Oliver Cromwell, much like the practice of brewing Whitsun ale.

Whitsun ales were special beers brewed in mediaeval times by the local churchwardens and then sold to raise money for the church. This was often accompanied by the holding of Robin Hood Games – an occasion which involved electing a May (or Summer) King and Queen, often also known as Robin Hood and Maid Marion (hence the

---

57 As evidence of the truth of this saying, one of the panes of glass in the village church is scratched with the message: 'C. Parker glazed this Church Mar. 2 1784 and glad of the job'.

festival name), who often acted as 'Lords of Misrule'. Because of the importance of archery in the Middle Ages these events may well also have served as clever pieces of marketing to promote archery practice. The Abingdon Parish Records during the mid-sixteenth century mention a payment of the princely sum of 18d for the setting up and decoration of a 'Robin Hood's Bower', presumably to act as a resting place for the newly elected king and queen. As with maypoles, these festivities were frowned upon by the puritans and largely disappeared after the civil war but some did persist: they were certainly taking place in Wantage as late as 1867.

Not all summer traditions were geared towards celebration and Midsummer's Eve in particular was seen as a time of ill omen when evil spirits ventured abroad to poison wells and generally do mischief, a belief which may explain why so many villages lit protective bonfires on that night of the year. Because Midsummer's Eve is also the eve of the Feast of St John the Baptist, it was customary in Watchfield to drape collars made from St John's Wort around the necks of small children at sundown to protect them from witches and ward off evil.

Once the summer was properly underway residents of the Vale were really free to enjoy themselves. To give one decidedly odd example, on the Saturday closest to 6 July, Grove held its annual duck races during which grown men chased live ducks along the Letcombe Brook beside the village green; each man who caught a duck was entitled to keep it. Today the tradition is kept alive with children's plastic-duck-racing from the village bridge.

Because of a quirk of geology the Vale is threaded with a seam of greensand, which makes the area especially suitable for fruit growing and it was once particularly renowned for the succulence of its cherry harvest. Cherries would be sold in the street at the Kingston Lisle Cherry Festival on the first Sunday after 6 July and Wantage held a Cherry Fair the same month. Most towns and villages held an annual feast of one kind or another and relatively major population centres would hold Mop (hiring) Fairs, usually around Michaelmas, at which various skilled (and unskilled) workmen would barter their service for a year with local employers. The term 'Mop Fair' comes from the badge, or mop, which each man would wear to identify his trade: after negotiations with a new employer were complete the mop would be replaced with ribbons to indicate that the workman was now gainfully employed, at least for the next year, and the party could begin. Faringdon's main Mop Fair was held on 18 October but there was an additional Runaway Fair on 29 October. This wasn't, as you might expect, another fair to fill positions vacated by unhappy appointees from the previous week but a second chance for those not chosen first time around to secure employment. A Mop-up Fair if you like.

There were also fairs specialising in other merchandise – for instance there were Horse Fairs at Faringdon and Abingdon and Sheep Fairs, mostly in villages up on the Downs above the Vale such as East Ilsley and Lambourn. The Lambourn Fair was held on St Clement's Day (23 November), possibly because St Clement was the patron saint of blacksmiths and was thus associated with Wayland the Smith. Until 1883, a special type of cake made from a unique dough, with butter, currants, spice, candied peel and sugar, called Clementing Cakes, were sold at these occasions. Many of the local towns still have carnivals or other celebrations over the same date as the original village fair or feast – the Harwell Whitsun Feast being the best-known example. Sometimes fairs allowed local people liberties they were otherwise denied, for example at Shrivenham anyone who placed a branch from a thorn bush outside their cottage door during the April Fair was entitled to sell ale to passers-by.

The Annual Feast was also the setting for a series of fairground-style games and competitions. Challow Feast on Trinity Sunday featured an odd competition in which the women of the village vied to drink the most cups of tea (the prize was a length of cloth) but more orthodox competitions were also available. In *The Scouring of the White Horse* Thomas Hughes describes some of these popular activities:

> There'll be backsword play and climmin the powl,
> And a race for a pig and a cheese;
> And us thinks as hisn's a dummel sowl
> As dwoan't care for zich spwoarts as these.

We have already mentioned cheese rolling in connection with the scouring but scrabbling after a pig was obviously an equally exciting and doubtless amusing spectator sport at any similar events. Climbing the (greasy) pole was such a popular spectacle that it was used as a metaphor by Benjamin Disraeli and eventually became the cliché we all know today. But what was backswording?

Berkshire folk clearly have an affinity for anything which involves sticks. The regional pub game is Aunt Sally, which is found only in the counties close around the Vale, and involves throwing a series of sticks at a wooden 'dolly' perched atop a pole in an attempt to knock it cleanly off its perch in a series of competitive rounds known as 'legs' (the final and most important of which is usually the 'beer leg'). While Aunt Sally[58] might be considered to be the acceptable face of stick-based entertainment, backswording is rather more combative and, in essence, involves two contestants attempting to brain each other with cudgels.

There were rules of course. The combat often took place on a large raised platform for the benefit of the audience, although any suitably marked area would suffice if necessary. Each protagonist, usually known as an 'Old Gamester', would be armed with a stout stick and the aim was simply to draw at least an inch of blood from the head of the opponent. There were two referees called 'sticklers' wielding long sticks with which to separate the fighters[59] but their role seems to have been simply to start the fight, to ensure that no grappling took place and to adjudicate on the winning wound if necessary. Technique was far less important that a stout swing and a sturdy blocking defence.

The prize money was often considerable for these tournaments and successful fighters could become real local celebrities, taking on all comers and doing their best to make sure that very little prize money made its way into the pockets of their amateur challengers. Alfred Williams relates an anecdote about a contest at the Coleshill Feast

---

58 The name probably arose because the dolly was originally a model of the head of an old woman smoking a clay pipe.

59 Hence the expression 'a stickler for the rules'.

when one of these unbeaten semi-professional backsword champions arrogantly offered the enormous sum of thirty shillings to any man who could defeat him. A young carter, eager to put an end to his boasting, leapt to the platform and addressed his friends. 'Well, gentlemen! What be I to do wi' this owl' man? Be I to break 'is 'ed or no?'. 'Ef 'e ool be obstinate, go at un,' roared the audience and, thus encouraged, the young man soundly defeated the champion and claimed his reward.

Thomas Hughes featured backswording in a number of his works, most notably in *Tom Brown's Schooldays*, but if reading about the sport is insufficiently exciting it is actually possible to watch a revived version of this old tradition. This is because the annual Uffington White Horse Show each August hosts the finals of the English Country Backswording Tournament, although it is worth mentioning that the modern rules have been somewhat changed to allow for head protection (three qualifying blows to the head will win a bout, with no blood required) and to stress that the Old Gamester's sticks should now be wielded skilfully like swords rather than forcefully as clubs. Both men and women take part in modern backswording: both emerge equally bruised and battered.

Moving away from armed combat and back to the gentler side of country life, if you would like a taste of rural life in the Vale in the seventeenth century then the local Vale Islanders dance group should be your first port of call. Named after the collective term for the villages around Charney Bassett, which would be effectively isolated during particularly wet periods, the Islanders perform Playford[60] English country dances in authentic period costume. While only part of their repertoire can be said to be truly home-grown, there is another form of

---

60 John Playford published *The English Dancing Master*, a compendium of 105 contemporary rural dances in 1651 and continued to update his catalogue throughout his life.

dancing which did have an individuality all of its own in the Vale: the local style of Morris dancing.

Morris dancing is generally considered to have originated with Moorish dancers at the royal Tudor court,[61] but quickly became popular in rural communities and is first recorded locally in the Vale at Abingdon in 1560, where churchwardens accounts record the purchase of 'two dossin of Morres belles', perhaps indicating that early Morris dancing was a church-sponsored activity along with those Whitsun ales. Shakespeare highlights the seasonal aspect of Morris dancing both in Henry V:

> And let us do it with no show of fear;
> No, with no more than if we heard that England
> Were busied with a Whitsun morris-dance.

and again in *All's Well That Ends Well*:

> As fit ... as a pancake for Shrove Tuesday, a morris for May-day,

As you might expect, Morris dancing was another of those activities banned by the Puritans but it was legalised again after the restoration of Charles II. While some dance sides operated purely locally it would seem that many travelled widely and danced to raise cash along the way. For example, Morris dancers from Abingdon are recorded by F. G. Waldron as having toured in both London and Surrey:

> In the summer of 1783, the editor saw at Richmond in Surrey, a company of Morris dancers from Abingdon ... The dancers and the fool were Berkshire husbandmen, taking an annual circuit; and collecting money from whoever would give them any.

Although it managed to survive in some places (Abingdon being one notable example), the popularity of Morris dancing declined with the rise of industrialisation. Luckily, largely through the encouragement and

---

61 This theory is cast into doubt by a reference to a payment to Morris Dancers in 1448. Oddly, John Cutting suggests a concordance between 'Moorish' and both 'traditional' *and* 'exotic'.

publicity from folklorists such as Cecil Sharp[62] (who became fascinated when he happened to look out of a window and see the Headington Morris Men dancing outside his house when he was on holiday in 1899), it saw a resurgence from the early years of the twentieth century.

There are a number of active Morris sides in the Vale area, most notably the Abingdon Traditional Morris Dancers (from the Ock Street area of the town) and the Icknield Way Morris Men in Wantage, although there are many more in the surrounding area; there are at least four around Oxford and another three in the village of Bampton alone. Alas, the wonderfully named BUMMs (Bishopstone Union of Morris Men) seem to have gone into hibernation and, to the best of my knowledge, danced their last in 2010, although I would be delighted to hear that they are still active in their field.[63] Morris sides, even those operating within the close geographical area of the Vale, tend to have their own individual repertoire of dances; the Icknield Way Morris Men are the guardians of the Stanton Harcourt tradition for example, whereas the Abingdon Traditional Morris Dancers have their own selection of historic and evolving sequences.

Part of the regalia of the Abingdon side is a curious artefact consisting of a garlanded ox skull mounted on a pole: the famous Ock Street Horns. The story behind the horns began after an ox roast in the town square in 1700, when an argument arose between the inhabitants of Ock Street and the nearby Vineyard (a road named for its proximity to the vineyards of Abingdon Abbey) over who should take possession of the skull after the party. A major scuffle broke out between the two communities; the Ock Street men eventually emerged victorious, claimed their prize, and the skull has been the symbol of the Ock Street Morris Men to this very day.

Abingdon is also the only place in the Vale to elect a mock mayor each year, in this case the Mayor of Ock Street, on the Saturday nearest to summer solstice. It is thought that electing a mock mayor, a local

---

62 Sharp also drew heavily on *The English Dancing Master*.

63 Or pub car park.

person with no civic power or duties at all, arose from the discontent of a largely disenfranchised urban population and allowed the new 'Mayor' a platform to criticise and generally mock the local authorities. In the case of the Mayor of Ock Street, the electorate consists of anyone living along the street itself, although the candidates are drawn from the rather limited pool of the Abingdon Traditional Morris Men. (Given that the winner becomes Squire of the Morris for the next year that seems only fair.) Once the election has taken place the successful candidate is carried shoulder-high up and down the street before the real business of dancing and drinking in the local pubs begins.

By the time winter came around and dancing lost its appeal in the colder weather, begging was back on the agenda. On St Thomas's Day (21 December) the poor widows of Uffington would traditionally call on their richer neighbours and beg for alms – a custom known locally as 'mumping'. This was practiced at various places across the country, the name deriving from the word 'mumper', colloquial slang for a tramp. A more widely observed local practice was the custom of wassailing, which involved a group of men carolling from house to house while carrying a wassail bowl, a large vessel which they expected to be filled with lamb's wool by the end of the evening. 'Lamb's wool' is, perhaps unsurprisingly, an alcoholic drink consisting of hot ale, sugar and spices, eggs, apples and cream. Tasty...

As the nights started to draw in, the enterprising local Morris Men did not just hang up their bells and retire to the nearest inn; instead they would begin practicing for the winter mumming play. The word 'mummer' shares a common origin with the German *mummerspiel*, meaning masquerade, and the plays draw heavily on the pagan midwinter concept of rebirth and renewal. While the ideas behind the plays' narratives are very ancient, most authorities tend to believe that the performances themselves, in their present format at least, probably date back no further than the mid-1800s. The Vale has a rich tradition of mumming plays, which were particularly popular in the eighteenth and nineteenth centuries, though interest waned until revived very recently – as late as 1977 in the case of the Wantage Mummers. The plot generally features an introduction from Father Christmas followed by a combat between St (or King) George and an enemy who is often portrayed as a Turkish knight, which results in the wounding or killing of the champion. A doctor then revives the hero who proceeds to defeat his foe in a thrilling rematch. after which a pauper character proceeds to collect contributions from the crowd.

Although the story remains fairly constant the characters vary wildly: the hero is, appropriately enough, King Alfred in the Wantage version but was King William at Long Wittenham, King George at Stanford-in-the-Vale and St George in Hatford; the villain was an 'Africky King' at Steventon, the Tipton Slasher in Cholsey, but Napoleon look-alike Beau Slasher at Brightwell-cum-Sotwell and Steventon. There were more mumming plays featuring the same basic cast with local variations at Stanford-in-the-Vale and Blewbury, as well as Ardington, the Hendreds, Sutton Courtenay... According to Malcolm Bee, writing in *Oxfordshire Local History*, there seems scarcely to have been a local village which didn't have a mumming group, although most are now little more than folk memories.

Thankfully it is still possible to watch revived mumming performances in the Vale as both the Abingdon Traditional Morris Dancers and the Wantage Mummers perform annually to raise money for charity. The Abingdon performance is based on a script from Sunningwell, just to the north of Abingdon, whereas the Wantage version is based on the play originally performed at Steventon. Mumming may also be seen occasionally in Uffington, where the words to the play were handed down from father to son for many generations and finally documented in 1972: the Uffington version is only performed on particularly special occasions.

You can catch the Abingdon Mummers at various locations in the town and surrounding villages before Christmas (including Drayton, where one of the performances is overlooked by Charles Sykes's painted George and Dragon on the side of the Gothic House). The Abingdon version of the play features King George and the French Bold Slasher rather than St George and the Dragon from the original Drayton version.

The Wantage Mummers' performance, full of contemporary references, takes place on Boxing Day in Faringdon, Wantage and Childrey.

And, as if mumming, Morris and Mock Mayors weren't enough, Abingdon has one final exuberance to impart: bun throwing. It probably started out as a simple dole, a charitable donation of bread to the local poor, but Abingdon was obviously unhappy with anything so mundane and to celebrate the coronation of King George III in 1761, and maybe even in the spirit of 'let them eat cake', the Corporation of Abingdon gathered together at the top of the Market House (better known as the County or Town Hall and now the town museum) to hurl buns down upon the eagerly gathered throng of townsfolk below. One participant, a gentleman by the name of John Waite, proudly recorded in his diary how he managed to catch one in the scramble in the town square, so it was clearly a popular entertainment. So much so in fact that it became a town tradition, repeated at King George's Golden Jubilee in 1810 and again at the coronation of George IV in 1821. By the time of William IV's accession to the throne ten years later, the spectacle was both well established and well attended. The Borough Minutes from the time record that 500 penny cakes were 'distributed' and the *Abingdon Herald* wrote that '500 cakes ... were thrown from the tops of houses into the dirt to be scrambled for, in accordance with ancient usage.'

The bun-throwing tradition has been followed ever since, most recently to commemorate the marriage of the Duke and Duchess of Cambridge and again for the Queen's Diamond Jubilee. I notice that bun-throwing also took place when the Queen visited the town in 1956: what she made of that is not recorded but interested parties can sometimes take a peek at a selection of the buns thrown since 1887 in periodic special exhibitions in the town museum itself.

And the weirdness just goes on. Swan Upping is not what you might expect (although indulging oneself as an amateur would still lead to an appointment with the local constabulary); it is in fact an ancient tradition which started back in the twelfth century at a time when the Crown laid claim to all the mute swans on the River Thames and decided both to catalogue its possessions and enforce its rights by marking each bird along the length of the river. If this seems a lot of work, then it is worth remembering that swans were a valuable addition to any royal banquet and, sheer size aside, there was doubtless considerable prestige in being the only personages able to eat such a regal bird.[64]

Permission to own swans was extended to the Worshipful Company of Vintners and the Worshipful Company of Dyers in the fifteenth century, presumably as reward for services rendered. Swans owned by the Dyers can be recognised by a single nick to the bill, whereas those owned by the Vintners have two nicks, one on each side; an unmarked bill therefore indicated royal possession. The Swan Upping ceremonies take place over five days in July and consist of a series of skiffs piloted by the three parties dressed in traditional costume proceeding northwards along the river from Sunbury Lock, catching, marking and making health checks on any swans found along the way. The procession finally reaches our region on the Friday and can be observed at Culham, Abingdon and all points in between.

Lest you feel that the origins of all the idiosyncrasies of the area lie in the past, there is one other event which proves that there is still a rich vein of eccentricity running through the local character: The World Pooh Sticks Championships at Day's Lock, Long Wittenham. This annual spring competition was started in 1984 by lock-keeper Lynn David as a way of raising funds for the RNLI and, as all devotees of Winnie-the-Pooh will know, it involves dropping sticks from one side of the lock bridge and racing to the other side to see which emerges first. After Lynn's retirement the event organisation was taken over by the local Rotary Club and now attracts teams from as far away as Australia

---

64 Swans are still banned from commoners' tables but, strictly off the record, I can reveal that they taste a little like osprey.

and Japan. Being an international event, the honours are not always restricted to the UK and a team from the Czech Republic was awarded the team championship in 2004 with the runners-up coming from Latin America! At the time of writing, due to the ever-increasing popularity of the event and the lack of access to Days Lock, the organisers were searching for a new venue for the event; shortly before going to print the first of the new championships was held at Langel Common, Witney.

Radcot

The bridge at Radcot crosses the Thames at what was once a confused muddle of split channels and marshy ground and it is at this somewhat mournful spot that the spirits of a band of survivors of the Civil War can be found on misty nights. They are said to be Levellers; a group of extreme political radicals who believed in a far greater degree of democracy and redistribution of wealth than most of their more orthodox brethren in the government and, because of this, they were viewed with distrust by the mainstream political elite of the Commonwealth. In those tense post-revolutionary times political tensions simmered but, ironically, it was a dispute over unpaid wages that finally sparked open conflict, with regiments based in the Thames Valley mutinying and gathering support from Abingdon, Wantage and other Vale towns and villages. Needless to say, with the future of the precarious new government at stake, not to mention considerable sums of money, the struggle was both inevitable and brutal.

On 14 May 1649 a large group of Leveller mutineers found themselves pursued by forces from the main parliamentarian army and sought to flee across the River Thames. Finding New Bridge garrisoned, they were forced to detour and so crossed the river at Radcot, finally stopping in the nearby Cotswold village of Burford to rest. Alas, their dogged pursuers were thus able to fall upon them unawares, whereupon the rebels were rounded up and imprisoned in the town church overnight.

Clemency was clearly not an option as Oliver Cromwell wanted to eradicate this particular challenge to his leadership and, in the traditional version of the tale, each man was led out to stand before the local churchyard wall the following morning and unceremoniously shot, an untimely end which may explain their continued post-mortem attempts to make a more successful escape across the river. All, that is, but one man by the name of Miles Sindercombe, who somehow managed to escape the general massacre by slipping away into the night. Sadly for the legend (if not the majority of the men involved) history records that only a cornet (a very junior officer) and two corporals were actually executed at that time as an example to the rest and many of the fugitives managed to escape the clutches of the army, even before Burford was surrounded. Cromwell is reported to have made a speech telling the surviving Levellers that, while they deserved to be decimated for their disloyalty to the new government, he had decided to show mercy and pardon them all. The incident effectively marked the end of the Leveller movement and organised opposition to the new Commonwealth.

Whichever version of the story you prefer to believe, it is clear that the loss of his comrades and his cause had burned a desire for revenge into Sindercombe's heart and he later joined a band of other malcontents who declared their intent to assassinate Cromwell. It has to be said that they were not terribly efficient assassins since they planned and abandoned four separate strategies to shoot the Lord Protector, before deciding to simply burn down Whitehall palace and everyone in it using a gunpowder-filled barrel as an incendiary bomb. They got as far as planting the device before they were betrayed and arrested; unwilling to accept that his fate was to be executed by Cromwell, Sindercombe swallowed poison while being held in the Tower of London, thus cheating the Lord Protector of his victory. And, just perhaps, after his death he re-joined his fellow fugitives back at Radcot Bridge to endlessly replay their doomed attempts to escape Cromwell and build the egalitarian society of which they dreamt.

Littleworth

The pub which used to be the Fox and Hounds at Littleworth, now a thriving restaurant, is haunted by the ghost of a man the pub regulars affectionately referred to as Samuel. According to Matt, a regular visitor, the ghost was occasionally glimpsed by pub employees, usually at the busiest times, which might suggest that he was making an appearance in a vain attempt to offer some assistance to the hard-pressed bar staff. Could he have been a previous landlord or was he instead an old customer hoping to snatch a free drink unnoticed in the rush?

Fernham

In the days when rural communities felt it important to police their local mores and moral standards, local people often displayed disapproval and organised homespun justice through the procedure known as 'rough music'. Rough music was generally a demonstration of collective disapproval, usually performed with a selection of domestic cookware outside the house of a transgressor, and was often invoked in cases of marital infidelity or promiscuity. There is a splendid documented example from Fernham in 1637, which demonstrates how villages managed to enforce their standards through this sort of communal action.

On this occasion, a local man by the name of Thomas Rickettes had taken advantage of the regular absences of the husband of Dorothy Greene to begin an affair with the lady in question, sneaking into her bedroom whenever her spouse was otherwise occupied in the fields. When the adulterous couple's behaviour came to the notice of the rest of the village these good folk were suitably outraged and, on catching the couple *in flagrante delicto,* subjected them to a bout of rough music, gathering outside the cottage window and creating a loud cacophony, 'some with a spice mortar, a platter and

a candlestick ringing and making a noise'. In an unusual development the crowd seems to have become carried away, because they then burst into the bedroom and attempted to drag Rickettes away to lock him in the stocks. There is no record of the outcome of this example of summary justice, nor how Mr Greene reacted when he found out about the incident.

There is another very similar case from Childrey, which took place within the living memory of the oldest residents and conforms much more closely to the usual rough-music practice. A woman from the Stowell end of the village (very much the down-market end in those days) was the victim. For three nights a 'rough band' played outside her house on an assortment of metal household items and on the last night an effigy of the woman was ceremonially burnt on her doorstep. Not surprisingly, the lady left the village shortly thereafter.

Badbury Hill

Badbury Hill, just to the west of Faringdon, is topped by another of the hillforts that are sprinkled liberally across the Vale. The actual physical walls have been largely destroyed over the years, but the place is noteworthy as being a possible site of one of King Arthur's battles against the invading Saxons. From the viewpoint of much of our local history, and having described sites in these pages associated with King Alfred fighting off invading Danes, it may seem strange to step back hundreds of years to a point where the Anglo-Saxons are cast in the role of invaders, but this is very much the case with the stories of King Arthur.

Needless to say, this is not the legendary King Arthur of the Knights of the Round Table, the Holy Grail and so on, but the (semi-)historical character from which the Camelot legends grew. This Arthur is generally seen as a sixth-century local Romano-Celtic leader defending the country against numerous barbarian invaders after the dying Roman Empire had abandoned its far-flung conquests in a desperate attempt to defend its traditional Mediterranean territories. According to legend Arthur and the defending Britons fought twelve great battles against the invaders and, as the front line ebbed and flowed, one particular confrontation is seen as being of particular importance: the twelfth and final clash known as *Mons Badonicus,* the Battle of Mount Badon. The monk Gildas, writing half a century after the battle, described a siege of some kind followed by a great victory for the Britons, cheerily calling it 'the last great slaughter'. Interestingly, Gildas' account

does not mention Arthur at all – his military leader is called Ambrosius Aurelianus, although this mysterious figure does go by the nickname of 'Bear' because of his habit of wearing a bearskin tunic. It can hardly be coincidence that the Celtic word for bear is *Artos*.

The inclusion of the name Arthur in the tale actually had to wait until the ninth-century *Historia Brittonum* compiled by Nennius, but when the king was finally named his arrival was dramatic:

> The twelfth was the most severe contest, when Arthur penetrated to the Hill of Badon. In this engagement, 940 fell by his hand alone, no one but the Lord offering him assistance.

Mons Badonicus was a great victory for the Britons and held up the advance of the invaders for a generation or more but, as history tells us, it was only a temporary reprieve. Of course those barbarian invaders eventually settled down to create the Saxon kingdoms we know so well, including the Wessex of King Alfred.

Whatever its long term consequences, the location of Mount Badon is a hotly debated question. Descriptions of the battle mention a besieged hillfort, but this hardly offers much of a clue to help us identify the site itself. Suggestions have included villages called Badbury in both Wiltshire and Dorset, as well as Bardon Hill in Leicestershire and the spa towns of Bath and Buxton, along with other sites as far-flung as Bowden Hill in West Lothian and Mynydd Baedan in Glamorgan. Nennius specifically mentions the 'Baths of Badon' in his *Historia Brittonum*, which may count against Badbury Hill[65] but, other assertions notwithstanding, it is surely self-evident that our local Badbury Hill, set amongst a defensive landscape of so

---

65 Although, if the Ginge *Whirllypool* can vanish into history, why not some local *Baths of Badon*?

many other hillforts, has a far more plausible claim than some of the other pretenders!

Badbury Camp is within easy reach of Great Coxwell and its magnificent Great Barn. While not exactly counting as folklore, it is worth mentioning that the enormous mediaeval structure, which was built by monks under the authority of Beaulieu Abbey, is generally (and erroneously) known as the Great Coxwell *Tithe* Barn, though it is unlikely that it was ever actually used for storing tithes. The barn, measuring a massive 144 ft (44 m) by 38 ft (12 m), was part of the monastic grange at Coxwell, effectively a tied farm owned by the parent monastery, and so is likely to have been a simple storage barn for produce from the farm itself.

Faringdon

Faringdon's most famous ghost story concerns the reluctant naval officer Hampden Pye, son of local landowner and MP Sir Robert Pye. Pye Senior had a rollercoaster career during and after the Civil War; during the conflict he had besieged his own father's holdings in Faringdon and managed to topple the church steeple with a cannonball during the assault. (Pye's role in all this may actually be a piece of local propaganda; the attacking forces were based at Folly Hill to the east of the town and the tower fell towards its south side, indicating that the offending cannonball is actually more likely to have come from the defenders.) Robert Pye married Anne Hampden, the daughter of John Hampden whom we met courtesy of The Plough at Clifton Hampden, and Hampden Pye was their eldest son.

The story of the young Hampden Pye was popularised in *The Ingoldsby Legends,* published in 1837 by clergyman Richard Harris Barham, writing under the pseudonym of Thomas Ingoldsby of Tappington Manor. Barham changed the name of the name of the luckless victim to Hamilton Tigue and spiced the bare bones of the tale with some extra detail, but even when it is shorn of its poetic metre,[66] the story is worth telling.

Hampden Pye enjoyed the life of the young carefree gentleman and was consequently something of a tribulation to his father and stepmother – especially his stepmother, who would have been more than happy to have her own young son stand as heir to the family fortune. While he was simply a drunkard and carouser they could comfort themselves with the thought that no long-term harm to the family reputation

---

66 If not poetic licence.

was likely to arise, but when the young Pye came home one day and announced that he had secretly married a highly unsuitable village girl, his family clearly felt that this was the last straw and had Hampden packed off to sea as a Naval cadet to fight in the War of the Spanish Succession under Admiral Sir George Rooke.

With the young man out of the way, his stepmother began to wonder if it might be better for all concerned, (and for Edmund, the son of her own blood, in particular) were Hampden not to return to Faringdon at all. Fortunately for her plans she was acquainted with the captain of the ship on which the young Pye was serving and so a dastardly plot was hatched. The captain recruited the services of one of his seamen (in *The Ingoldsby Legends* this was a scurvy wretch by the name of Hairy-faced Dick), who in the heat of a confrontation with a Spanish warship somehow managed to push Hampden in front of a cannon, which promptly blew his head off his shoulders, killing him instantly.

Back home in Faringdon the grieving (or, in the case of his stepmother, secretly pleased) family arranged to hold a memorial service in his honour, but Hampden was not about to let a small thing like the lack of a head prevent him from revealing the truth about his death. As his stepmother climbed into the coach to proceed to the church she was confronted by Hampden's ghost, complete with his head held securely in his lap, sitting in the coach awaiting her arrival. Her terrified screams brought family servants running but none of them could see anything but an empty seat. In the poem this terrible spectre follows the wicked Lady Pye around for the rest of her life, and similarly haunts both the captain and Hairy-faced Dick to distraction, but in other versions of the story his stepmother is so shocked to see this fearsome apparition that she blurts out the story of her guilt in an attempt to get Hampden to leave her in peace.

Whatever the effects on Lady Pye's future, Hampden's ghost was subsequently seen haunting the north side of the churchyard at Faringdon where, according to some accounts, he had been buried. This is interesting in its own right because the north side was traditionally considered to be the Devil's domain (possibly because the sun never shone directly onto that part of the ground) and no burials took place there – although sometimes suicide victims might be an exception to this rule. This belief may be connected with the small 'Devil's door' or *fuga daemonum*, which was set into the wall on the north side of a church. In mediaeval times it was left open during baptisms so that the Devil could use it to leave the church after the actual moment of baptism had taken place, once he realised that he had no immediate hope of claiming the child's soul. Whatever the reason for Pye favouring this area, his ghost eventually became something of a nuisance and a century or so later the local priest laid his spirit to rest with bell, book and candle.

I ought to point out that, from a historical perspective, many of the actual details of the story as related above are somewhat less than accurate. The major problem with the legend is that there was never a wicked stepmother, since Robert Pye and his wife Anne both died in 1701. Worse still, the war in which Pye was supposed to have died didn't start until the following year, an awkward circumstance unless Pye was actually killed in an earlier conflict. All of which begs the question: if Pye was the ghost in the churchyard then why was he there and, if not, who was it? Obviously, since the ghost was exorcised many years ago, all such speculations are now just so much Pye in the sky...

A later member of the family, Henry James Pye, also of Faringdon House (though financial mismanagement meant he later had to sell the property), achieved fame in an entirely different way when in 1790 he became Poet Laureate to King

George III. He was actually the first poet laureate to be paid for his services and the first to be nominated by the Prime Minister but, alas, his selection was more of a political than a literary appointment, as his poetry was not of the highest order. His 'Ode to His Majesty's Birthday 1807' was so full of avian metaphor and was so badly received that it may well have been the inspiration for the nursery rhyme:

> Sing a song of sixpence,
> A pocket full of rye.
> Four and twenty blackbirds,
> Baked in a Pye.
> When the Pye was opened,
> The birds began to sing;
> Wasn't that a dainty dish,
> To set before the king?

Whether you revere or revile his poetry, Pye loved the town of his birth and was well aware of the role his ancestors had played in its history:

> Contract the prospect now, and mark more near
> Fair Faringdon her humble turret rear,
> Where once the tapering spire conspicuous grew,
> Till civil strife the sacred pile o'erthrew:
> —*Faringdon Hill.* Book II – Henry James Pye

Appropriately enough, Pye's ghost is said to haunt the grounds of Faringdon House, which he himself had erected in 1790. Fittingly, the spirit of Gerald Hugh Tyrwhitt-Wilson, aka Lord Berners, may also be glimpsed here on occasion. One can only imagine the scene should the visits of these two eccentric spirits ever coincide.

And, while on the subject of Faringdon and its hills, we cannot fail to mention Folly Hill, site of the famous Faringdon Folly but so named long before the tower was erected. The name probably comes from the ferny foliage which clings to its slopes, but there is an alternative explanation which claims that Sir Henry Unton once wished to improve the view from Faringdon House and planted numerous trees on top of the hill in an attempt to do so. They failed to thrive in the thin soil of the hillside and when they had finally died the hill was known thereafter as Unton's Folly. There was a hillfort here before the Romans reached our shores and a royal Anglo-Saxon and later a Norman castle as well; apart from being a Royalist base during the Siege of Faringdon, the site mostly slept the years away until Lord Berners built his famous folly many years later.

A snippet of local custom, recorded by Fred Thacker in *The Stripling Thames*, describes how in feudal times the law had, in his words,

> a short way with frail women. Every tenant's daughter who strayed from virtue was compelled to forfeit forty pence, a considerable sum in early times, to the lord of the manor. This fine could be commuted by the girl's appearance in his court carrying a black sheep across her back and making confession: 'Ecce porto pudorem posterioris mei'.

An approximate translation of this confession might be 'Behold, I am carrying my shame behind me'.[67]

In 1996, following a series of renovations and alterations to the building, the management and staff of The Bell Hotel in the town square began to experience a series of unsettling events which led them to believe that they were being haunted by the ghost of a monk: repeated appearances of a figure in the attic and other parts of the hotel did little to dispel this belief.

The Bell is certainly a prime candidate to host a haunting

---

67 Possibly an appropriate statement to make as we approach the end of this book.

since it may well date back as far as the year 1202, when King John granted land in Faringdon to the monks of the order of St Mary of Citeaux in Burgundy, more usually called the Cistercians. No monastery was ever built, but by the fourteenth century the building which is now the hotel was already in active use as a *hospicium*, or guesthouse, run by the monks and by the seventeenth century it was in private hands as a thriving coaching inn catering for travellers heading to and from London. In fact the original chapel is now the restaurant, complete with thick and uneven walls, which often cause considerable logistical difficulties for the present staff; the shell of the original inn comprises the main part of the hotel.

Given its monastic background, the idea of having a phantom monk in residence probably did not seem so outlandish as might be expected, and indeed prior to 1996 there had been occasional reports of strange figures glimpsed at The Bell, but clearly the building works in that year led to an increase in activity sufficient to cause unease amongst the staff. The ghostly monk was seen on several occasions walking across the rooms in the attic, and also along the corridor on the floor below where the guest rooms are located. A temporary manager told how she got up and went into the bathroom in the middle of the night, only to feel something brush against her in the semi-dark; looking around to try and identify what might have touched her, she saw the monk walking away from her across the attic before disappearing through a closed door. More frighteningly, the regular manager woke up one night to find the cowled figure of a monk standing beside his bed looking down at him: when he put out his arm to touch the apparition, his hand went right through the apparition and struck the wall.

The figure was described by one witness as being fairly short, about five feet tall, with a slightly pointed cowl, brown in colour. Since monks of the Cistercian order wore white habits this may indicate that the ghost is that of a novice or visitor to the hospital or, as we noted at Charney Manor, that the apparition pre-dates the general rule of wearing white robes in the Order. The apparition appeared to be aware of his surroundings because he was observed looking around the attic and holding on to the staircase handrail (although it is interesting to speculate how he was able to physically grasp a handrail and yet walk insubstantially through a door). Thuds and bangs were also sometimes heard coming from an alcove in the upper floor of the hotel.

It was not just the monk who made appearances. A female ghost was also reported, although this spirit seemed to be far more mischievous as she was described as playing 'peek-a-boo' with the kitchen staff, who would sometimes catch fleeting glimpses of her peering at them around doorways. Despite her playful reputation, the staff thought that this female ghost might have been connected with a former landlady who hanged herself at the inn in the nineteenth century.

Perhaps if the manifestations had limited themselves to the behind-the-scenes parts of The Bell, the staff would just have shrugged off their ghostly encounters, but when guests started to report strange occurrences in the bedrooms, ranging from unexplained noises and cold spots to one visitor actually being pinned down to the bed, it was clear that business might start to suffer. Consequently, a medium was invited to the hotel to take a look around; disappointingly, rather than attempt any kind of 'cleansing' the psychic simply reported that The Bell had six ghosts, adding that only two would cause any trouble, before (presumably) departing with a cheery wave and leaving the staff at The Bell no happier than before.

Doubtless feeling rather let down, the manager and the assistant manager, who shared the staff quarters in the attic, then contacted paranormal research group ASSAP[68] to ask for their advice. As a result of this second plea for help, ASSAP held an overnight investigation at The Bell in October 1996 to try to confirm some of the stories they had been told. They also hoped to discover anything which might explain the strange noises being heard in the hotel. Unfortunately, while they were able to experience some of the phenomena for themselves, they couldn't find anything which might help to explain them. During the night, strange sounds were heard on numerous occasions by various members of the team, especially from the alcove that the staff had pointed out as a special locus of activity but, despite some minor structural investigation, no-one could explain the odd banging noises, nor the sudden startling crash that sounded from the sloping roof outside halfway through their stay.

As with the visit from the psychic, this may well have been a frustrating outcome for the staff at The Bell but, as is so often  the case, the phenomena started to die down shortly afterwards and business at the hotel returned (mostly) to normal. Following more building work in 1998 there was a brief resurgence in activity, with two guests reporting seeing the monk in their rooms. Rather more worryingly, one night a new manager reported hearing footsteps moving along the corridor and then pausing outside her door before moving on again. When she finally plucked up the courage to check the corridor it was empty and the doors at each end were firmly locked.

---

68 ASSAP: more properly the mildly mouth-mangling Association for the Scientific Study of Anomalous Phenomena (hence the acronym).

Since that time The Bell has been largely quiet. Some staff still occasionally report hearing unexplained bangs and crashes but, apart from that, it seems that we will need to await further redevelopment of the building before we encounter this particular monastic manifestation once more.

Just across the square from The Bell sits another pub with (despite the conservative 1664 date on the front) an even longer history and even more ghostly residents. Down in the cellars of the Old Crown Coaching Inn some of the foundations are said to date back to Roman times, indicating that some sort of structure may have been here for almost two thousand years. In fact there is also a blocked-up doorway in the cellar, which is clearly visible along with an ancient wooden beam above it serving as a lintel, but in a graphic demonstration of how ground levels change over the course of time, the beam barely reaches waist height. Remember the ankle-up soldiers from the Ginge barn? I suspect that if any such apparition were ever to be seen at the Crown we would be lucky to glimpse more than heads and shoulders. There is also a priest-hole to be seen off the main bar and a tradition of two tunnels running from the pub, one across the town square and another towards the church. It may be unfair to call this a tradition, since the start of both of these passageways can be seen but not followed due to blockages and the danger of collapse.

During the heyday of The Bell it seems that the Crown was also run as a way station by the monks of Beaulieu. However, by the time of the Civil War it too was an independent business although, in addition to being a simple inn, the Crown also hosted the various assizes that passed through the town. The present conference room, with its splendidly decorated ceiling, was used as a court room by the infamous Judge Jeffreys, the Hanging Judge, although he is not involved with haunting this place. In fact Jeffreys, who hanged three hundred men in Lyme Regis at the Bloody Assizes following the Monmouth

Rebellion of 1685, is said to haunt the Great House at Lyme where he dined before the trials of his victims. Some versions of the tale depict him gnawing on a bloody bone, an apt testament to his brutality.

The ghosts of the Crown are of a far lesser station in life than the illustrious judge, although their stories are intimately tied up with his. Every Hanging Judge needs a hangman and Jeffreys found a willing accomplice in Faringdon. There is a peep-hole, now blocked up but still visible, into the courtroom through which the executioner could peer; if he saw the Judge don his black cap the verdict was death and the hangman would hurry to the scaffold in the square to be ready to administer justice. Or at least such justice as existed in former times.

This hangman had apartments in the loft of the pub, where he lived with his wife and baby in comparative luxury, kept busy by the demands of his office. Things took a downward turn following the defeat of King James by William of Orange and the subsequent fall from grace of Jeffreys, and so the family fell on hard times. A hangman makes few friends in a community and few people would have come forward to help the newly impoverished executioner. Given his lack of both friends and prospects he is said to have entered a room which used to be known as the Henrietta Room and hanged himself from a beam with his own rope. The beam can still be seen in the room – it is easily identifiable by the notch from which the rope was slung.

It is the spirit of this hangman who is the first of the Crown's ghosts. Even today, the bulbs placed in the ceiling spotlight nearest the notched beam refuse to last any length of time although, as a previous landlady Kerry wryly observed, this is as likely to be due to faulty electrics as any baleful supernatural influence.

The room next door to the old Henrietta Room is known as the Court Room and is directly below the hangman's old apartments, which are now used as an attic space – generally locked and containing nothing more than a heating boiler. The ceiling of this room has a small gap between one beam and the wall and a number of guests staying here have described a disconcerting feeling of being watched; a number have reported seeing an eye peering down at them from above. Could this be the same executioner who committed suicide next door or could this be another restless spirit? No-one can say for sure.

The second ghost haunts the upstairs flat of the building. Surprisingly, considering the number of condemned men  who have passed through the Crown, this ghost is not thought to be one of the victims although, as you might expect, there is a link to the violent past of the place. The story told is that the wife of one of the men executed in the square watched aghast from an upstairs window with her young child as her husband was hanged. After he was dead, she hurled the child from the window before throwing herself to the flagstones below and it is her tortured spirit which can be sensed by those with the skill. Certainly Kerry told me her young son once spent an evening staring at an unseen something in the lounge of the flat and occasionally laughed as if amused by the antics of someone no-one else could see.

Finally, there have been numerous sightings of a dark-coated man sitting by the window to the right of the main door to the front part of the bar. Strangely for a regular pub ghost, he makes his appearance at 7 am and consequently is generally encountered by live-in staff and cleaners. He is evidently a very lifelike phantom as one cleaner became noticeably agitated on seeing him, fearing that a strange man had somehow managed to find his way into the bar. His long coat and top hat mark him out as a Victorian gentleman of distinction so he may have been a previous publican, manager or even a resident. Whatever his origin he does not like changes to his environment; whenever the chairs are moved from that part of the bar glasses are found shattered or optics are broken. After a few abortive attempts at reorganisation, the layout of tables is now firmly settled in a pattern which suits the unknown gentleman. I did suggest deliberately clearing the area by way of an experiment but this idea was not universally well received...

Despite all these strange happenings around them, none of the staff at the Crown, whether they live at the hotel or elsewhere, are overly worried by any of the various ghosts to be found in the building despite continuing reports of footsteps thought to be caused by an unknown coachman climbing the stairs at night. Whether any of the guests disturbed by the staring eye would agree with their opinion that the spirits are generally benign is, of course, another matter.

Not all of the ghosts of Faringdon are rooted so deeply in the past; one particularly inexplicable series of events took place as relatively recently as the 1960s in a small tied farm cottage on the outskirts of the town.

Norman Wheeler had lived at Oriel Cottage with his wife Dorothy and his four children for 16 years while he was employed as a farm labourer at Fernham Manor farm. They were a perfectly ordinary family with no history of attracting strange phenomena, although the presence of a teenage daughter in the house (Betty Wheeler was 15 at the time) may have some bearing on the situation. As we have previously noted, some researchers have pointed to the role of girls of this age acting as a catalyst for weird happenings and, as we shall see, the happenings at Oriel Cottage were decidedly weird.

The first sign of anything out of the ordinary was the sighting of barely glimpsed shadows flitting around the house accompanied by doors slamming and mysterious knockings from within the walls. These would typically begin at around 11 pm and continue until the early hours of the morning and would be accompanied by an unpleasant clammy cold sensation, which could be felt even when a roaring fire was built up downstairs. It was these persistent knocking sounds that disturbed the family most; if the family tapped on a wall, the ghost would tap back and sometimes when the 19-year-old son Colin played his mouth organ the ghost would beat time in accompaniment! In any case their first action was to call in the local police. An officer from Faringdon duly arrived and investigated the situation but, apart from confirming the reality of what was happening, he was powerless to intervene. 'There is no doubt that there are strange noises there. I don't know what they are but there is nothing the police can do,' he observed. A few days later a plumber and two carpenters who examined the pipework and the floorboards of the house were also singularly unsuccessful in finding a mundane cause for the noises.

As the events in the cottage continued, it became a source of increasing interest in the local community. At one point a group of twenty-one local people gathered at the house in an attempt to investigate the haunting and were suitably impressed to see a shadowy shape and feel a cold wind blow across the floor and around their feet. Following this well-attested confirmation that all was not well, George Fields, a local architect, visited the house and proceeded to lift floorboards and examine the structure of the cottage in another attempt to identify the cause of the banging:

I have been to the house and heard these noises. I just can't make them out – they seem to move from place to place. I just can't understand them. I thought it might be an animal trapped in the roof, but this possibility is ruled out because the noises come from all over the place, even the downstairs walls.

Finally, he too left, unable to offer any explanation for what was happening.

As you might expect, after suffering all this disruption for some weeks the family began to show signs of strain. The younger children refused to go upstairs under any circumstances and the whole household took to sleeping huddled together in the front room (even so their unseen tormentor would not let them sleep and kept to its nightly routine). Finally, their doctor prescribed sedatives to help them all get some much-needed rest.

As we have seen in so many cases of this kind, once the strain became unbearable the family decided to seek spiritual help and contacted a medium from Swindon. She visited the house and declared that although the cottage itself had no history of violent death on the premises it was haunted by the spirit of a former lodger who had stayed briefly with the family some years before and who had later killed himself at Uffington. 'We think he is trying to get revenge because we only let him stop with us for a week. He was a real trouble-maker,' commented Mr Wheeler. The lodger had in fact jumped in front of a train at Uffington station on the very night the Wheelers had asked him to leave.

Rather than removing the ghost herself as might have been expected, this medium suggested contacting a priest, so the vicar of Faringdon came and performed a 30-minute exorcism ceremony in the cottage. Fortunately this seems to have been a successful intervention; the manifestations ceased and peace at last descended on the family home.

Unfortunately this all came too late for the Wheelers; the farmer who owned the tied property resented the bad publicity the haunting was generating, as well as the time off work Mr Wheeler was having to take to look after his family, and made Mr Wheeler redundant. The Wheelers were faced with eviction and left the area to find work elsewhere and, although they said that they were sad to be leaving Faringdon, they were obviously pleased to escape from the scene of so many traumatic experiences. As Dorothy Wheeler told the *Oxford Mail* before she left: 'We don't want to stay in the house anymore anyway. The children could never settle down here after the shock.'

So what could have caused all these upsets? As with so many of the mysterious events we have observed in the pages of this book, no rational explanation was ever found, though a number of suggestions were put forward. We have already noted that Betty Wheeler was 15 and, according to some theories at least, a possible source of paranormal activity, but if that was indeed the case why should an exorcism make any difference? Numerous visits from assorted experts failed to uncover any kind of 'rational' cause for the strange noises and draughts, but no-one is infallible and perhaps one of them managed to overlook some important clue which might have explained at least some of the phenomena which plagued the Wheelers. It was widely suggested that the whole haunting was a hoax, although given the effect it had on the family – even to the point of losing them their home – this would have been either a spectacularly badly misfiring trick or a particularly well-executed and cruel campaign. Which leaves the possibility that this may have been caused by an actual, genuine ghost – or sensory distortions caused by the seepage of gas into the property, mass-hysteria, pixies... The list could go on, with each 'explanation' more outlandish than the last.

In the end I think we just have to look at the situation the Wheelers were forced to endure, as well as the events in the Long Wittenham Co-Op, Uffington Church, Longworth Lodge Cottage, in the skies above Abingdon and beside the rivers across the Vale, as just part of the natural order of things; perhaps a part we do not yet understand but one which we can approach with a sense of wonder even as we try to unravel its various mysteries.

One day, not soon perhaps but eventually, we may be able to incorporate the strange phenomena we have encountered across the region into our view of the universe, but until then let us simply enjoy the strange, the unexplained and the downright frightening and take pleasure in their ability to both puzzle and scare us. The Vale may remain veiled a while yet. I will cede the closing lines to Emily Dickinson, who made the point far more elegantly and succinctly than I ever could:

> But nature is a stranger yet;
> The ones that cite her most
> Have never passed her haunted house,
> Nor simplified her ghost.

Bibliography

36 Strange Tales from Oxford and Shire, John Richardson. J Hannon (1981)
A Berkshire Village its History and Antiquities, Rev. Lewin G. Maine. J. Parker (1866)
A Dictionary of Fairies, Katharine Briggs. Viking (1976)
A Glossary of Berkshire Words and Phrases, Major Barzillai Lowsley. Trübner (1888)
A History of the County of Berkshire, P.H. Ditchfield & W. Page (eds). Victoria County History (1907)
A Short History of Hanney, Diana Bowder. D.R. Bowder (1989)
Abingdon Abbey, John Hudson. Clarendon Press (2002)
Annals of Windsor, Robert Richard Tighe & James Edward Davis. Longman, Brown, Green, Longmans and Roberts (1858)
Ceawa's Burial Mound, Hazel and Clive Brown. Garden Shed Publications (2007)
Childrey: A Village in the Vale of the White Horse, June Maxwell Drummond. Privately Published (1989)
English Jests and Anecdotes Collected from Various Sources, William Peterson. Edinburgh (1880)
English Villages, P. H. Ditchfield. Methuen & Co (1889)
Essays, Wray Hunt. Privately printed by Hatchards (1899)
Folklore of Oxfordshire, Christine Bloxham. The History Press (2005)
Folklore, Myths and Legends of Britain, Readers Digest. Readers Digest Association (1973)
Folk-Memory or, the Continuity of British Archaeology, Sydney Harrowing et al. Clarendon Press, (1908)
Ginge Brook, Frank Poller.
Harwell, the Enigma Revealed, Nick Hance. Enhance Publishing (2006)

Haunted England: A Survey of English Ghostlore, Christina Hole. Trafalgar Square (1990)
Highways and Byways in Berkshire, James Edmund Vincent. Macmillan and Co (1906)
Highways and Byways in Oxford and the Cotswolds, Herbert Arthur Evans. Macmillan (1905)
History and the Morris Dance, John Cutting. Dance Books Ltd (2010)
Lewis's Topographical Dictionary of England, Samuel Lewis (ed). S Lewis (1848)
Lines in the Landscape, Barclay, Lambrick, Moore and Robinson. Oxford Archaeology (2003)
Longcot: A Village in the Vale, Guy Richards and Shirley Dalton-Morris. Shirley Dalton-Morris (1999)
Lord Berners: The Last Eccentric, Mark Amory. Faber and Faber (2009)
Lost Gods of Albion, Paul Newman. Sutton Publishing (1997)
May Day to Mummers, Christine Bloxham. Wychwood Press (2002)
Oxford and County Ghost Stories, John Richardson. J Hannon (1977)
Oxfordshire Customs, Sports & Traditions, Marilyn Yurdan. The History Press (2011)
Oxfordshire Stories of the Supernatural, Betty Puttick. Countryside Books (2003)
Ridings, Rough Music and the 'Reform of Popular Culture' in Early Modern England, Martin Ingram. Oxford University Press (1984)
Round About the Upper Thames, Alfred Williams. Duckworth & Co (1922)
The Berkshire Book, 2e Berkshire Federation of Women's Institutes (1951)
The History of Ashbury, D. & E. Disbury. David & Edna Disbury (1966)

The Janos People, Frank Johnson Neville. Spearman Ltd (1980)
The Length of the Road, Maud Ody. Wessex Press (1985)
The Ley Hunter's Companion, Paul Devereux and Ian Thompson. Thames and Hudson (1979)
The Life of John Milton, David Masson. Gould & Lincoln (1859)
The Lives and Portraits of Curious and Odd Characters, Compiled, 1852. Reprint. London: Forgotten Books (2013)
The Scouring of the White Horse, Hughes. Thomas (1859)
The Story of My Life , Augustus John Cuthbert Hare Dodd. Mead & Co (1896–1901)
The Stripling Thames, Fred S. Thacker. Fred S. Thacker (1909)
The Sun and the Serpent, Paul Broadhurst and Hamish Miller. MYTHOS (1990)
The Witch Figure, Venetia Newall (ed). Routledge (2013)
Travels Round our Village: A Berkshire Book, Eleanor G. Hayden Smith. Elder & Co (1908)
True Ghost Stories, Marchioness Townshend and M. M. C. Ffoulkes. Hutchinson (1936)
Vanishing England, P. H. Ditchfield. Methuen & Co (1910)
Villages of the Vale, Alfred Williams. Nonsuch Publishing (2007)
Wiltshire Folklore and Legends, Ralph Whitlock. Robert Hale Ltd (1992)
Witch Hunts in Europe and America: an Encyclopedia, William E. Burns. Greenwood Press (2003)
Witchcraft in England, 1558–1618, Barbara Rosen. University of Massachusetts Press (1991)
Witchcraft in the Thames Valley, Tony Barham. Spurbooks Ltd (1974)

Newspapers

New Jersey Herald
Oxford Mail
Wantage Herald

Websites

Abingdon Traditional Morris Dancers
   http://www.abingdonmorris.org.uk
BBC Domesday project
   http://www.bbc.co.uk/history/domesday
British History Online
   http://www.british-history.ac.uk
David Nash's (incomparable) History of Berkshire
   http://www.berkshirehistory.com
Icknield Way Morris Men
   http://www.icknieldwaymorrismen.org.uk
Neil Maw's A Chronicle of a Village
   http://neil-maw.co.uk/watchfield.chronicle

Index of place names

Numbers in bold indicate a section dedicated to that place.

Abingdon, 29, 55, **80–92**, 138, 139, 181, 235, 238–42, 243
Aldbourne, 101
Alfred's Castle, 1
Ardington, 22, **123**, 177, 241
Ashbury, 101, 177, **197**, 217
Ashdown, 1
Ashdown House, **194–6**
Aston Tirrold, **20–21**, 232
Badbury Hill, **250–2**
Bampton, 44n, 139, 239
Baulking, *see* Hatford and Baulking
Binsey, 126–7
Bishopstone, 102, **200**, 239
Blewburton Hill, **66**, 101
Blewbury, 22, 55, **62–65**, 137, 232, 241
Brightwell-cum-Sotwell, **9–10**, 24, 99, 241
Buckland, 29, **163**
Burford, 54, **245–6**
Buscot, 29, **230**
Carswell, 55
Charney Bassett, 1, 29, **144–9**, 165, 177, 180, 199, 237
Cherbury Camp, 1, 165
Childrey, **186–7**, 233, 242, 249
Chilton, **67–68**
Cholsey, 9, **24–27**, 241
Churn Knob, 24, 101
Clanfield, 140
Clifton Hampden, **41–46**, 101, 253
Coleshill, 158, **227–9**, 236
Culham, 53, **79**, 243

Denchworth, **179–80**
Didcot, **47–50**, 51, 102
Dorchester, 24, 28
Dorchester Abbey, 41, 43, 101, 152
Dragon Hill, 99, 210, 211
Drayton, **75**, 102, 180, 241
East Challow, 117, 118, 119, 174, **179–80**, 235
East Hagbourne *see* Hagbourne, East and West
East Hanney *see* Hanney East and West
East Hendred *see* Hendred, East and West
East Ilsley, 175, 235
Ewelme 10, 99
Faringdon, 57, 59, 76, 149, 235, 242, **253–268**
Farnborough, 101
Fernham, **248–9**
Frilford, **94**
Fyfield, 106n, **151–4**, 155, 233
Ginge, **124–8**, 233
Goosey, 150
Great Coxwell, 252
Grim's Ditch, **22–23**, 32, 132, 186
Grove, **104–7**, 234
Hagbourne, East and West, **51–52**, 57, 75, 175
Hanney, East and West, 74, **95–97**, 149, 177, 219
Harwell, 57, 67, 68, 235
Hatford and Baulking, **171–4**, 241
Hendreds, The, 102, 123, 125, **130–1**, 149, 175, 231, 233, 241
Highworth, **223–6**
Hinton Parva, **201–5**
Hinton Waldrist, **160–2**
Hungerford, 232
Icknield Way, 61, 132
Idstone, **198–9**
Kingston Lisle, 54, **191–3**, 234

INDEX OF PLACE NAMES

Lambourn, 217, 235
Letcombe, Regis and Bassett, 1, 61, 102, 173, **181–5**
Littleworth, 247
Lockinge, 102, **129**
Long Wittenham, **34–40**, 44, 49, 99, 101, 113, 149, 202n, 233, 241, 243
Longcot, **217–8**, 233
Longworth, 56, **156–9**, 162
Mackney, 9
Marcham, **93**
Marsh Gibbon, 138
Milton, 58
Moulsford 55, 99
North Moreton, **11–16**, 89n, 101, 149
Oxfordshire, 1, 2, 56, 57, 60, 80, 132, 153, 178
Pusey, **164–6**
Radcot, **245–6**
Ridgeway, 1, 2, 22, 60, 61, 64, 101, 132, 181, 184, 197, 216
River Thames *see* Thames, River
Rowstock, **69–71**
Scutchamer Knob, 22, 32, **132–4**
Segsbury Camp, 1
Segsbury Castle, 184
Shrivenham, 219, **221–2**, 231, 235
South Fawley, 101
South Moreton, **17–19**, 101, 214
Sparsholt, 101, 178, **188–90**, 192
Stanford-in-the-Vale, 74, 150, **167–70**, 218, 241
Steventon, 5, 57, **72–74**, 241
Sutton Courtenay, 28, 47, **76–78**, 102, 138, 178, 241
Thames, River, 2, 28, 29, 44, 45, 98, 139, 243, 245
Thames Valley, 24, 54, 59, 67, 245
Tubney, 58, **155**
Uffington, 61, 99, 101, 149, 165, **175–6**, 189, 206, 217, 240, 241, 266, 268

Uffington White Horse, 1, 28, 149, 192, 205, **206–211**, 213, 214, 215, 216
Upton, 68, 103
Wallingford, **3–8**, 59, 63, 99, 103, 133, 232
Wantage, 53, 54, 57, 60, 74, 76, 87, 106, 107, **108–122**, 123, 130, 143, 179n, 232, 234, 239, 240, 241, 242, 245
Watchfield, **219–20**, 234
Wayland's Smithy, 1, 61, **212–6**
West Hagbourne *see* Hagbourne, East and West
West Hendred *see* Hendred, East and West
Westcot, 53
White Horse *see* Uffington White Horse
White Horse Hill, 60, 172, 189, 221
Witney, 244
Wittenham Clumps, **31–33**, 99, 101, 134
Woolstone, 178, 206, 210, 213

General Index

Numbers in bold indicate whole sections dedicated to the topic. The term ghost appears throughout and has not been indexed.

Abingdon Abbey, 28, 34, 80, 145, 148, 150, 163, 239
Abbot of Abingdon, 85, 144
Anglo-Saxons, 3, 24, 76, 81, 102, 108, 133, 164–5, 181, 207, 212, 232, 250
animals, 50, **53–61**, 89, 209, 141
   badgers, 58
   bees, 198–9
   cats, 13, 53–57, 74, 179, 227–8
   dogs, 26, 61, 66, 86, 110, 140, 188, 198, 224
   dragons, 148–9, 207–8, 211
   horses, 17, 19, 34, 52, 64, 67, 68, 95–96, 106, 141, 161, 183, 185, 202, 212, 213, 216, 225, 228, 229, 235
   pigs, 51–52
   sheep, 10, 58–60, 215, 235, 257
   wallabies, 57, 58
Aubrey, John, 156, 207
backswording, 236–7
badgers, 58
battles, 10, 125, 132, 157, 165, 181, 191, 207, 250–1
bees, 198–9
Berners, Lord, 140–3, 256–7
Betjeman, John, 141, 189
Birinus, St *see* St Birinus
Bronze Age, 1, 3, 31, 132
cats, 13, 53–57, 74, 179, 227–8
celebrations, 231–4
Cromwell, Oliver, 156, 171, 233, 245–6
Civil War, 4, 52, 125–6, 171, 245, 253
crop circles, 204
crop marks, 29, 180

curses, 11, 12n, 62, 88, 89, 139, 201
cursuses, **28–30**
customs, 167, 231–244, 257
Danes, 1, 3, 81, 133, 165, 181, 191, 250
Devil, 22, 73, 95, 132, 158, 186, 255
dogs, 26, 61, 66, 86, 110, 140, 188, 198, 224
Dorchester Abbey, 41, 43, 101, 152
dragons, 148–9, 207–8, 211
eccentrics, **135–143**, 156
fairies, 133, 134
fairs, 234–5
familiars, 13, 89
festivals, 233, 234, 235
Forkbeard, Sweyn, 3, 165
hillforts, 1, 31, 66, 184, 211, 250, 252, 257
horse riders, 52, 66, 67, 68, 75, 77, 183–4, 186
horses, 17, 19, 34, 52, 64, 67, 68, 95–96, 106, 141, 161, 183, 184, 202, 212, 213, 216, 225, 228, 229, 235
Iron Age, 3, 22, 31, 47, 66, 209, 214
King Alfred, 1, 3, 47, 108, 111, 164, 191, 207, 241, 250
King Arthur, 164, 210, 212, 250–1
King Charles I, 3, 156
King Cynegils, 24
ley lines, **98–103**
meteors, 60, 174–5
monks, 80, 144, 145–6, 150, 201–3, 224–5, 250, 252, 257–60, 261
Morris dancing, 238–41
Mummers, 240–2
Nine Men's Morris, 102
Odin, 22, 188–189
Oxford Archaeological Unit, 29, 206, 209
pigs, 51–52
Pooh sticks, 140, 243–4
railways, 19, 25–26, 47–48

GENERAL INDEX

rough music, 248
St Birinus, 24
St George, 99, 103, 149, 207–8, 211, 241
Saxons, *see* Anglo-Saxons
sheep, 10, 58–60, 215, 235, 257
Swan Upping, 242–3
traditions, 232–245
Uffington Castle, 1, 99, 165, 206, 211
UFOs, 87, 98, 119, 168–9, 198, 204
wallabies, 57, 58
Wayland the Smith, 212–3, 215, 235
witches, 11, 12–14, 88–89, 139, 154, 155, 161, 201, 214, 226, 234
witch marks, 73

Two Rivers Press has been publishing in and about Reading since 1994. Founded by the artist Peter Hay (1951–2003), the press continues to delight readers, local and further afield, with its varied list of individually designed, thought-provoking books.